PENGUIN CLASSICS

FACUNDO: OR, CIVILIZATION AND BARBARISM

Domingo Faustino Sarmiento was born in the Province of San Juan, Argentina, in 1811. A statesman, essayist, biographer, and poet, he is best remembered for his devotion to improving education in Argentina, a topic about which he wrote extensively, as well as for his polemic *Facundo*. In 1827, as Argentina's civil war raged, he joined the army, and was thrown in jail. He escaped to Chile, where he lived in exile for two years, and to which he would return many times over the next several decades. He was back in San Juan in 1829, when Juan Manuel de Rosas became governor of the Buenos Aires province. In 1839, Sarmiento published *Prospecto de un establecimiento de educación para señoritas dirigido por D. Domingo F. Sarmiento*, and in 1845 he published two biographies, *General Fray Félix Aldao* and *Civilización y barbarie: Vida de Don Facundo Quiroga*, popularly known as *Facundo*. The following year he began a journey that would take him to Europe, the United States—where he met the educator Horace Mann—and other parts of Latin America. In 1849 he published a book on his travels and *Educación popular*, which was influenced by Mann, and in 1850 *Argirópolis*, in which he attacked the Rosas regime, and his autobiography, *Recuerdos de provincia*. Over the next few years, he served as public relations officer of the Argentine army, Chile's director of education, senator and then governor of San Juan, and Argentina's ambassador to the United States. He published several more books, including *Ambas Américas* and *Vida de Abrán Lincoln*. In 1867 he translated the *Life of Horace Mann* into Spanish, and the following year Mary Peabody Mann's English translation of *Facundo* was published under the title *Life in the Argentine Republic in the Days of the Tyrants; or, Civilization and Barbarism*. That same year, 1868, Sarmiento was named president of the Argentina Republic, a post he held until 1874. He was appointed director of the schools of the province of Buenos Aires in 1875 and general super̶i̶n̶̶̶̶̶̶ ̶A̶r̶gentina's schools in 1881. Sarmiento d̶i̶e̶d̶ ̶

Ilan Stavans teaches at Amherst College. His books include *Growing Up Latino* (1993), *Tropical Synagogues* (1994), *The Hispanic Condition* (1995), *The One-Handed Pianist and Other Stories* and *Art and Anger: Essays on Politics and the Imagination* (both 1996), *The Oxford Book of Latin American Essays* (1997), and *The Riddle of Cantinflas: Essays on Hispanic Popular Culture* (1998). He has been a National Book Critics Circle Award nominee, a Guggenheim fellow, and the recipient of the Latino Literature Prize.

FACUNDO

OR, CIVILIZATION AND BARBARISM

———————

DOMINGO F. SARMIENTO

TRANSLATED BY MARY MANN
INTRODUCTION BY ILAN STAVANS

PENGUIN BOOKS

PENGUIN BOOKS

Published by the Penguin Group

Penguin Group (USA) Inc., 375 Hudson Street, New York, New York 10014, U.S.A.

Penguin Group (Canada), 90 Eglinton Avenue East, Suite 700, Toronto,
Ontario, Canada M4P 2Y3 (a division of Pearson Penguin Canada Inc.)

Penguin Books Ltd, 80 Strand, London WC2R 0RL, England

Penguin Ireland, 25 St Stephen's Green, Dublin 2, Ireland (a division of Penguin Books Ltd)

Penguin Group (Australia), 250 Camberwell Road, Camberwell,
Victoria 3124, Australia (a division of Pearson Australia Group Pty Ltd)

Penguin Books India Pvt Ltd, 11 Community Centre, Panchsheel Park, New Delhi – 110 017, India

Penguin Group (NZ), cnr Airborne and Rosedale Roads,
Albany, Auckland 1310, New Zealand (a division of Pearson New Zealand Ltd)

Penguin Books (South Africa) (Pty) Ltd, 24 Sturdee Avenue,
Rosebank, Johannesburg 2196, South Africa

Penguin Books Ltd, Registered Offices: 80 Strand, London WC2R 0RL, England

First published in the United States of America as *Life in the Argentine
Republic in the Days of the Tyrants; or, Civilization and Barbarism* by Hurd
and Houghton 1868

This edition with an introduction by Ilan Stavans published in Penguin
Books 1998

11 13 15 17 19 20 18 16 14 12

Copyright © Ilan Stavans, 1998
All rights reserved
Originally published in Argentina as *Civilización y barbarie* in 1845.

LIBRARY OF CONGRESS CATALOGING-IN-PUBLICATION DATA
Sarmiento, Domingo Faustino, 1811–1888.
[Facundo. English]
Facundo: or, civilization and barbarism/Domingo F. Sarmiento;
translated by Mary Mann; introduction by Ilan Stavans.
   p.   cm.
ISBN 0 14 04.3677 4
   1. Argentina—History—1817–1860. 2. Argentina—Description
and travel. 3. Quiroga, Juan Facundo, 1790–1835. 4. Rosas, Juan
Manuel José Domingo Ortiz de, 1793–1877. I. Mann, Mary Tyler
Peabody, 1806–1887. II. Stavans, Ilan. III. Title.
F2846.S2472   1998
982'.04—dc21   98-3712

Printed in the United States of America
Set in Bembo
Designed by Claire O'Keeffe

CONTENTS

INTRODUCTION

Posterity forgets or acclaims.
—WALTER BENJAMIN

"On ne tue point les idées." Around this quotation Domingo
Faustino Sarmiento built not only the brief "Author's Notice"
that served as entryway to the original edition of *Facundo: or,
Civilization and Barbarism*, but also the book as a whole—and
even his entire life. The quotation is at once a code of honor
and a key to the elaborate labyrinth of intentions, inventions,
and misappropriations that Sarmiento left for his readers to de-
code, a challenge that even today they will find nowhere more
rewarding than in reading *Facundo*, his most influential and enduring creation, the one that made him a household name in
his native Argentina as well as in the entire Hispanic world.

To understand the quotation fully, though, one must first
realize the scope of the book and the conditions under which
it came to be. Written hastily, *Vida de Quiroga*, as it was known
at first, originally appeared serially between May 12 and June
21, 1845, in the newspaper *El Progreso* of Santiago, Chile; later
that year it was published in book form. The complete title, as
stated in the frontispiece of the first edition printed in Santiago
by Imprenta del Progreso, was *Civilización i barbarie. Vida de
Juan Facundo Quiroga, i aspecto físico, costumbres y ámbitos de la
República Argentina*. From the beginning the reception was
mixed: some members of the circle of Argentine émigrés living
in Chile embraced it enthusiastically, while others approached
it with deep, uncompromising suspicion, criticizing its accu-
racy, technique, style, and spelling. But the clash between these
two views only enhanced its stature and influence, and soon
the volume became a veritable center of gravity in Argentina,

one around which the debate on identity and culture rotated. By the late nineteenth century, its influence had spread even farther into Latin America, where it began to be called *"el Quijote de América."* In the United States and Europe, French, American, and Italian translations introduced it in an altogether different light.

It is sometimes mentioned that *Facundo* was actually conceived as the second installment of a trilogy. The first was a biography written shortly before on the Argentine friar and caudillo general Fray Félix Aldao. This book, popular in the circles of Argentine exiles in Chile, encouraged Sarmiento to continue his literary endeavors along the same pattern. The third installment was *El Chacho*, about another gaucho leader and sometimes partner of Facundo against whom Sarmiento himself, while governor of the San Juan province, fought in 1864. And yet, while the three volumes are all about civilization and barbarism, the literary value of the first and third is inferior to that of *Facundo*. At the time of the book's first publication, Sarmiento was thirty-four, an active idealist, a presumptuous and self-centered intellectual (his contemporaries nicknamed him *Don Yo*, Mr. I). Prominent as a fighter in the war for freedom and against tyranny in Argentina, he was condemned to an exile hundreds of miles away from home. His nemesis was Juan Manuel de Rosas, the unyielding Argentina dictator, but his struggle had a wider spiritual reach: he saw his true enemies as silence and consent; and his hope was to stir emotions, to persuade, to verbalize the collective hatred and instigate a rebellion based not on bullets but on ideas. Sarmiento conceived his volume as a study in collective psychology, what the essayist Ezequiel Martínez Estrada would decades later call "an X ray," or an ethnographic and sociological examination of the impact of the Argentine landscape on its people and vice versa. He set out not only to debunk Rosas, but also, perhaps more urgently, to explain what had brought him to power—to illustrate the natural and social conditions in Argentina that allowed such a tyrant to emerge triumphant. He would do so by balancing the tension between the particular and the universal: that is, through his portrayal of the life of a single "barbarous" individual, the tumultuous caudillo Juan Facundo Quiroga, whose military career inspired awe and hatred in the mind of an entire generation, Sarmiento would offer a diagnosis of what was wrong and right with the country and how its collective psyche was the result of a fierce battle between the forces of darkness and light. Facundo, the gaucho barbarian, represented the former; Sarmiento, the civilized thinker, educator, and forger of a nation, the latter.

He also wished to produce a political pamphlet—a weapon to debunk the autocratic regime of Rosas, "the Robespierre of Argentina"—albeit one of a very personal nature, allowing him to advance his cause by interjecting as many of his own values and anecdotes as possible. The result is a bifunctional one, with the subject a subterfuge, a pretext, since the actual motivation to write it, as the distinguished twentieth-century *sarmentista* Alberto Palcos once argued, was anything but biographical. In fact, according to Palcos, Sarmiento had five main impulses which led him to embark on the project: to discredit Rosas and caudillismo, not only in Argentina but also in Chile, where Sarmiento had sought asylum five years earlier; to give meaning to the life of the Argentine émigrés fighting for justice and democracy; to give them a doctrine to interpret their condition; to allow Sarmiento's literary talents to find a pure mode of expression; and to make his name ubiquitious in the struggle to liberate Argentina from oppression.

In short, *Facundo* was conceived as many books in one, and the end product is something of a hybrid. Biography was an extremely popular genre in mid-nineteenth-century Argentina, but it was dramatically different from the way we think of it today. It was a branch of history which allowed the observer to interject his own interpretations of historical events. The biographer might introduce peripheral themes and explore issues apparently irrelevant to the main concern of his intellectual enterprise. The objective was to create a mélange, a conglomeration of views rather than a linear and progressive narrative. This form exactly suited Sarmiento. "The biography of a man who played an illustrious role in his day and age and as a citizen of his country," he observed, "is a summary of contemporary history, illustrated by the bright colors that reflect the costumes and habits of a nation, the dominating ideas, the tendencies of civilization and the especial direction the genius of a great man imprints in society." And, Sarmiento added, biography "is the compendium of the many historical hiatuses that is most accessible to the people and that allows for a more direct and clear instruction. It is quite hard to comprehend the connection between the multiple human events that happen simultaneously; but nothing is simpler, nor is there anything that excites us more and better engages our ardent sympathy than the particular history of a man. . . ." If, as he saw it, to make history more palatable, more convincing, one needed to establish a marriage between historical information and imaginative, fabricated ingredients, between fact and fiction, so be it: impartiality, he trusted, was less important and made worse literature than partisanship. This surely explains why for some *Facundo* is a history lesson and for others it is the true beginning of Argentine fiction. "What differentiates it from other modern biographies," Manuel Gálvez, author of the popular *Vida de Sarmiento*, argued, "is its ferociously libelous character and the excessive abundance of sociology. Except for some moments, the author is constantly present in the pages replete with personal items." And Miguel de Unamuno, the Spanish philosopher, argued: "I never took [it] as a historical work, nor do I think it can be very highly valued in that regard. I always thought of it as a literary work, as a historical novel."

That, precisely, is why Sarmiento's quotation in the "Author's Notice," attributed to the French intellectual Hippolyte Fortoul and roughly translated as "Ideas cannot be killed," is so mystifying—because, like much of what follows, it is memorable yet inaccurate. Fortoul never actually said it; and neither did Constantin Volney, to whom it was attributed by the critic and librarian Paul Groussac. According to scholar Diana Sorensen Goodrich, who, among a handful of other modern scholars, has traced the quotation's origins, the closest we can get to it is a sentence by Diderot, *"On ne tue pas de coups de fusil aux idées,"* which Sarmiento probably read around 1832 in the *Revue Encyclopédique*, in an article by Charles Didier. In English translation Diderot's words read: "Man can be beheaded, ideas cannot" (in Spanish: *"El hombre puede ser decapitado, las ideas no"*). But its meaning is considerably less important than Sarmiento's manipulation of it. This type of manipulation is at the heart of Argentine letters, with Borges as its consummate and effectual master. It signals an approach to data that is irreverent and beguiling. In a different context, one could see it as evidence of carelessness and inaccuracy; in the pens of Sarmiento and his successors, though, it is much more: an act of appropriation of foreign knowledge, an attempt to reinvent culture in the New World by transmuting and distorting what was brought from Europe. The quote is a palimpsest, a glimpse at Latin America, a region whose self-perception is based on a loss in translation.

Sarmiento does two things in his "Author's Notice": first, he acknowledges, even tries to justify, the many errors in the book, both historical and stylistic, as resulting from the urgency behind it, for the author was in a hurry, "far from the theater of events and [writing] on a subject matter about which nothing had been written until then." Second, he relates an anecdote. As we come to this part of the note, Sarmiento states, in Diana Sorensen Goodrich's translation:

Toward the end of 1840, I was leaving my homeland, a pitiful exile, ruined, full of bruises, kicks, and blows received the previous day in one of those bloody bacchanals of low soldiers and *mazorqueros*. As I passed the baths of Zonza . . . I wrote these words in charcoal:

On ne tue point les idées.

The government, which had been made aware of this, sent a commission in charge of deciphering the hieroglyph, which was said to contain base outpourings, insults and threats. Having heard the translation, they said, "So, what does it mean?" It meant simply that I was on my way to Chile, where freedom still shined, and that I had made up my mind to project the lighting that its printing presses emitted all the way to the other side of the Andes. Those who know my behavior in Chile know if I have been able to live up to my promise.

Even in exile, Sarmiento, like his fellow Argentine émigrés, is at the mercy of Rosas's forces, but he carries with himself his most enviable weapon: human reason. His corrupt enemy may have weapons more dangerous and deadly, but his is unconquerable; he may get killed, but his dream for the liberation of his homeland, for the establishment of democracy, will never perish. And yet the inaccuracy of the quotation throws a different light on the entire book: Sarmiento touts freedom and knowledge, but his knowledge is equally corrupt. Should one explain the inaccuracy as a perversion of memory? If Sorensen Goodrich is right, Sarmiento read it some eight years before being forced out of his homeland. But even if he could only remember a portion of Diderot's complete line, the device is symptomatic. To advance his argument, to sharpen his weapon, the man of letters in Argentina—and for that matter, in other corners of Latin America as well—inherits packaged ideas and intellectual forms from abroad, what Flaubert, in *Bouvard et*

Pécuchet, called *"idées fixes,"* and manipulates them at will. Sarmiento has encrypted the code that not only explains the tension between barbarism and civilization in the Americas but also, and subliminally, the metabolism of the colonial mentality in a land where individual concepts and even whole systems of thought are reframed and reinvented so as to fit the idiosyncratic needs of the region. *On ne tue point les idées* isn't a quote from Fortoul, Diderot, or any other French intellectual; it is a creation of Sarmiento, an attempt to legitimize his views by establishing a tangible lineage that links him to Europe. As one incisive reader after another, from Juan Bautista Alberdi to Martínez Estrada and Noé Jitrik, has claimed, it is as fictional as his biography of Juan Facundo Quiroga; based on reality, but an unequivocal figment of his imagination nonetheless.

Sarmiento used the tools of the historian to paint a panoramic canvas of Argentina, but he lacked an essential attribute: neutrality. He was an impassioned essayist, one of the most lucid and provocative ever to come out of the Hispanic orbit, one who knew how to put ideas to work so as to advance a political cause. This manipulative approach has its roots in the manichean scheme, the dialectical game of opposites still applicable today. Sarmiento was among the first to employ it in describing the real tension between civilization and barbarism. The conjunction "and"—the "*y*" in *Civilización y barbarie*—should not be ignored, for the dialectical opposition is based on mutual need: civilization is to barbarism what darkness is to light—its opposite, its other side. The young Sarmiento, like his fellow members of the so-called Asociación de Mayo or Asociación de la Jóven Generación Argentina, the intellectual group created by Esteban Echeverría that opposed Rosas, was influenced by the views of Montesquieu and Adam Smith, and his utopianism was inspired by Claude Saint-Simon and Charles Fourier. He believed that institutions could foster democracy, and only through education could a nation become civilized.

The role of the government was to increase the population and spread it across deserted areas of the country, and to bring literacy to the masses so as to make them less barbaric.

What did Sarmiento mean by "civilization" and "barbarism"? The terms were not really his; he appropriated them from the jargon of various intellectual sources. "Civilization" was a buzzword in the eighteenth century, particularly in France, England, and Germany, where it was used by intellectuals like Samuel Johnson, Jean-Jacques Rousseau, and Alexander von Humboldt. During the Enlightenment it defined a level of civil and political sophistication that came as a result of centuries of accumulated knowledge—an ascent with reason as its banner. On the other hand, "barbarism," its roots in Aristotle but coined by Mirabeau, meant a descent in the opposite direction, and was synonymous with savagery, wildness, and even evil inclinations. For Sarmiento, the consummate Europeanized Latin American intellectual, these two words described a land torn by a divided loyalty: the desire to emulate Europe and the urge to pursue the unruly, chaotic behavior symbolized by the primitivism of the Americas.

He was obviously biased. He viewed the European colonization of the Americas as a worthy and much needed enterprise but was distressed that Spain, a primitive, barbarous nation, had been the one to conquer and establish viceroys in the River Plate. In his eyes Spain, "the backward daughter of Europe," had inflicted enormous ills in its colonies through the Catholic Church, especially through the Holy Inquisition, an absolutist, repressive religious institution. An altogether different story would have taken shape had the French, Dutch, or British settled in the Southern Hemisphere. And thus, a central query permeates Facundo: Is the República Argentina, known as Provincias Unidas del Río de la Plata when Sarmiento was a child, an ad hoc habitat to the highest forms of civilization? Is it forever doomed by virtue of its peripheral location, far from the centers of intellectual sophisticated in the Old Continent, and by its awkward Spanish heritage?

"The vast tract which occupies [the extremities of the Argentine Republic]," Sarmiento writes, "is altogether uninhabited, and possesses navigable rivers as yet unfurrowed even by a frail canoe." This leads him to conclude that "Its own extent is the evil from which [it] suffers." Vastness, then, is a sign of barbarism, for life in the fringes of society, on the edge, is unstable and uncouth. The antidote: immigration and urbanism. Immigration is only hinted at as a solution in *Facundo*, but as time went by, it became a leitmotif in Sarmiento's political career. Immigrants, especially those from "enlightened" European nations, are seeds of progress. They can make the countryside prosperous, slowly turning it into a landscape of cities. "Growing and expanding, we shall build, if we have not already built, a Tower of Babel in America, its workmen speaking all tongues, not blending them together in the task of construction," he once wrote. As a legislator in 1878, in spite of the opposition of the Catholic Church, he proposed laws favoring religious freedom and intermarriage. But his most audacious thesis was his endorsement in 1845 of the Argentine city as a conduit for civilization; anything beyond or outside it was barbaric. "[The] constant insecurity of life outside the towns," Sarmiento claims in *Facundo*, "stamps upon the Argentine character a certain stoical resignation to death by violence, which is regarded as one of the inevitable probabilities of existence. Perhaps this is the reason why they inflict death or submit to it with so much indifference, and why such events make no deep or lasting impression upon the survivors." The "they" is in sharp contrast to the "we" introduced by him a bit later on: "they" are the feudal criollos, owners of huge portions of Argentine countryside and of an archaic tradition, and also the gauchos, uncivilized dwellers on the fringes of civil behavior, instinctual and brute; "we" are the urbanites, rational ones, capable of assimilating European good manners. The dialectic brings to mind not only the chronicles of Spanish missionaries in Central and South America, but also the travel writing by European scientific explorers such as Humboldt about the "equinoctial regions" of the New Continent; it also invokes the language used during the explorations of the American Southwest and manifest in the novels of James Fenimore Cooper. This is as it should be, for *Facundo*, if anything, is the byproduct of a quintessential insider parading as outsider.

The book is roughly divided into three parts, all varying in quality and length. The first is concerned with the Argentine geography and its impact on the social and human scene, particularly on the gaucho, a social type in the pampas often described as an equivalent to the American cowboy. The second part is devoted to chronicling the upbringing and political and military adventures of Juan Facundo Quiroga, ending with his assassination in 1835, exactly a decade before the publication of *Facundo*. The third part, the shortest and one eliminated from the second and third editions of 1851 and 1868, is also the most overtly political: it focuses on Rosas's tyranny and offers some pragmatic views on the future of Argentina.

The first part, clear, vivid, and engaging and the most popular among readers, illustrates the tension between urban and rural life in Argentina in the context of the struggle between the country's pre-Columbian past and its present journey, across numerous obstacles, toward modernity. To illustrate this journey, Sarmiento elaborates a hierarchy, with the gaucho representing the most maladroit of social types. He describes four types of gauchos: the *rastreador* or track finder, the *baquiano* or pathfinder, the *gaucho malo* or outlaw, and the *cantor* or minstrel. His portraits are so inspired that generations of readers have excerpted these sections to highlight Sarmiento's talents as a *costumbrista*, an artist intoxicated by the beauty and contradictions of nature, human and otherwise. Still, his disapproval of the Argentine countryside comes through, for he simultaneously admires and condemns the gaucho, whom he sees as "independent of every want, under no control, with no notion of government, all regular and systematic order being wholly impossible among such people." (Allison Williams Bunkley, Sarmiento's English-language biographer, described him as "a lifelong enemy of *gauchocracy*.") And yet the gaucho is unique, a poet by ancestry, with an enduring musicality of spirit, a vessel of tradition, a knight courageous to the core, always carrying his guitar around as well as the knife he "inherited from the Spaniard." He is a hero unafraid of death, sovereign of his own destiny.

The gaucho is a national symbol deeply embedded in the fabric of Argentine culture and identity, and ubiquitious in literature, from the collection of vignettes *The Jewish Gauchos of the Pampas*, by Alberto Gerchunoff, to the contributions by Jorge Luis Borges, most memorably the short story "Biography of Tadeo Isidoro Cruz [1829–1854]," included in *The Aleph and Other Stories*; the essay "La poesía gauchesca," collected in *Discusión*; and the two-volume anthology *Poesía gauchesca*, edited with Adolfo Bioy Casares. The classics of the genre, though, are *Martín Fierro*, by poet Miguel Hernández, and its sequel, *La vuelta de Martín Fierro*; as well as the poetry of Bartolomé Hidalgo, Hilario Ascasubi, and Estanislao del Campo; the novels of Ricardo Güiraldes, Benito Lynch, and Eduardo Gutiérrez; and the nonfiction of William Henry Hudson, Paul Groussac, Leopoldo Lugones, and Ricardo Rojas. For the most part, this literature was produced by urban criollos who tended to romanticize the gaucho and have shaped what has come to be known as *la literatura gauchesca*. The concept is problematic and is different from *la literatura gaucha*: whereas the latter, as rudimentary as it might be, is a byproduct of the gaucho himself, the former is an appropriation by a remote observer, a nonparticipant often from the city and infatuated with gaucho ways. Curiously, *Facundo* is neither one nor the other, although in spirit it is surely closer to *la literatura gauchesca*. At the time of its writing, Sarmiento had neither been to the pampa nor had he ever spent time among the gauchos. His is a sociological description of gaucho manners, not an attempt to re-create gaucho folklore and mentality poetically. Even when Sarmiento does not address gaucho themes, the *gauchesco* strategy suits him well, for he fashions himself as an egocentric ethnographer, an objective observer; he turns the gaucho into an artifact—alien, exotic, and eradicable. (This ambiguity and his adopting the role of ethnographer might explain why *Martín Fierro*, and not *Facundo*, is considered by Argentines "the book closest to the nation's soul." Does this prove Sarmiento right? Has the country chosen barbarism over civilization?)

All this explains why the first part of *Facundo*, in spite of its magnificence, is also so controversial. Sarmiento's ambiguous feelings toward this archetype prevent him from endorsing the most radical of measures to assure civilization and progress: annihilation. As a socialist, he never falls into the trap of calling for the elimination of the gaucho, although he certainly portrays him as an obstacle in the road to progress. Nor does he hesitate to support the city, and not the country, as locus of reason and morality. Both Facundo and Rosas are gauchos, caudillos from the provinces; their predominance cannot but bring about a reign of terror. (In Sarmiento's argument, the military leader who represents civilization and urban culture is General José María Paz, and as such he is depicted in *Facundo* as a representative of the city, "in spirit a European soldier, even to the arms he used; he was an artillery officer, and therefore mathematical and scientific.")

Race, then, is at the core of Sarmiento's argument. He attributes Argentina's failure as a nation, says literary historian Nicolas Shumway, "to the inadequacy of the area's 'races,' " a term "used to connote culture as well as bloodlines." These races have intermingled through miscegenation, producing, in Sarmiento's eyes, a people "typified by love for idleness and incapacity for industry, except when education and the demands of a social position succeed in spurring it out of its customary crawl." Comments such as these are offensive to today's sensibilities, and perhaps even racist too. But they don't make Facundo the instrument of a fascist ideology. On the contrary, Sarmiento's trust in education as the road to civilization makes him a romantic, an idealist in the fullest sense of the word. It is useful to note that Argentina and Uruguay, on the banks of the River Plate, had almost a total absence of Indian population at the time of the Spanish colonization. This made for a whiter, more Europeanized social texture and a culture largely based on emigration from places like Italy and England. In Mexico, in comparison, the encounter between the Iberian conquistador and the native people resulted in what the philosopher and minister of education José Vasconcelos called *la raza de bronce*, the mestizo race. There, until the early twentieth century, for reasons not altogether different in scope, *el indio*, the Indian, assumed the role the gaucho had in Argentina: the parasite, an agent of retardation and savagery. (In 1883, five years before his death, Sarmiento, already a recognized thinker and statesman whose intellectual pursuits had pushed him to make broader, more daring reflections not only on Argentina but on the whole Hispanic Americas, would ponder the issue of *el indio* in his book *Conflictos y armonías de las razas en América*.) To move forward, the nation had either to marginalize the gaucho or else incorporate him into the modernization process. During the late nineteenth century and the dawn of the twentieth, *gauchesco* literature held an enormous appeal in Argentina, largely as a result of the nostalgia generated by modernity: the gaucho, it was recognized, had been pushed to the fringes, his tradition on the verge of extinction. *Facundo* is still at the early stages of this alienation; its author is not a victim of nostalgia, although, as time went by, the book clearly served as an instrument to justify the preponderance of European presence at the expense of autochthonous manifestations.

The first three chapters of *Facundo* are devoted to analyzing the gaucho scene. It is only in Chapter IV, as he addresses the revolution of 1810, a war largely fought in, for, and around the cities, that Sarmiento reaches his real subject matter. And with Chapter V, Juan Facundo Quiroga, known as *el tigre de los llanos*, the Tiger of the Plains, becomes the volume's true protagonist, as Sarmiento chronicles his life and military adventures—his rise and fall—in brilliant novelistic detail. Argentina in 1845 was sharply polarized between federalists and unitarians, one side believing in the autonomy of provincial life while the other favored a more centralized model of government. One side would have to predominate, Sarmiento felt, and determine the country's future. Pessimistically, he saw that Facundo Quiroga, a magnetic national symbol, carried too much weight in the collective psyche. Born in 1788 into a powerful family of La Rioja, Facundo had fought against the unitarian views of Bernardino Rivadavia. Shouting the slogan *"¡Religión o muerte!,"* he had wisely organized the peasantry and in 1826 triumphantly consolidated a bloc of provinces (Cuyo, La Rioja, Córdoba, Santiago de Estero), making himself a decisive political figure. He entered Buenos Aires in 1830 and after a series of treaties, defeated the unitarian forces led by Lamadrid in the *ciudadela* of Tucumán. But he then made a decisive allegiance with Rosas that brought about his demise. He was assassinated in an ambush in Barranca Yaco, at the age of fifty-seven, by, not surprisingly, "a gaucho-outlaw," one Santos Pérez. The cruel event, for Sarmiento a model of the type of barbarism that had also brought Facundo glory, is described vigorously in Chapter XIII. The protagonist, traveling to Córdoba in a carriage, has been notified in advance of a plot against his life. "The man is not born who will kill Quiroga," he replies. Notice how Sarmiento interconnects the opposing parties:

Daylight came at last, and the carriage started, accompanied by two postilions, one of whom was a mere lad and nephew of one of the company which lay in wait for them; two couriers who accidentally joined the party, and the negro who went on horseback. They soon reached the fatal spot, two discharges were fired into the carriage from each side of the road, but without wounding any one; then the soldiers rushing up sword in hand, disabled the horses in a moment, and cut to pieces the driver and couriers. Quiroga meanwhile put his head out of the window and said to the commander of the company, "What is all this?" His only answer was a ball through his head. Santos Pérez then passed his sword several times through the body, and when the butchery was completed, had the carriage filled with dead bodies, and dragged into the woods, with the murdered postilion still on his seat. The young lad alone was alive, and Pérez seeing him, asked who he was. His sergeant replied, that the boy was a nephew of his, and that he would answer for him with his life. Without a word, Pérez walked up to the sergeant, shot him through the heart, and then seizing the boy by the arm, threw him on the ground and cut his throat in spite of his childish cries for mercy.

Sarmiento's portrait of Facundo is not altogether negative: he idealizes his character's valor and decisiveness; but, most important, he uses historical details to enhance his own capabilities as a chronicler.

However, the statesman Juan Bautista Alberdi, a member of the Asociación de Mayo and Sarmiento's one-time friend and acerbic foe, described this section of *Facundo* as "a fable decked out as a document." He sharply criticized its pseudohistoriography, claiming it was based on tradition and popular legend, "which usually results in a history that is the product of vanity, a sort of *political mythology* with a political base." He discredited Sarmiento's authority as a biographer because of his sketchy research and careless, inconsistent approach to his subject and portrayed his style as formless and his persona as self-centered and exploitative. And he was not alone: Valentín Alsina, another prominent unitarian exile from the Asociación de Mayo, wrote a letter in Montevideo in 1846 to Sarmiento in an attempt to correct, in the form of fifty-one notes, the many errors and inexactitudes. (The letter is reproduced in the Biblioteca Ayacucho edition of 1977.) And indeed, Sarmiento, living in Santiago, far from his subject's immediate locale, narrated the life of Facundo out of memory and with the limited resources at his disposal. But neither Alberdi nor Alsina ever addressed the structural problems of the three sections of the book. The weakest criticism is leveled at the style, which the Spanish scholar Américo Castro once compared to Goya's *Caprichos* in its obsession with "horror in all its negative greatness." Though often rough, vague, even amorphous, Sarmiento's style is nevertheless energetic and skillful. (In this he calls to mind *Don Quixote*, for both Sarmiento and Cervantes are extraordinary fabulists but poor stylists.) The strongest criticism, on the other hand, and perhaps a more tangible one, is the one Alberdi directed toward Sarmiento's obsessive allegorizing: "To present Facundo Quiroga—one of the most wicked men in world history—as . . . the mirror image of the Argentine Republic, is the greatest insult flung at this good and honest nation. . . ." One may ask: Is Facundo really the archetype Sarmiento wants him to be? And is "the system of caudillos" truly the "fruit of the desert tree and the colonial past" in Argentina? My own answer to both questions is yes: like Melville's *Moby-Dick, Facundo* is a cosmic metaphor of good versus evil and human reason against chaos.

After the death of Facundo, Rosas, a *porteño* five years

younger than the Tiger of the Plains and a tyrant who first was governor of the province of Buenos Aires and later ruled Argentina for decades with an iron fist, becomes the central focus in *Facundo*. This is peculiar because throughout the whole book Rosas is an unequivocal presence, a topic that obsesses Sarmiento more than Facundo Quiroga, but which he refuses to address directly. So the question arises: why didn't Sarmiento write a biography of Rosas himself? Why use the subterfuge of a sit-in? The answer is that he was courageous but not a fool: Rosas's strength, as Sarmiento in his Chilean exile understood quite well, extended far beyond national boundaries; and so, while talking about him, he imposed a dose of self-censorship—but only a small dose, for his device is anything but cowardly. Rosas, in Sarmiento's view the ultimate caudillo, the quintessential *gaucho malo*, is the ghost on his shoulder, the everlasting enemy against whom he sets out to fight. Dethroned by Justo José de Urquiza in 1853, he died in England in 1877, exactly eleven years before Sarmiento. Fate had synchronized the chemistry of both men. Just as the name Rosas in Latin America is widely understood as a synonym of oppression in a way that only Paraguay's Gaspar Rodríguez de Francia and Chile's Augusto Pinochet would rival, so has the name Sarmiento been metamorphosed into a synonym for freedom and progress. Sarmiento himself could see that he and Rosas—author and subject—one day would come to personify the opposition between civilization and barbarism.

Their respective records speak for themselves. Rosas established a policy of protectionism in Argentina. He fought against France, accentuated the centralized role that Buenos Aires played in national politics, and endorsed the principle of self-determination of Latin American states. His success, of course, came at the expense of freedom, democracy, and human rights. Sarmiento, on the other hand, became known as an advocate of intellectual clarity and sophistication. Instinct and reason, primitivism and civilization—therein we see the authentic story of *Facundo*: neither a picture of Argentina, nor the life and death of Juan Facundo Quiroga, but an internal battle, the struggle of one single man, a cabalistic *Adam Kadmon*, with his doppelgänger. The passages devoted to Rosas in Chapters XIV and XV of the original edition are harsh: "Don Juan Manuel Rosas, before being a public man, had made his residence a sort of asylum for homicides without ever extending his protection to robbers," Sarmiento writes. And elsewhere, symptomatically, he states that Rosas "applied the knife of the gaucho to the culture of Buenos Aires, and destroyed the work of centuries—of civilization, law and liberty." On and on, Sarmiento's hatred pours out: Rosas's policies are treacherous; he has turned Buenos Aires into a "theater of blood," and polarized the Argentine citizenry. Salvation is to be found in the French quotation: man can be beheaded, ideas cannot; the written word, the book itself, is the best weapon against tyranny. But the reader cannot be fooled: these passages are about Sarmiento himself, whom Alberdi described as "a mythmaker," for he and Rosas, the emancipated and the inhuman, complement each other and are two sides of the same coin.

This is not to say, of course, that had the author of *Facundo* the power on his side, he would transform himself into another Rosas. Happily, power did not corrupt him. In fact, having traveled from the periphery as an exile to center stage as a minister of education, senator, governor of the province of San Juan, ambassador to the United States, and, ultimately, as president of Argentina between 1868 and 1874, Sarmiento's political mandate was about enlightenment. He was much concerned with alleviating the tension between the two opposing forces. He implemented and endorsed innovative pedagogical methods, consolidated Buenos Aires as a platform of progress and cosmopolitanism, and pushed Argentina toward more cultural, social, and economic openness. Alleviating, though, is the right word to describe his effort, for the tension between the opposing forces of civilization and barbarism is constant and inevitable: Argentina, for Sarmiento, was and always would be divided. Similarly, he and Rosas—or, as time goes on, whoever comes to represent them—will always struggle for control of the nation's psyche.

Like the French quotation around which the "Author's Notice" is built, Mary Mann's 1868 English translation of *Facundo* gives us a surprising opportunity to understand the book. During his first trip to the United States in 1847, a couple of years after the first Spanish edition was released, Sarmiento had been introduced to Horace Mann, the famed Massachusetts educator, by a mutual acquaintance. This trip, which took him to Spain, Majorca, Central Europe, and finally North America, had come about when the Chilean government, fearing that Sarmiento's activism against Rosas and his prestige among Argentine exiles would strain foreign relations between Chile and Argentina, sent him abroad. He seized the opportunity and went sightseeing, met an array of personalities, and kept notes that would eventually serve as the basis of a travelogue unlike any other produced by a Latin American up to that time, one that reads like both an echo of and a response to Humboldt. He met Horace Mann in East Newton; they talked about politics and pedagogy, with Mann's wife Mary as their interpreter, and the encounter proved fruitful. Sarmiento would apply many of Mann's ideas on education to the Argentine education system; and in 1867, years after his friend's death, he would edit and translate into Spanish the *Life of Horace Mann*. Mann was very fond of Sarmiento, but it was his wife, who admired Sarmiento tremendously and loved him in secret, who served as his liaison with the New England intelligentsia. On his second trip to the United States in 1866, she introduced him to Emerson, Longfellow, and Hawthorne, among other leading thinkers and writers of the day; and it was she, at his request, who embarked on a translation of parts of his autobiography *Recuerdos de provincia*, as well as of *Facundo*.

Their partnership is a classic case of unequal gender relations, an affair where the personal and the professional intertwine. The author came to depend on his translator and she nurtured his work and career as she worshiped him. Though courteous and gentlemanly, Sarmiento was always aware that through Mary Mann he could find success, a wider audience, and international prestige. Latin Americans knew as well then as they do today that only after success had been achieved in the United States would their fellow countrymen appreciate their endeavor, and Sarmiento, in using Mary Mann, took this truth to heart. He talked of her in religious terms: as a woman whose love "saved" him from treachery and disenchantment, as "my angel of yore!" and as an "incarnation of maternal love." In a letter to a third party, drafted in Boston in 1865, Sarmiento wrote: "She outdoes herself for me to help me and protect me. Her first question to anyone who approaches is 'Do you know the Argentine Minister?' and the eulogy begins." In return, Mary Mann treated him as a living legend. Her admiration was unqualified. "Be assured, my dear sir," she wrote him in 1866, "that one day your name will be the magic wand which will be working even after your ashes sleep among the remains of your ancestors." To a mutual acquaintance, she wrote:

You will be surprised when I confess to you that I am so presumptuous that I have undertaken to write the biography of our noble friend Mr. Sarmiento. I have been reading his *Voyages*, his book *Civilization and Barbarism*, his noble thoughts on *The Monitor*, *The Annals*, his great work *Popular Education* and I am dejected, as his compatriots have not yet said to him: "Take our hand and do with us what you believe we are capable of doing because your admirable intellectual work, your glories and the distinguished acts of your life give you the power to guide the legislation as well as the education of the people. . . ." As for intellectual culture I have never seen a more wonderful case than [his], for at a very early age, by himself he has transported himself to each pole of the earth and has understood the politics of nations and the exact reason for their culture and prosperity. What a pity that such a man should grow old! We would need to have him live a few generations to spread the wisdom he possesses.

"To me you are not a man, but a nation," she added in a sentence that outlived her and Sarmiento, and might be read not only as the motto of their friendship—he the idol, she the idolator—but also of the entire era. For Sarmiento, particularly after Mary Mann introduced him to an English-speaking audience, underwent the same type of allegorical metamorphosis he had applied to Facundo: he ceased to be a mortal and became an emblem.

Her translation of *Facundo* was done with meticulous care. She corresponded with him profusely to clarify details and vagueness, scattered footnotes throughout the book, and composed a preface and a 120-page biographical sketch of Sarmiento that might have been conceived as a cornerstone for a full-blown biography she would write one day. Since her knowledge of Argentine history and politics was insubstantial, she depended on him for advice and verification. But an author like Sarmiento, who admitted that he wrote impulsively and extravagantly, is hardly the best fact checker, which explains why the factual mistakes of the original reappear in the translation. More important, by the time Mary Mann embarked on the project—"a labor of love," as she described it once—Sarmiento was no longer the youthful agitator exiled in Chile but an established legislator, a man of power, widely known in

diplomatic and intellectual circles, on the road to becoming
Argentina's president. Indeed, her translation appeared the same
year the nation's Congreso Nacional elected him for the highest
office with a vote of 131 to 79. (He was sworn in on October 12, Columbus Day, a date known throughout the Hispanic
world as *El día de la raza*, the day of racial miscegenation.) This
change of stature and climate needed to be reflected in the
book in some way, particularly in an edition to be read by U.S.
government figures and political pundits. Therefore Sarmiento,
Mann, and their publisher, Hurd and Houghton, consciously
decided to stress certain elements while eclipsing others. Consciously, because Sarmiento, ready to reinvent himself, was fully
aware of what was lost and gained in the English translation.
The title page, for instance, was signed by "Domingo F. Sarmiento, L.L.D., Minister Plenipotentiary from the Argentine
Republic to the United States." Mann's preface stressed his
career as a rebel only as the foundation for his extraordinary
career as politician ready to fix all wrongs. She also explained
how *Facundo* came to be written, its early reception at home
and in France, and offered a microhistory of Argentina's political fortunes, from the founding of Buenos Aires in 1535 to
Sarmiento's "heroic" presidency. After detailing his military
and ideological ups and downs, the rancor within the ruling
elite, and the like, she writes: "The disastrous history of the last
few years has proved that he was in the right, and his countrymen, by the light of the conflagration of civil war, have at last
seen that he was their best guide, and the only prominent man
that has clearly mastered the situation. Their wild cry of agony
now summons him to their aid." A messianic antidote, with
Sarmiento as the one and only savior.

Also at issue was the title. *Facundo*, both Mary Mann and
her publisher believed, made reference to an obscure Argentine
figure no American could recognize; the title needed to be
more dramatic and topical. They kept *Civilization and Barbarism*

as a subtitle but sought something more enticing to precede it. The replacement, *Life in the Argentine Republic in the Days of the Tyrants*, did the job but also reconfigured the overall content: this, it short, was no longer a biography but a travel book of sorts, an exotic vista of a foreign land refined for an English-speaking audience. The caudillo Facundo Quiroga would be just a character in the costume drama of a banana republic struggling to become modern. The renaming serves two purposes: to recast Sarmiento as an extraordinary diplomat and writer; and to reinvent his book, emphasizing to American readers that knowledge of Hispanic civilization ought to be based on generalities and not on in-depth analysis.

To achieve this end, Sarmiento and his translator decided to release the English version in abridged form. Since the text was based on the third Spanish edition, the "Author's Notice" was eliminated. This meant excluding not only the comments on the various corrections suggested after the installments were published in *El Progreso* but also, and more meaningfully, Sarmiento's triumphant if symbolic revenge against Rosas's soldiers when he wrote the French quote on a wall in Zonza. Also, the English translation left out Chapters XIV and XV, entitled *"Gobierno unitario"* and *"Presente y pornevir"* respectively. The reason was simple: these sections offered a programmatic view of how Argentina should cure itself from the maladies that affect it, a component that the elder Sarmiento, now that his political career was well established, did not want to see in the volume. He wanted to be free to rule without being held accountable for youthful, utopian passions. Instead, Mann's text introduced a new Chapter XIV, a section from Sarmiento's biography of General Fray Félix Aldao which would clarify the link between the two gaucho leaders. And, at the translator's request, an appendix was added in the form of a letter on politics and education to a U.S. senator in which Sarmiento complains of the imminent disappearance of the national department of education. This last ingredient, in support of Horace Mann's concept of the "common school," displays the Argentine's remarkable talent for comparative if flawed political thinking: as the United States is just recovering from a bloody Civil War and mourning the death of Abraham Lincoln, Sarmiento takes the opportunity to recycle his concepts of barbarism and civilization to explain the struggle between the Union and the Confederacy. "The greatest antagonism between the Southern States and the Northern," he ventures to write, "has come, in my judgment, from the Southern following the same plan as that of ancient society in Europe and South America, and the Northern advancing in new and peculiar ways." For the country to move forward, he concludes, the North must prevail—not only with military might but through educational supremacy.

The book, in other words, was repackaged, rearranged so as to please an audience with little interest in but much pity for the complications of the Hispanic psyche. Diana Sorensen Goodrich, preeminently among other scholars, has researched the critical impact of Mann's English translation, particularly the way in which it was read as a south-of-the-border replica of the scenario that gave rise to the American Civil War. And indeed, rather than using the book as a touchstone to understand what novelist Arturo Uslar Pietri calls *"la otra América,"* the other America, reviewers applauded Sarmiento's adulation of the United States. *The Christian Examiner*, for example, described it as venerating "the glory, intelligence, and strength of this republic"; *The Nation*, intriguingly, compared the awkward gauchos "as a class, to Southern slaveholders"; and the *New Englander* claimed: ". . . nor can it be without advantage to us to see ourselves reflected in this mirror, and to get some oblique light cast upon our American civil liberty from the image set up on those South American plains." Sarmiento's biography of Juan Facundo Quiroga was now a hymn to *el coloso del Norte*, an explanation of what makes the United States victorious and Latin America so disgraceful and corrupt.

All of which makes Mary Mann's translation invaluable. It is both a manipulated rendition of Sarmiento's work as well as a rebirth. Her rhythmic prose and attention to detail are commendable, especially when one is aware of the silent yet fiery passion that palpitates behind its pages. When Ralph Waldo Emerson read the book, he purportedly said: "If I wrote thus for my public, I would be read." Should we blame Mann today for reinventing the original when it was Sarmiento himself who orchestrated the whole operation? Besides, isn't that what every translator does? A hundred and thirty years after its first appearance, her English-language *Facundo* is almost as important as the Spanish original, for it fostered Sarmiento's stature as a distinguished Latin American man of the pen and the sword, legitimizing his standing at home in Argentina and consolidating his posterity abroad. A less "adaptive," more integral translation would have portrayed Sarmiento as vengeful and uncongenial. Mann, savvy in public relations, helped him in a crucial battle: the conquest of world fame.

Her job, like that of all brilliant translators, is done invisibly, in the shadow. Today few even remember her name. Sarmiento gets all the credit. Not only did he turn a French quotation into the key to begin deciphering Hispanic culture on this side of the Atlantic, he also produced an excellent kaleidoscopic volume merging the boundaries of history, memory, and literature. To this day, Argentina celebrates its Teacher's Day on September 11, the day of Sarmiento's death. In schools across the nation, children sing the *"Himno a Sarmiento,"* recalling his struggle "with the pen, with the sword, with the word." His legacy is ubiquitious: his picture hangs in bureaucratic offices and is framed in stamps, paper currency, tourism advertisements, and on the covers of the scores of reprints of

Facundo. The view of Latin America as a wastebasket and re-cycling machine of plagiarized ideas begins with him, the true and only author of *"On ne tue point les idées."* Borges once described Facundo as "the most memorable character of [Argentine] literature." He is mistaken: our everlasting admiration ought to be placed in Sarmiento the falsifying genius, Sarmiento the ultimate chameleon. He, more than Facundo, is his own best creation.

Ilan Stavans

CHRONOLOGY

1811   Faustino Valentín Sarmiento is born in San Juan, Argentina, on February 15. (He will later adopt the name Domingo.) The country is in the midst of a war of independence.

1816   Sarmiento enrolls in the Escuela de la Patria. His father joins the army and travels to the Andes in the fight against Spain.

1825   Argentina breaks away from Spain. General Fray José Félix Aldao conquers Mendoza.

1826   Bernardino Rivadavia becomes Argentina's first president. A war between Argentina and Brazil is declared.

1827   Sarmiento works as a clerk in an aunt's store. He joins the
−28   army, quits and ends up in jail. Later on, he escapes to Chile. Juan Facundo Quiroga (1788–1835) emerges as a crucial political figure in Argentina, as the country makes peace with Brazil.

1829   Sarmiento lives in San Juan, where he translates into Spanish major works of French literature. Juan Manuel de Rosas (1793–1877) becomes governor of the Buenos Aires province.

1831   After a series of defeats, Quiroga conquers Mendoza, consolidating his power. Sarmiento seeks his second exile in Chile. He becomes the principal of a municipal school in Santa Rosa, where he applies a progressive pedagogical method.

1832   Sarmiento organizes another school. Emilia Faustina, his first daughter, is born. (Her mother's identity remains a mystery.) He travels to Valparaíso.

1833   He works as a miner in Copiapó, on the bank of the Copiapó River. England takes control of the Falkland Islands.

1834   Still in Copiapó, he writes a feuilleton with a plan to colonize the valley on the bank of the Colorado River with emigrants from San Juan and Mendoza.

1835   Quiroga is assassinated in Barranca Yaco. Rosas's military and political power goes unchallenged, persecuting many unitarians and military officers whom he characterizes as "traitors."

1836   Sarmiento returns to San Juan, where he organizes a theater troupe.

1837   Argentina gets ready for war against Bolivia. Sarmiento writes poetry.

1838   He organizes a library society and sends Juan Bautista Alberdi his poem "Canto a Zonda." France orchestrates a blockade of Buenos Aires.

1839   Sarmiento publishes *Prospecto de un establecimiento de educación para señoritas dirigido por D. Domingo F. Sarmiento.*

1840   Peace with France. A unitarian subversion takes place in Mendoza, followed by a countersubversion that threatens to put many unitarians in jail, Sarmiento among them. He travels to Chile. On his way out, Sarmiento writes his famous French misquote: *"On ne tue point des idées."*

1841   He sells books for a living, writes for the newspaper *El Mercurio,* and is on staff at *El Nacional.*

1842   He writes for *El Progreso*.

1843   He publishes *Mi defensa* and becomes a founding member of the Facultad de Filosofía y Humanidades of the Universidad de Chile. He proposes a series of spelling alterations to the Spanish language. In Santiago, he also founds a private school for rich children.

1845   His biographies *General Fray Félix Aldao* and *Civilización y barbarie: Vida de Don Facundo Quiroga* are published, first in newspaper installments and then in book form. Sarmiento becomes a friend of Esteban Echeverría, an important writer of the Asociación de Mayo and author of *The Slaughterhouse*.

1846   Sarmiento travels to Spain and Majorca.

1847   He visits Italy, Switzerland, Germany, and other European countries. He travels to Canada and the United States, where he meets Horace Mann in East Newton, Massachusetts. He also travels to Cuba, Panama, and Peru, then returns to Chile.

1848   He marries Betina Martínez Pastoriza and adopts her son, Dominguito.

1849   He publishes *Travels to Europe, Africa, and America* and *Educación popular*, the latter influenced by Horace Mann.

1850   He publishes *Argirópolis*, once again attacking the Rosas regime. In it he suggests establishing the capital of the "Provincias Unidas del Río de la Plata," as Argentina was known at the time, in a convenient port, an idea Brazil would adopt a century later in Brasília. But Sarmiento's proposal is considered ludicrous by his fellows and rejected. During the same year he also brings out his autobiography, *Recuerdos de provincia*.

1851   Back in Argentina, he is appointed public relations officer of the army.

1852   He returns to Chile. He publishes *Campaña del Ejército Grande* and becomes director of education. He also holds an acerbic debate with Alberdi that will continue for years.

1853   Rosas is defeated and seeks asylum in England. The French translation of *Facundo*, by A. Giraud, appears in Paris under the title *Civilisation et barbarie: Moeurs, coutumes, caractères des peuples argentins. Facundo Quiroga et Aldao.*

1854   Sarmiento returns to Argentina. He is imprisoned, and once again leaves for Chile.

1855   He returns to Buenos Aires and is elected senator.

1856   He creates thirty-six new schools and orchestrates the translation into Spanish of major works on such subjects as religion, grammar, and arithmetic.

1857   He holds a debate with poet José Mármol.

1861   Bartolomé Mitre becomes the president of Argentina.

1862   Sarmiento is named governor of his native province of San Juan. He fights against El Chacho Peñaloza, a leading military man about whom he will write a biography, considered to be the third installment of the trilogy *Civilización y barbarie* that includes *General Fray Félix Aldao* and *Facundo*.

1863   El Chacho is assassinated.

1864   Sarmiento is sent on a diplomatic mission to Chile and Peru. He becomes Argentina's ambassador to the United States and settles in Washington, D.C. He publishes *Ambas Américas* and *Vida de Abrán Lincoln*, among other books.

1865   Andrew Johnson, president of the United States, receives him in the White House. Sarmiento founds the newspaper *Ambas Américas*. Argentina, Brazil, and Uruguay battle Paraguay in the War of the Triple Alliance.

1866   His stepson Dominguito dies in the war against Paraguay. Sarmiento visits Mary Peabody Mann and is introduced to Emerson and Longfellow, among other U.S. writers and intellectuals.

1867   Sarmiento translates the *Life of Horace Mann* into Spanish. He travels to the International Exhibition in Paris and then visits New York, where he meets Ida Wickersham, with whom he has an affair and begins a long-lasting correspondence.

1868   Bartolomé Mitre invites Sarmiento to become minister of the interior and senator. He rejects the offer. Soon after, he is named president of the Argentina Republic by the Congreso Nacional in a vote of 131 to 79. Mary Mann's English translation appears in New York under the title *Life in the Argentine Republic in the Days of the Tyrants; or, Civilization and Barbarism*.

1869   The Allies occupy Asunción, Paraguay.

1874   Sarmiento leaves the presidency after an attempt on his life.

1875   He is appointed director of the schools of the Province of Buenos Aires. During the same year, he is wrongly accused of orchestrating the assassination of El Chacho.

1879   He runs unsuccessfully for the presidency.

1881   He is appointed general superintendent of Argentina's schools.

1883   *Conflictos y armonías en las razas en América* is published. Sarmiento travels to Montevideo.

1884   He visits Chile. His *Complete Works*, in fifty-two volumes plus an index, subsidized by the Argentine government, begin to appear in France and Argentina.

1885   He is defeated as candidate for governor of the San Juan province.

1886   He publishes *Vida de Dominguito*, a biography of his martyred stepson, and *Condición del extranjero en América*. An epidemic of cholera spreads throughout Argentina. Sarmiento is designated president of the relief operation.

1888   Domingo Faustino Sarmiento dies in Paraguay on September 11. He is buried in Buenos Aires.

SUGGESTIONS FOR FURTHER READING

The primary and secondary material on Domingo Faustino Sarmiento and his *Facundo* is extensive in Spanish, less so in English. This list is limited to important editions, scholarly studies, and literary essays. For a more complete bibliography, the reader should consult the notes and chronology of Nora Dottori and Silvia Zanetti in *Facundo: o, Civilización y barbarie* (Caracas: Biblioteca Ayacucho, 1977), as well as Horacio Jorge Becco's "Bibliografía de Sarmiento," in *Humanidades* XXXVII, 2 (1961): 119–44; Guillermo Ava's "Las ediciones de *Facundo*" in *Revista Iberoamericana* 23 (1958): 375–94; the bibliography in Allison Williams Bunkley's *The Life of Sarmiento* (Princeton: Princeton University Press, 1952); and Ricardo Rojas's *Bibliografía de Sarmiento* (Universidad Nacional de La Plata, 1911).

Academia Argentina de Letras. *Sarmiento: Centenario de su muerte*. Buenos Aires: Biblioteca de la Academia Argentina de Letras, 1988.

Alberdi, Juan Bautista. *Obras completas*. 8 vols. Buenos Aires: La Tribuna Nacional, 1886.

———. *Cartas quillotanas. Polémica con D.F. Sarmiento*. Buenos Aires: Claridad, 1922.

———. *La barbarie histórica de Sarmiento*. Buenos Aires: Pampa y Cielos, 1964.

———. *Facundo y su biógrafo: notas paras servir a un estudio*. Tucumán: Ediciones de Signo, 1988.

Altamirano, Carlos, with Beatríz Sarlo. *Ensayos argentinos: De Sarmiento a la vanguardia.* Buenos Aires: Centro Editor de América Latina, 1983.

Anderson Imbert, Enrique. *Genio y figura de Sarmiento.* Buenos Aires: Eudeba, 1967.

————. *Una aventura amorosa de Sarmiento.* Buenos Aires: Losada, 1968.

Ara, Guillermo. "Las ediciones de *Facundo*," *Revista Iberoamericana* 23 (1958): 375–94.

Arciniegas, Germán. "Sarmiento," *Revista Iberoamericana* 23 (1958): 395–416.

Barcos, Julio R. *El civilizador Sarmiento. Síntesis del pensamiento vivo.* Buenos Aires: Eds. Antonio Zamora, 1961.

Barisani, Blas. *En torno a Sarmiento.* Buenos Aires: Reina y Madre, 1955.

Barrenechea, Ana María, and Beatríz R. Lavandera. *Domingo Faustino Sarmiento.* Buenos Aires: Centro Editor de América Latina, 1967.

Bethell, Leslie, ed. *Argentina Since Independence.* New York and London: Cambridge University Press, 1993.

Borges, Jorge Luis. "Recuerdos de provincia" and "Facundo," in *Prólogos. Con un prólogo de prólogos.* Buenos Aires: Torres Agüero Editor, 1975.

Botana, Natalio R. *Domingo Faustino Sarmiento.* Buenos Aires: Fondo de Cultura Económica, 1996.

Bunge, Carlo Octavio. *Sarmiento.* Madrid: Espasa-Calpe, 1926.

Bunkley, Allison W., ed. *A Sarmiento Anthology.* Translated by Stuart Edgar Grummon. Princeton: Princeton University Press, 1948.

————. *The Life of Sarmiento*. Princeton: Princeton University Press, 1952.

Castro, Américo: "En torno al *Facundo* de Sarmiento," *Sur* VIII (1938): 26–34.

Correas, Edmundo. *Sarmiento and the United States*. Gainesville: University of Florida Press, 1961.

Crowley, Frances G. *Domingo Faustino Sarmiento*. New York: Twayne Publishers, 1972.

Fogelquist, James Donald. "Cooper y Sarmiento: el tema de la civilización y la barbarie," *Cuadernos americanos* 234 (1981): 95–112.

Gálvez, Manuel. *Vida de Sarmiento: el hombre de autoridad*. Buenos Aires: Emecé, 1945.

González Echevarría, Roberto. *Myth and Archive: A Theory of Latin American Narrative*. Cambridge and New York: Cambridge University Press, 1990.

————, and Enrique Pupo-Walker. *The Cambridge History of Latin American Literature*. 3 vols. Cambridge and New York: Cambridge University Press, 1996.

Halperín Donghi, Tulio. *El revisionismo histórico argentino*. Mexico: Siglo XXI, 1971.

————, ed. *Proyecto y construcción de una nación: Argentina 1846–1880*. Caracas: Biblioteca Ayacucho, 1980.

————, and Iván Jaksić, Gwen Kirkpatrick, and Francine Masiello, eds. *Sarmiento: Author of a Nation*. Berkeley: California University Press, 1994.

Henríquez Ureña, Pedro. "Perfil de Sarmiento," *Cuadernos americanos* XXIII, 5 (1945): 199–206.

Jitrik, Noé. *Muerte y resurrección de "Facundo."* Buenos Aires: Centro Editor de América Latina, 1968.

Jones, C.A. *Facundo*. London: Grant & Cutler, 1974.

Katra, William H. *Domingo Faustino Sarmiento: Public Writer* (Between 1839 and 1852). Tempe: Center for Latin American Studies, Arizona State University, 1985.

Ludmer, Josefina. *El género gauchesco. Un tratado sobre la patria*. Buenos Aires: Sudamericana, 1988.

Lugones, Leopoldo. *Historia de Sarmiento*. Buenos Aires: Ernesto Tornquist, 1911.

Martínez Estrada, Ezequiel. *Los invariantes históricos del Facundo*. Buenos Aires: Viau, 1947.

———. *Radiografía de la pampa*. Buenos Aires: Losada, 1957.

———. *Meditaciones sarmientinas*. Chile: Editorial Universitaria, 1968.

———. *Sarmiento*. Buenos Aires: Sudamericana, 1969.

Molloy, Sylvia. *At Face Value: Autobiographical Writing in Spanish America*. Cambridge and New York: Cambridge University Press, 1991.

Montt, Luis. *Homenaje a Sarmiento*. Santiago: Imprenta Gutemberg, 1888.

Ocampo, Victoria. "Con Sarmiento," *Sur* VIII (1938): 7–9.

Palcos, Alberto. *Sarmiento: la vida, la obra, el genio*. Buenos Aires: El Ateneo, 1938.

Paoli, Pedro de. *Facundo: Vida del Brigadier General Don Facundo Quiroga, víctima suprema de la impostura*. Belgrano and Buenos Aires: Ciordia and Rodríguez Editores, 1952.

Patton, Elda Clayton. *Sarmiento in the United States*. Evansville, Indiana: University of Evansville Press, 1976.

Peña, David. *Juan Facundo Quiroga*. Buenos Aires: Editorial Universitaria de Buenos Aires, 1968.

Peña de Matsushita, Marta E. *El impacto de la experiencia norteamericana en el pensamiento de Sarmiento*. Nagoya, Japan: Centro de Estudios de América Latina, University of Nanzan, 1989.

Picón Salas, Mariano. *Sarmiento, Lugones, Mallea*. Buenos Aires: Embajada de Venezuela, 1977.

Piglia, Ricardo. *Artificial Respiration*. Translated by Daniel Balderston. Durham and London: Duke University Press, 1994.

Ponce, Aníbal. *Sarmiento: Constructor de la nueva Argentina*. Buenos Aires: Editores Iglesias y Materia, 1950.

————. *La vejez de Sarmiento*. Buenos Aires: H. Mattera, 1951.

Prieto, Adolfo. *La literatura autobiográfica argentina*. Rosario: Editorial Biblioteca, 1968.

————. *El discurso criollista en la formación de la Argentina moderna*. Buenos Aires: Sudamericana, 1988.

Revista Iberoamericana 54, no. 143 (April–June 1988).

Rojas, Ricardo. *Sarmiento, el profeta de la Pampa*. Buenos Aires: Losada, 1945.

Romero, José Luis. *A History of Argentine Political Thought*. Introduction and translation by Thomas F. McGann. Stanford: Stanford University Press, 1963.

Sarmiento, Domingo Faustino. *Obras completas*. 52 volumes and an index. Compiled by Luis Montt and Augusto Belín Sarmiento. Paris, Belin, and Buenos Aires: Márquez, Zaragoza and Cía., 1884–1903.

————. *Conflictos y armonías de las razas en América*. Buenos Aires: La Cultura Argentina, 1915.

————. *Cartas de Sarmiento a la Señora María Mann*. Buenos Aires: Imprenta de la Universidad, 1936.

————. *Facundo: Civilización y barbarie. Vida de Don Facundo Quiroga* (1845). Editions in charge of: (1) Alberto Palcos (La Plata: Universidad Nacional de La Plata, 1938, revised edition, 1961); (2) Joaquín González (Buenos Aires: Rosso, 1939); (3) Delia S. Etcheverry (Buenos Aires: Ediciones Estrada, 1940); (4) Raúl Moglia (Buenos Aires: Ediciones Pauser, 1955); (5) Emma Susana Speratti Piñero (Mexico: Universidad Nacional Autónoma de México, 1957); (6) Raimundo Lazo (Mexico: Editorial Porrúa, 1966); (7) Benito Varela Jacome (Barcelona: Editorial Bruguera, 1969); (8) Roberto Yahni (Madrid: Alianza, 1970); (9) Pedro Henríquez Ureña (Buenos Aires: Losada, 1971); (10) Jorge Luis Borges (Buenos Aires: Librería "El Ateneo" Editorial, 1974); (11) Luis Ortega Galindo (Madrid: Editora Nacional, 1975); (12) Noé Jitrik (Caracas: Biblioteca Ayacucho, 1977). Translations: *Civilisation et barbarie: Moeurs, coutumes, caractères des peuples argentins. Facundo Quiroga et Aldao*, by A. Giraud (Paris: Arthus Bernard, 1853); *Life in the Argentine Republic in the Days of the Tyrants; or, Civilization and Barbarism*, by Mary Peabody Mann (New York: Hurd and Houghton, 1868); *Facundo o civilità e barbarie*, by F. Fontana de Phillippis Milano (1881). Small sections of *Facundo* in other English translations are also available: "Argentine Tracker," *Scholastic* XLIX (November 1945); and *Facundo*, Part 1, Chapters I–III, Part 2, Chapters II–IV and VI, and Part 3, Chapters I–II, *A Sarmiento Anthology*, edited by A.W. Bunkley (Princeton: Princeton University Press, 1948).

————. *Vida de Abrán Lincoln*. New York: Appleton, 1861; Buenos Aires: Editorial Alba, 1941.

————. *Recuerdos de provincia*. Pologue and notes by Jorge Luis Borges. Buenos Aires: Emecé, Colección El Navío, 1944; also, with prologue by Enrique Anderson Imbert. Buenos Aires: Editorial de Belgrano, 1981.

————. *Travels: A Selection.* Translated by Inés Muñoz. Washington, D.C.: Pan-American Union [Organization of American States], 1963; also, *Travels in the United States in 1847.* Translation and introductory essay by Michael Aaron Rockland. Princeton: Princeton University Press, 1970.

Scobie, James R. *Argentina: A City and a Nation.* New York: Oxford University Press, 1971.

Shumway, Nicolas. *The Invention of Argentina.* Berkeley: University of California Press, 1991.

Sommer, Doris. *Foundational Fictions: The National Romances of Latin America.* Berkeley: University of California Press, 1991.

Sorensen Goodrich, Diana. *Facundo and the Construction of Argentine Culture.* Austin: University of Texas Press, 1996.

Stavans, Ilan. *Art and Anger: Essays on Politics and the Imagination.* Albuquerque: University of New Mexico Press, 1996.

————. *The Oxford Book of Latin American Essays.* New York and Oxford: Oxford University Press, 1997.

Zalazar, Daniel E. *La evolución de las ideas de Domingo F. Sarmiento.* Somerville, N.J.: Spanish Literature in the U.S.A., 1986.

Zea, Leopoldo. "El proyecto de Sarmiento y su vigencia," *Cuadernos americanos* 13 (1988): 85–96.

A NOTE ON THE TEXT

This edition is based on the Hafner Press reprint of the first American edition of *Life in the Argentine Republic in the Days of the Tyrants; or, Civilization and Barbarism* (New York: Hurd and Houghton, 1868), translated into English by Mary Peabody Mann. A number of errata in the text have been corrected. Since the information in Mann's preface is all but outdated, it has been omitted, as have her biographical sketch of Sarmiento, made to a large extent of long juxtaposed quotes from *Recuerdos de provincia* and *Viajes por Europa, Africa y América* with very little connection to *Facundo*, and the appendixed letter from Sarmiento to Senator Sumner.

Mann based her text on the third Spanish edition: *Facundo: civilización i barbarie en las pampas arjentinas* (New York: A. Appleton y Compañía, 1868), which excluded the introduction and last two chapters of the first edition of 1845 and, in turn, included the section *Aldao y El Chacho, último caudillo de la montonera de los llanos. Episodio de 1863*. Mann's translation also excluded the introduction and last two chapters of the first Spanish edition, but replaced them with a different text listed as Chapter XIV: "Friar José Felix Aldao, Brigadier General and Governor." Today, the standard Spanish edition of *Facundo* is the one edited by Alberto Palcos (Universidad Nacional de La Plata, 1938), on which the authoritative critical edition of Noé Jitrik in Biblioteca Ayacucho (Venezuela, 1977) is based.

Finally, the author's notice from the 1845 edition has been translated, and appears as an appendix.

FACUNDO:

OR,

CIVILIZATION AND BARBARISM

CONTENTS

CHAPTER I.

CHAPTER II.

CHAPTER III.

CHAPTER IV.

CHAPTER V.

CHAPTER VI.

CHAPTER VII.

CHAPTER VIII.

CHAPTER IX.

CHAPTER X.

CHAPTER XI.

CHAPTER XII.

CHAPTER XIII.

Idea of Government
Rosas Governor of Buenos Ayres
Rosas and Facundo
Facundo at Buenos Ayres
Facundo's New Plans
Facundo's Secret Opposition to Rosas
Facundo's Presentiments
Facundo's Obstinacy
Facundo's Individuality
Facundo's Death
Santos Perez

CHAPTER XIV.

FRIAR JOSÉ FELIX ALDAO, BRIGADIER–GENERAL AND GOVERNOR.   206

Lieutenant José Aldao
The Catholic Party and Religion
Aldao Captain under San Martin
Aldao at Mendoza
The Aldao Triumvirate
Future Destiny of the Republic
Barcala, the Educated Slave
Facundo's Palace
Tablada
El Pilar
Aldao and Facundo
Petition of Mendoza
General Paz Lassoed
Card-playing
Rodriguez the Soldier
Brizuela
Acha
Rodeo del Medio
Aldao's Harem
Death of Aldao
What Mendoza gained from Aldao's Government

CHAPTER I

Physical Aspect of the Argentine Republic, and the Forms of Character, Habits, and Ideas Induced by It

The extent of the Pampas is so prodigious that they are bounded on the north by groves of palm-trees and on the south by eternal snows.

—HEAD

The Continent of America ends at the south in a point, with the Strait of Magellan at its southern extremity. Upon the west, the Chilian Andes run parallel to the coast at a short distance from the Pacific. Between that range of mountains and the Atlantic is a country whose boundary follows the River Plata up the course of the Uruguay into the interior, which was formerly known as the United Provinces of the River Plata, but where blood is still shed to determine whether its name shall be the Argentine Republic or the Argentine Confederation. On the north lie Paraguay, the Gran Chaco, and Bolivia, its assumed boundaries.

The vast tract which occupies its extremities is altogether uninhabited, and possesses navigable rivers as yet unfurrowed even by a frail canoe. Its own extent is the evil from which the Argentine Republic suffers; the desert encompasses it on every side and penetrates its very heart; wastes containing no human dwelling, are, generally speaking, the unmistakable boundaries between its several provinces. Immensity is the universal characteristic of the country: the plains, the woods, the rivers, are all immense; and the horizon is always undefined, always lost in haze and delicate vapors which forbid the eye to mark the point in the distant perspective, where the land ends and the sky begins. On the south and on the north are savages ever on the watch, who take advantage of the moonlight nights to fall like packs of hyenas upon the herds in their pastures, and upon the defenseless settlements. When the solitary caravan of wagons, as it sluggishly traverses the pampas, halts for a short period of rest, the men in charge of it, grouped around their scanty fire, turn their eyes mechanically toward the south upon the faintest whisper of the wind among the dry grass, and gaze into the deep darkness of the night, in search of the sinister visages of the savage horde, which, at any moment, approaching unperceived, may surprise them. If no sound reaches their ears, if their sight fails to pierce the gloomy veil which covers the silent wilderness, they direct their eyes, before entirely dismissing their apprehensions, to the ears of any horse standing within the firelight, to see if they are pricked up or turned carelessly backwards. Then they resume their interrupted conversation, or put into their mouths the half-scorched pieces of dried beef on which they subsist. When not fearful of the approach of the savage, the plainsman has equal cause to dread the keen eyes of the tiger, or the viper beneath his feet. This constant insecurity of life outside the towns, in my opinion, stamps upon the Argentine character a certain stoical resignation to death by violence, which is regarded as one of the inevitable probabilities of existence. Perhaps this is the reason why they inflict death or submit to it with so much indifference, and why such events make no deep or lasting impression upon the survivors.

The inhabited portion of this country—a country unusually favored by nature, and embracing all varieties of climates—may be divided into three sections possessing distinct characteristics, which cause differences of character among the inhabitants, growing out of the necessity of their adapting themselves to the physical conditions which surround them.

In the north, an extensive forest, reaching to the Chaco, covers with its impenetrable mass of boughs a space whose extent would seem incredible if there could be any marvel too great for the colossal types of Nature in America.

In the central zone, lying parallel to the former, the plain and the forest long contend with each other for the possession of the soil; the trees prevail for some distance, but gradually dwindle into stunted and thorny bushes, only reappearing in belts of forest along the banks of the streams, until finally in the south, the victory remains with the plain, which displays its smooth, velvet-like surface unbounded and unbroken. It is the image of the sea upon the land; the earth as it appears upon the map—the earth yet waiting for the command to bring forth every herb yielding seed after its kind. We may indicate, as a noteworthy feature in the configuration of this country, the aggregation of navigable rivers, which come together in the east, from all points of the horizon, to form the Plata by their union, and thus worthily to present their mighty tribute to the Ocean, which receives it, not without visible marks of disturbance and respect. But these immense canals, excavated by the careful hand of Nature, introduce no change into the national customs. The sons of the Spanish adventurers who colonized the country hate to travel by water, feeling themselves imprisoned when within the narrow limits of a boat or a pinnace. When their path is crossed by a great river, they strip themselves unconcernedly, prepare their horses for swimming, and plunging in, make for some island visible in the distance, where horse and horseman take breath, and by thus continuing their course from isle to isle, finally effect their crossing.

Thus is the greatest blessing which Providence bestows upon any people disdained by the Argentine gaucho, who regards it rather as an obstacle opposed to his movements, than as the most powerful means of facilitating them; thus the fountain of national growth, the origin of the early celebrity of Egypt, the cause of Holland's greatness, and of the rapid development of North America, the navigation of rivers, or the use of canals, remains a latent power, unappreciated by the inhabitants of the banks of the Bermejo, Pilcomayo, Paraná, and Paraguay. A few small vessels, manned by Italians and adventurers, sail up stream from the Plata, but after ascending a few leagues, even this navigation entirely ceases. The instinct of the sailor, which the Saxon colonists of the north possess in so high a degree, was not bestowed upon the Spaniard. Another spirit is needed to stir these arteries in which a nation's life-blood now lies stagnant. Of all these rivers which should bear civilization, power, and wealth, to the most hidden recesses of the continent, and make of Santa Fé, Entre Rios, Corrientes, Cordova, Salta, Tucuman, and Jujui, rich and populous states, the Plata alone, which at last unites them all, bestows its benefits upon the inhabitants of its banks. At its mouth stand two cities, Montevideo and Buenos Ayres, which at present reap alternately the advantages of their enviable position. Buenos Ayres is destined to be some day the most gigantic city of either America. Under a benignant climate, mistress of the navigation of a hundred rivers flowing past her feet, covering a vast area, and surrounded by inland provinces which know no other outlet for their products, she would ere now have become the Babylon of America, if the spirit of the Pampa had not breathed upon her, and left undeveloped the rich offerings which the rivers and provinces should unceasingly bring. She is the only city in the vast Argentine territory which is in communication with European nations; she alone can avail herself of the advantages of foreign commerce; she alone has power and revenue. Vainly have the provinces asked to receive through her, civilization, industry, and European population; a senseless colonial policy made her deaf to these cries. But the provinces had their revenge when they sent to her in Rosas the climax of their own barbarism.

Heavily enough have those who uttered it, paid for the saying, "The Argentine Republic ends at the Arroyo del Medio."

It now reaches from the Andes to the sea, while barbarism and violence have sunk Buenos Ayres below the level of the provinces. We ought not to complain of Buenos Ayres that she is great and will be greater, for this is her destiny. This would be to complain of Providence and call upon it to alter physical outlines. This being impossible, let us accept as well done what has been done by the Master's hand. Let us rather blame the ignorance of that brutal power which makes the gifts lavished by Nature upon an erring people of no avail for itself or for the provinces. Buenos Ayres, instead of sending to the interior, light, wealth, and prosperity, sends only chains, exterminating hordes, and petty subaltern tyrants. She, too, takes her revenge for the evil inflicted upon her by the provinces when they prepared for her a Rosas!

I have indicated the circumstance that the position of Buenos Ayres favors monopoly, in order to show that the configuration of the country so tends to centralization and consolidation, that even if Rosas had uttered his cry of "Confederation or Death!" in good faith, he would have ended with the consolidated system which is now established. Our desire, however, should be for union in civilization, and in liberty, while there has been given us only union in barbarism and in slavery. But a time will come when business will take its legitimate course. What it now concerns us to know is, that the progress of civilization must culminate only in Buenos Ayres; the pampa is a very bad medium of transmission and distribution through the provinces, and we are now about to see what is the result of this condition of things.

But above all the peculiarities of special portions of the country, there predominates one general, uniform, and constant character. Whether the soil is covered with the luxuriant and colossal vegetation of the tropics, or stunted, thorny, and unsightly shrubs bear witness to the scanty moisture which sustains them; or whether finally the pampa displays its open and monotonous level, the surface of the country is generally flat and unbroken—the mountain groups of San Luis and Cordova in the centre, and some projecting spurs of the Andes toward the north, being scarcely an interruption to this boundless continuity.

We have, in this fact, a new element calculated to consolidate the nation which is hereafter to occupy these great solitudes, for it is well known that mountains and other natural obstacles interposed between different districts, keep up the isolation and the primitive peculiarities of their inhabitants. North America is destined to be a federation, not so much because its first settlements were independent of each other, as on account of the length of its Atlantic coast, and the various routes to the interior afforded by the St. Lawrence in the north, the Mississippi in the south, and the immense system of canals in the centre. The Argentine Republic is "one and indivisible."

Many philosophers have also thought that plains prepare the way for despotism, just as mountains furnish strongholds for the struggles of liberty. The boundless plain which permits the unobstructed passage of large and weighty wagons by routes upon which the hand of man has only been required to cut away a few trees and thickets, and which extend from Salta to Buenos Ayres, and thence to Mendoza, a distance of more than seven hundred leagues, constitutes one of the most noteworthy features of the internal conformation of the Republic. The exertions of the individual, aided by what rude nature has done already, suffice to provide ways and means of communication; if art shall offer its assistance, if the forces of society shall attempt to supply the strength lacking in the individual, the colossal dimensions of the work will repel the most enterprising, and insufficiency of labor will be an obstacle. Thus in the matter of roads, untamed nature will long have control, and the action of civilization will continue weak and inoperative.

Moreover, these outstretched plains impart to the life of the interior a certain Asiatic coloring, which we may even call very decided. I have often mechanically saluted the moon, as it rose calmly and brightly, with these words of Volney in his description of the Ruins: "La pleine lune à l'Orient s'élévait sur un fond bleuâtre aux plaines rives de l'Euphrate." There is something in the wilds of the Argentine territory which brings to mind the wilds of Asia; the imagination discovers a likeness between the pampa and the plains lying between the Euphrates and the Tigris; some affinity between the lonely line of wagons which crosses our wastes, arriving at Buenos Ayres after a journey lasting for months, and the caravan of camels which takes its way toward Bagdad or Smyrna. The wagons which make such journeys among us, constitute, so to speak, squadrons of little barks, the crews of which have a peculiar dress, dialect, and set of customs, which distinguish them from their fellow-countrymen, just as the sailor differs from the landsman. The head of each party is a military leader, like the chief of an Asiatic caravan; this position can be filled only by a man of iron will, and daring to the verge of rashness, that he may hold in check the audacity and turbulence of the land pirates who are to be directed and ruled by himself alone, for no help can be summoned in the desert. On the least symptom of insubordination, the captain raises his iron *chicote*, and delivers upon the mutineer blows which make contusions and wounds; if the resistance is prolonged, before resorting to his pistols, the help of which he generally scorns, he leaps from his horse, grasps his formidable knife, and quickly reëstablishes his authority by his superior skill in handling it. If any one loses his life under such discipline, the leader is not answerable for the assassination, which is regarded as an exercise of legitimate authority.

From these characteristics arises in the life of the Argentine people the reign of brute force, the supremacy of the strongest, the absolute and irresponsible authority of rulers, the administration of justice without formalities or discussion. The caravan of wagons is provided, moreover, with one or two guns to each wagon, and sometimes the leading one has a small piece of artillery on a swivel. If the train is attacked by the savages, the wagons are tied together in a ring, and a successful resistance is almost always opposed to the blood-thirsty and rapacious plunder of the assailants. Defenseless droves of pack-mules often fall into the hands of these American Bedouins, and muleteers rarely escape with their lives. In these long journeys, the lower classes of the Argentine population acquire the habit of living far from society, of struggling singlehanded with nature, of disregarding privation, and of depending for protection against the dangers ever imminent upon no other resources than personal strength and skill.

The people who inhabit these extensive districts, belong to two different races, the Spanish and the native; the combinations of which form a series of imperceptible gradations. The pure Spanish race predominates in the rural districts of Cordova and San Luis, where it is common to meet young shepherdesses fair and rosy, and as beautiful as the belles of a capital could wish to be. In Santiago del Estero, the bulk of the rural population still speaks the Quichua dialect, which plainly shows its Indian origin. The country people of Corrientes use a very pretty Spanish dialect. "Dame, general, una chiripá," said his soldiers to Lavalle. The Andalusian soldier may still be recognized in the rural districts of Buenos Ayres; and in the city foreign surnames are the most numerous. The negro race, by this time nearly extinct (except in Buenos Ayres), has left, in its zambos and mulattoes, a link which connects civilized man with the denizen of the woods. This race mostly inhabiting cities, has a tendency to become civilized, and possesses talent and the finest instincts of progress.

With these reservations, a homogeneous whole has resulted from the fusion of the three above-named families. It is characterized by love of idleness and incapacity for industry, except when education and the exigencies of a social position succeed in spurring it out of its customary pace. To a great extent, this unfortunate result is owing to the incorporation of the native tribes, effected by the process of colonization. The American aborigines live in idleness, and show themselves incapable, even under compulsion, of hard and protracted labor. This suggested the idea of introducing negroes into America, which has produced such fatal results. But the Spanish race has not shown itself more energetic than the aborigines, when it has been left to its own instincts in the wilds of America. Pity and shame are excited by the comparison of one of the German or Scotch colonies in the southern part of Buenos Ayres and some towns of the interior of the Argentine Republic; in the former the cottages are painted, the front-yards always neatly kept and adorned with flowers and pretty shrubs; the furniture simple but complete; copper or tin utensils always bright and clean; nicely curtained beds; and the occupants of the dwelling are always industriously at work. Some such families have retired to enjoy the conveniences of city life, with great fortunes gained by their previous labors in milking their cows, and making butter and cheese. The town inhabited by natives of the country, presents a picture entirely the reverse. There, dirty and ragged children live, with a menagerie of dogs; there, men lie about in utter idleness; neglect and poverty prevail everywhere; a table and some baskets are the only furniture of wretched huts remarkable for their general aspect of barbarism and carelessness.

This wretched manner of life of a people already on the decrease, and belonging to the pastoral districts, doubtless gave rise to the words which spite and the humiliation of the English arms drew from Sir Walter Scott: "The vast plains of Buenos Ayres," he says, "are inhabited only by Christian savages

known as Guachos" (gauchos, he should have said), "whose
furniture is chiefly composed of horses' skulls, whose food
is raw beef and water, and whose favorite pastime is running horses to death. Unfortunately," adds the good foreigner,
"they prefer their national independence to our cottons and
muslins."★

It would be well to ask England to say at a venture how
many yards of linen and pieces of muslin she would give to
own these plains of Buenos Ayres!

Upon the boundless expanse above described stand scattered
here and there fourteen cities, each the capital of a province.
The obvious method of arranging their names would be to
classify them according to their geographical position: Buenos
Ayres, Santa Fé, Entre Rios, and Corrientes, on the banks of
the Paraná; Mendoza, San Juan, Rioja, Catamarca, Tucuman,
Salta, and Jujui, being on a line nearly parallel to the Chilian
Andes; with Santiago, San Luis, and Cordova, in the centre.
But this manner of enumerating the Argentine towns has no
connection with any of the social results which I have in view.
A classification adapted to my purpose must originate in the
ways of life pursued by the country people, for it is this which
determines their character and spirit. I have stated above that
the proximity of the rivers makes no difference in this respect,
because the extent to which they are navigated is so trifling as
to be without influence upon the people.

All the Argentine provinces, except San Juan and Mendoza,
depend on the products of pastoral life; Tucuman avails itself
of agriculture also, and Buenos Ayres, besides raising millions
of cattle and sheep, devotes itself to the numerous and diver-
sified occupations of civilized life.

The Argentine cities, like almost all the cities of South

★*Life of Napoleon Bonaparte*, vol. ii., chap. 1.

America, have an appearance of regularity. Their streets are laid out at right angles, and their population scattered over a wide surface, except in Cordova, which occupies a narrow and confined position, and presents all the appearance of a European city, the resemblance being increased by the multitude of towers and domes attached to its numerous and magnificent churches. All civilization, whether native, Spanish, or European, centres in the cities, where are to be found the manufactories, the shops, the schools and colleges, and other characteristics of civilized nations. Elegance of style, articles of luxury, dress-coats, and frock-coats, with other European garments, occupy their appropriate place in these towns. I mention these small matters designedly. It is sometimes the case that the only city of a pastoral province is its capital, and occasionally the land is uncultivated up to its very streets. The encircling desert besets such cities at a greater or less distance, and bears heavily upon them, and they are thus small oases of civilization surrounded by an untilled plain, hundreds of square miles in extent, the surface of which is but rarely interrupted by any settlement of consequence.

The cities of Buenos Ayres and Cordova have succeeded better than the others in establishing about them subordinate towns to serve as new foci of civilization and municipal interests; a fact which deserves notice. The inhabitants of the city wear the European dress, live in a civilized manner, and possess laws, ideas of progress, means of instruction, some municipal organization, regular forms of government, etc. Beyond the precincts of the city everything assumes a new aspect; the country people wear a different dress, which I will call South American, as it is common to all districts; their habits of life are different, their wants peculiar and limited. The people composing these two distinct forms of society, do not seem to belong to the same nation. Moreover, the countryman, far from attempting to imitate the customs of the city, rejects with disdain its luxury and refinement; and it is unsafe for the costume. of the city people, their coats, their cloaks, their saddles, or anything European, to show themselves in the country. Everything civilized which the city contains is blockaded there, proscribed beyond its limits; and any one who should dare to appear in the rural districts in a frock-coat, for example, or mounted on an English saddle, would bring ridicule and brutal assaults upon himself.

The whole remaining population inhabit the open country, which, whether wooded or destitute of the larger plants, is generally level, and almost everywhere occupied by pastures, in some places of such abundance and excellence, that the grass of an artificial meadow would not surpass them. Mendoza, and especially San Juan, are exceptions to this general absence of tilled fields, the people here depending chiefly on the products of agriculture. Everywhere else, pasturage being plenty, the means of subsistence of the inhabitants—for we cannot call it their occupation—is stock-raising. Pastoral life reminds us of the Asiatic plains, which imagination covers with Kalmuck, Cossack, or Arab tents. The primitive life of nations—a life essentially barbarous and unprogressive—the life of Abraham, which is that of the Bedouin of to-day, prevails in the Argentine plains, although modified in a peculiar manner by civilization. The Arab tribe which wanders through the wilds of Asia, is united under the rule of one of its elders or of a warrior chief; society exists, although not fixed in any determined locality. Its religious opinions, immemorial traditions, unchanging customs, and its sentiment of respect for the aged, make altogether a code of laws and a form of government which preserves morality, as it is there understood, as well as order and the association of the tribe. But progress is impossible, because there can be no progress without permanent possession of the soil, or without cities, which are the means of developing the capacity of man for the processes of industry, and which enable him to extend his acquisitions.

Nomad tribes do not exist in the Argentine plains; the stock-raiser is a proprietor, living upon his own land; but this condition renders association impossible, and tends to scatter separate families over an immense extent of surface. Imagine an expanse of two thousand square leagues, inhabited throughout, but where the dwellings are usually four or even eight leagues apart, and two leagues, at least, separate the nearest neighbors. The production of movable property is not impossible, the enjoyments of luxury are not wholly incompatible with this isolation; wealth can raise a superb edifice in the desert. But the incentive is wanting; no example is near; the inducements for making a great display which exist in a city, are not known in that isolation and solitude. Inevitable privations justify natural indolence; a dearth of all the amenities of life induces all the externals of barbarism. Society has altogether disappeared. There is but the isolated self-concentrated feudal family. Since there is no collected society, no government is possible; there is neither municipal nor executive power, and civil justice has no means of reaching criminals. I doubt if the modern world presents any other form of association so monstrous as this. It is the exact opposite of the Roman municipality, where all the population were assembled within an inclosed space, and went from it to cultivate the surrounding fields. The consequence of this was a strong social organization, the good results of which have prepared the way for modern civilization. The Argentine system resembles the old Slavonic Sloboda, with the difference that the latter was agricultural, and therefore more susceptible of government, while the dispersion of the population was not so great as in South America. It differs from the nomad tribes in admitting of no social reunion, and in a permanent occupation of the soil. Lastly, it has something in common with the feudal system of the Middle Ages, when the barons lived in their strongholds, and thence made war on the cities, and laid waste the country in the vicinity; but the baron and the feudal castle are wanting. If power starts up in the country, it lasts only for a moment, and is democratic; it is not inherited, nor can it maintain itself, for want of mountains and strong positions. It follows from this, that even the savage tribe of the pampas is better organized for moral development than are our country districts.

But the remarkable feature of this society, viewed in its social aspect, is its affinity to the life of the ancients—to the life of the Spartans or Romans; but again a radical dissimilarity appears when the subject is considered from another side. The free citizen of Sparta or of Rome threw upon his slaves the weight of material life, the care of providing for his subsistence, while he lived, free from such cares, in the forum or in the public place of assembly, exclusively occupied with the interests of the State—peace, war, and party contests. The stock-raiser has his share of the same advantages, and his herds fulfill the degrading office of the ancient Helot. Their spontaneous multiplication constitutes and indefinitely augments his fortune; the help of man is superfluous; his labor, his intelligence, his time, are not needed to the preservation and increase of the means of life. But though he needs none of these forces for the supply of his physical wants, he is unable to make use of them, when thus saved, as the Roman did. He has no city, no municipality, no intimate associations, and thus the basis of all social development is wanting. As the land-owners are not brought together, they have no public wants to satisfy; in a word, there is no *res publica*.

Moral progress, and the cultivation of the intellect, are here not only neglected, as in the Arab or Tartar tribe, but impossible. Where can a school be placed for the instruction of children living ten leagues apart in all directions? Thus, consequently, civilization can in no way be brought about. Barbarism is the normal condition,* and it is fortunate if domestic customs preserve a small germ of morality. Religion feels the consequences of this want of social organization. The offices of the pastor are nominal, the pulpit has no audience, the priest flees from the deserted chapel, or allows his character to deteriorate in inactivity and solitude. Vice, simony, and the prevalent barbarism penetrate his cell, and change his moral superiority into the means of gratifying his avarice or ambition, and he ends by becoming a party leader. I once witnessed a scene of rural life worthy of the primitive ages of the world, which preceded the institution of the priesthood. In 1838 I happened to be in the Sierra de San Luis, at the house of a proprietor whose two favorite occupations were saying prayers and gambling. He had built a chapel where he used to pray through the rosary on Sunday afternoons, to supply the want of a priest, and of the public divine service of which the place had been destitute for many years. It was a Homeric picture: the sun declining to the west; the sheep returning to the fold, and rending the air with their confused bleatings; the service conducted by the master of the house, a man of sixty, with a noble countenance, in which the pure European race was evident in the white skin, blue eyes, and wide and open forehead; while the responses were made by a dozen women and some young men, whose imperfectly broken horses were fastened near the door of the chapel. After finishing the rosary, he fervently offered up his own petitions. I never heard a voice fuller of pious feeling, nor a prayer of purer warmth, of firmer faith, of greater beauty, or better adapted to the circumstances, than that which he uttered. In this prayer he besought God to grant rain for the fields, fruitfulness for the herds and flocks, peace

---

*In 1826, during a year's residence at the Sierra de San Luis, I taught the art of reading to six young people of good families, the youngest of whom was twenty-two years old.

for the Republic, and safety for all wayfarers. I readily shed tears, and wept even with sobs, for the religious sentiment had been awakened in my soul to intensity, and like an unknown sensation, for I never witnessed a more religious scene. I seemed to be living in the times of Abraham, in his presence, in that of God, and of the nature which reveals Him. The voice of that sincere and pure-minded man made all my nerves vibrate, and penetrated to my inmost soul.

To this, that is, to natural religion, is all religion reduced in the pastoral districts. Christianity exists, like the Spanish idioms, as a tradition which is perpetuated, but corrupted; colored by gross superstitions and unaided by instruction, rites, or convictions. It is the case in almost all the districts which are remote from the cities, that when traders from San Juan or Mendoza arrive there, three or four children, some months or a year old, are presented to them for baptism, confidence being felt that their good education will enable them to administer the rite in a valid manner; and on the arrival of a priest, young men old enough to break a colt, present themselves to him to be anointed and have baptism *sub conditione* administered to them.

In the absence of all the means of civilization and progress, which can only be developed among men collected into societies of many individuals, the education of the country people is as follows: The women look after the house, get the meals ready, shear the sheep, milk the cows, make the cheese, and weave the coarse cloth used for garments. All domestic occupations are performed by women; on them rests the burden of all the labor, and it is an exceptional favor when some of the men undertake the cultivation of a little maize, bread not being in use as an ordinary article of diet. The boys exercise their strength and amuse themselves by gaining skill in the use of the lasso and the bolas, with which they constantly harass and pursue the calves and goats. When they can ride, which is as soon as they have learned to walk, they perform some small services on horseback. When they become stronger, they race over the country, falling off their horses and getting up again, tumbling on purpose into rabbit* burrows, scrambling over precipices, and practicing feats of horsemanship. On reaching puberty, they take to breaking wild colts, and death is the least penalty that awaits them if their strength or courage fails them for a moment. With early manhood comes complete independence and idleness.

Now begins the public life of the gaucho, as I may say, since his education is by this time at an end. These men, Spaniards only in their language and in the confused religious notions preserved among them, must be seen, before a right estimate can be made of the indomitable and haughty character which grows out of this struggle of isolated man with untamed nature, of the rational being with the brute. It is necessary to see their visages bristling with beards, their countenances as grave and serious as those of the Arabs of Asia, to appreciate the pitying scorn with which they look upon the sedentary denizen of the city, who may have read many books, but who cannot overthrow and slay a fierce bull, who could not provide himself with a horse from the pampas, who has never met a tiger alone, and received him with a dagger in one hand and a poncho rolled up in the other, to be thrust into the animal's mouth, while he transfixes his heart with his dagger.

This habit of triumphing over resistance, of constantly showing a superiority to Nature, of defying and subduing her, prodigiously develops the consciousness of individual consequence and superior prowess. The Argentine people of every class, civilized and ignorant alike, have a high opinion of their national importance. All the other people of South America throw this vanity of theirs in their teeth, and take offense at their presumption and arrogance. I believe the charge not to be wholly

* *Viscachas.*

unfounded, but I do not object to the trait. Alas, for the nation without faith in itself! Great things were not made for such a people. To what extent may not the independence of that part of America be due to the arrogance of these Argentine gauchos, who have never seen anything beneath the sun superior to themselves in wisdom or in power? The European is in their eyes the most contemptible of all men, for a horse gets the better of him in a couple of plunges.*

If the origin of this national vanity among the lower classes is despicable, it has none the less on that account some noble results; as the water of a river is no less pure for the mire and pollution of its sources. Implacable is the hatred which these people feel for men of refinement, whose garments, manners, and customs, they regard with invincible repugnance. Such is the material of the Argentine soldiery, and it may easily be imagined what valor and endurance in war are the consequences of the habits described above. We may add that these soldiers have been used to slaughtering cattle from their childhood, and that this act of necessary cruelty makes them familiar with bloodshed, and hardens their hearts against the groans of their victims.

Country life, then, has developed all the physical but none of the intellectual powers of the gaucho. His moral character is of the quality to be expected from his habit of triumphing over the obstacles and the forces of nature; it is strong, haughty, and energetic. Without instruction, and indeed without need of any, without means of support as without wants, he is happy in the midst of his poverty and privations, which are not such to one who never knew nor wished for greater pleasures than

---

*General Mansilla said, in a public meeting during the French blockade, "What have we to apprehend from those Europeans, who are not equal to one night's gallop?" and the vast plebeian audience drowned the speaker's voice with thunders of applause.

are his already. Thus if the disorganization of society among the gauchos deeply implants barbarism in their natures, through the impossibility and uselessness of moral and intellectual education, it has, too, its attractive side to him. The gaucho does not labor; he finds his food and raiment ready to his hand. If he is a proprietor, his own flocks yield him both; if he possesses nothing himself, he finds them in the house of a patron or a relation. The necessary care of the herds is reduced to excursions and pleasure parties; the branding, which is like the harvesting of farmers, is a festival, the arrival of which is received with transports of joy, being the occasion of the assembling of all the men for twenty leagues around, and the opportunity for displaying incredible skill with the lasso. The gaucho arrives at the spot on his best steed, riding at a slow and measured pace; he halts at a little distance and puts his leg over his horse's neck to enjoy the sight leisurely. If enthusiasm seizes him, he slowly dismounts, uncoils his lasso, and flings it at some bull, passing like a flash of lightning forty paces from him; he catches him by one hoof, as he intended, and quietly coils his leather cord again.

CHAPTER II

Originality and Peculiarities
of the Argentine People

*Ainsi que l' ocean, les Steppes remplessent
l'esprit du sentiment de l'infini.*
—HUMBOLDT

*Like the ocean, the Pampas fill the mind
with the impression of the infinite.*
—HUMBOLDT

If from the conditions of pastoral life, such as colonization and neglect have constituted it, rise serious obstacles in the way of creating any political organization, and much more for the introduction of European civilization and institutions, as well as their natural results, wealth, and liberty, it cannot be denied, on the other hand, that this state of things has its poetic side, and possesses aspects worthy of the pen of the romancer. If any form of national literature shall appear in these new American societies, it must result from the description of the mighty scenes of nature, and still more from the illustration of the struggle between European civilization and native barbarism, between mind and matter—a struggle of imposing magnitude in South America, and which suggests scenes so peculiar, so characteristic, and so far outside the circle of ideas in which the European mind has been educated, that their dramatic relations would be unrecognized machinery, except in the country in which they are found.

The only North American novelist who has gained a European reputation is Fenimore Cooper, and he succeeded in doing so by removing the scene of the events he described from the settled portion of the country to the border land between civilized life and that of the savage, the theatre of the war for the possession of the soil waged against each other, by the native tribes and the Saxon race.

It was in this manner that our young poet Echevarria succeeded in attracting the attention of the literary world of Spain by his poem entitled "The Captive." The subjects of "Dido and Argea" which his predecessors the Varelas had treated with classic art and poetic fire, but without success and ineffectively, because they added nothing to the stock of European ideas, were abandoned by this Argentine bard, who turned his eyes to the desert. In its immeasurable and boundless spaces, in its wastes traversed by wandering savages, in the distant belt of flame which the traveller sees approaching when a fire has broken out upon the plains, he found the inspiration derived by the imagination from the sight of such natural scenery as is solemn, imposing, unusual, and mysterious; and from this the echo of his verses resounded, and was applauded even in the Spanish Peninsula.

A fact which explains many of the social phenomena of nations deserves a passing notice. The natural peculiarities of any region give rise to customs and practices of a corresponding peculiarity, so that where the same circumstances reappear, we find the same means of controlling them invented by different nations. Thus, in my opinion, is to be explained the use of bows and arrows among all savage nations, whatever may be their race, their origin, and their geographical position. When I came to the passage in Cooper's "Last of the Mohicans," where Hawkeye and Uncas lose the trail of the Mingos in a brook, I said to myself: "They will dam up the brook." When the trapper in "The Prairie" waits in irresolute anxiety while the fire is threatening him and his companions, an Argentine would have recommended the same plan which the trapper finally proposes,—that of clearing a space for immediate pro-

tection, and setting a new fire, so as to be able to retire upon
the ground over which it had passed beyond the reach of the
approaching flames. Such is the practice of those who cross the
pampa when they are in danger from fires in the grass.

When the fugitives in "The Prairie" arrive at a river, and
Cooper describes the mysterious way in which the Pawnee
gathers together the buffalo's hide, "he is making a *pelota*," said
I to myself,—"it is a pity there is no woman to tow it,"—for
among us it is the women who tow *pelotas* across rivers with
lassos held between their teeth. The way in which a buffalo's
head is roasted in the desert is the same which we use for
cooking★ a cow's head or a loin of veal. I omit many other
facts which prove the truth that analogies in the soil bring with
them analogous customs, resources, and expedients. This explains our finding in Cooper's works accounts of practices and
customs which seem plagiarized from the pampa; thus, too, we
find reproduced among American herdsmen, the serious countenance, the hospitality, and the very garments of the Arab.

The country consequently derives a fund of poetry from its
natural circumstances and the special customs resulting from
them. To arouse the poetic sense (which, like religious feeling,
is a faculty of the human mind), we need the sight of beauty,
of terrible power, of immensity of extent, of something vague
and incomprehensible; for the fables of the imagination, the
ideal world, begin only where the actual and the commonplace end.

Now, I inquire, what impressions must be made upon the
inhabitant of the Argentine Republic by the simple act of fixing
his eyes upon the horizon, and seeing nothing?—for the deeper
his gaze sinks into that shifting, hazy, undefined horizon, the
further it withdraws from him, the more it fascinates and con-
fuses him, and plunges him in contemplation and doubt. What

★*Batear.*

is the end of that world which he vainly seeks to penetrate? He knows not! What is there beyond what he sees? The wilderness, danger, the savage, death! Here is poetry already; he who moves among such scenes is assailed by fantastic doubts and fears, by dreams which possess his waking hours.

Hence it follows that the disposition and nature of the Argentine people are poetic. How can such feelings fail to exist, when a black storm-cloud rises, no one knows whence, in the midst of a calm, pleasant afternoon, and spreads over the sky before a word can be uttered? The traveller shudders as the crashing thunder announces the tempest, and holds his breath in the fear of bringing upon himself one of the thousand bolts which flash around him. The light is followed by thick darkness; death is on every side; a fearful and irresistible power has instantaneously driven the soul back upon itself, and made it feel its nothingness in the midst of angry nature; made it feel God himself in the terrible magnificence of his works. What more coloring could the brush of fancy need? Masses of darkness which obscure the sun; masses of tremulous livid light which shine through the darkness for an instant and bring to view far distant portions of the pampa, across which suddenly dart vivid lightnings, symbols of irresistible power. These images must remain deeply engraved on the soul. When the storm passes by, it leaves the gaucho sad, thoughtful, and serious, and the alternation of light and darkness continues in his imagination, as the disk of the sun long remains upon the retina after we have been looking at it fixedly.

Ask the gaucho, "Whom does the lightning prefer to kill?" and he will lead you into a world of moral and religious fancies, mingled with ill-understood facts of nature, and with superstitious and vulgar traditions. We may add that if it is certain that the electric fluid enters into the economy of human life and is the same as the so-called nervous fluid, the excitement of which rouses the passions and kindles enthusiasm, imaginative exertion ought to be well suited to the temper of a people living under an atmosphere so highly charged with electricity that one's clothes sparkle when rubbed, like a cat's fur stroked the wrong way.

How can he be otherwise than a poet who witnesses these impressive scenes?

> *Jira en vano, reconcentra*
> *Su inmensidad, i no encuentra*
> *La vista en su vivo anhelo*
> *Dó fijar su fugaz vuelo,*
> *Como el pájaro en la mar.*
> *Doquier campo i heredades*
> *Del ave i bruto guaridas;*
> *Doquier cielo i soledades*
> *De Dios solo conocidas,*
> *Que él solo puede sondear.*
> —Echevarría

Or he who thus sees Nature in her gala dress?

> *De las entrañas de América*
> *Dos raudales se desatan;*
> *El Paraná, faz de perlas,*
> *I el Uruguai, faz de nácar.*
> *Los dos entre bosques corren*
> *O entre floridas barrancas,*
> *Como dos grandes espejos*
> *Entre marcos de esmeraldas.*
> *Salúdanlos en su paso*
> *La melancólica pava,*
> *El picaflor i jilguero,*
> *El zorzal i la torcaza.*
> *Como ante reyes se inclinan*
> *Ante ellos seibos i palmas,*
> *I le arrojan flor del aire,*

Aroma i flor de naranja.
Luego en el Guazú se encuentran
I reuniendo sus aguas,
Mezclando nácar i perlas,
Se derraman en el Plata.
                    —Dominguez

But this is cultivated poetry, the poetry of the city. There is another poetry which echoes over the solitary plains—the popular, natural, and irregular poetry of the gaucho.

Music, too, is found among our people. It is a national taste recognized by all our neighbors. When an Argentine is first introduced to a Chilian family, they at once invite him to the piano, or hand him a guitar, and if he excuses himself on the ground that he does not know how to play, they express wonder and incredulity, saying, "An Argentine, and not understand music!" This general supposition bears witness to our national habits. It is the fact, that the young city people of the better classes, play the piano, flute, violin, or guitar; the half-breeds devote themselves almost wholly to music, and many skillful composers and players have sprung up among them. Guitars are constantly heard at the shop-doors on summer evenings; and late in the night, one's sleep is pleasantly disturbed by serenades and peripatetic concerts.

The country people have songs peculiar to themselves. The "Triste," prevalent among the people of the northern districts, is a fugue melody expressive of lamentation, such as Rousseau considers natural to man in his primitive state of barbarism.

The "Vidalita" is a popular song with a chorus, accompanied by the guitar and tabor, in the refrain of which the bystanders join, and the number and volume of the voices increase. I suppose this melody originated with the aborigines, for I once heard it at an Indian festival at Copiapo, held to celebrate Candlemas. As a religious song it must be very old, and the Indians of Chili can hardly have adopted it from the Spaniards of the Argentine Republic.

The "Vidalita" is the popular measure for songs about the topics of the day, or for warlike odes; the gauchos compose the words which they sing, and trust to the associations which the song arouses, to make them understood by the people. Thus, then, amidst the rudeness of the national customs, two arts which embellish civilized life and give vent to many generous passions, are honored and favored, even by the lowest classes, who exercise their uncultured genius in lyrical and poetic composition.

In 1840, Echevarria, then a young man, lived some months in the country, where the fame of his verses upon the pampa had already preceded him; the gauchos surrounded him with respect and affection, and when a new-comer showed symptoms of the scorn he felt for the little minstrel,* some one whispered, "He is a poet," and that word dispelled every prejudice.

It is well known that the guitar is the popular instrument of the Spanish race; it is also common in South America. The *majo* or troubadour, the type of a large class of Spaniards, is still found there, and in Buenos Ayres especially. He is discoverable in the gaucho of the country, and in the townsman of the same class. The *cielito*, the dance of the pampas, is animated by the same spirit as the Spanish *jaleo*, the dance of Andalusia; the dancer makes castañets of his fingers; all his movements disclose the *majo;* the action of his shoulders, his gestures, all his ways, from that in which he puts on his hat, to his style of spitting through his teeth, all are of the pure Andalusian type.

From these general customs and tastes are developed remarkable peculiarities, which will hereafter embellish the national dramas and romances, and give them an original shade

---

*Cajeteija, little musical box.

of color. I propose at present only to notice a few of these special developments, in order to complete the idea of the customs of the country, and so to explain subsequently the nature, causes, and effects of its civil wars.

THE RASTREADOR

The most conspicuous and extraordinary of the occupations to be described, is that of the Rastreador, or track-finder. All the gauchos of the interior are Rastreadores. In such extensive plains, where paths and lines of travel cross each other in all directions, and where the pastures in which the herds feed are unfenced, it is necessary often to follow the tracks of an animal, and to distinguish them among a thousand others, and to know whether it was going at an easy or a rapid pace, at liberty or led, laden or carrying no weight.

This is a generally understood branch of household knowledge. I once happened to turn out of a by-way into the Buenos Ayres road, and my guide, following the usual practice, cast a look at the ground. "There was a very nice little Moorish mule in that train," said he, directly. "D. N. Zapata's it was—she is good for the saddle, and it is very plain she was saddled this time; they went by yesterday." The man was travelling from the Sierra de San Luis, while the train had passed on its way from Buenos Ayres, and it was a year since he had seen the Moorish mule, whose track was mixed up with those of a whole train in a path two feet wide. And this seemingly incredible tale only illustrates the common degree of skill;—the guide was a mere herdsman, and no professional Rastreador.

The Rastreador proper is a grave, circumspect personage, whose declarations are considered conclusive evidence in the inferior courts. Consciousness of the knowledge he possesses, gives him a certain reserved and mysterious dignity. Every one treats him with respect; the poor man because he fears to offend one who might injure him by a slander or an accusation; and the proprietor because of the possible value of his testimony. A theft has been committed during the night; no one knows anything of it; the victims of it hasten to look for one of the robber's footprints, and on finding it, they cover it with something to keep the wind from disturbing it. They then send for the Rastreador, who detects the track and follows it, only occasionally looking at the ground as if his eyes saw in full relief the footsteps invisible to others. He follows the course of the streets, crosses gardens, enters a house, and pointing to a man whom he finds there, says, coldly, "That is he!" The crime is proved, and the criminal seldom denies the charge. In his estimation, even more than in that of the judge, the Rastreador's deposition is a positive demonstration; it would be ridiculous and absurd to dispute it. The culprit accordingly yields to a witness whom he regards as the finger of God pointing him out. I have had some acquaintance myself with Calibar, who has practiced his profession for forty consecutive years in one province. He is now about eighty years old, and of venerable and dignified appearance, though bowed down by age. When his fabulous reputation is mentioned to him, he replies, "I am good for nothing now; there are the boys." The "boys," who have studied under so famous a master, are his sons. The story is that his best horse-trappings were once stolen while he was absent on a journey to Buenos Ayres. His wife covered one of the thief's footprints with a tray. Two months afterwards Calibar returned, looked at the footprint, which by that time had become blurred, and could not have been made out by other eyes, after which he spoke no more of the circumstance. A year and a half later, Calibar might have been seen walking through a street in the outskirts of the town with his eyes on the ground. He turned into a house, where he found his trappings, by that time blackened by use and nearly worn out. He had come upon the trail of the thief nearly two years after the robbery.

In 1830, a criminal under sentence of death having escaped from prison, Calibar was employed to search for him. The unhappy man, aware that he would be tracked, had taken all the precautions suggested to him by the image of the scaffold, but they were taken in vain. Perhaps they only assured his destruction; for as Calibar's reputation was hazarded, his jealous self-esteem made him ardent in accomplishing a task which would demonstrate the wonderful sharpness of his sight, though it insured the destruction of another man. The fugitive had left as few traces as the nature of the ground would permit; he had crossed whole squares on tiptoe; afterwards he had leaped upon low walls; he had turned back after crossing one place; but Calibar followed without losing the trail. If he missed the way for a moment, he found it again, exclaiming, "Where are you?" Finally, the trail entered a water-course in the suburbs, in which the fugitive had sought to elude the Rastreador. In vain! Calibar went along the bank without uneasiness or hesitation. At last he stops, examines some plants, and says, "He came out here; there are no footprints, but these drops of water on the herbage are the sign!" On coming to a vineyard, Calibar reconnoitered the mud walls around it, and said, "He is in there." The party of soldiers looked till they were tired, and came back to report the failure of the search. "He has not come out," was the only answer of the Rastreador, who would not even take the trouble to make a second investigation. In fact, he had not come out, but he was taken and executed the next day.

In 1831, some political prisoners were planning an escape; all was ready, and outside help had been secured. On the point of making the attempt, "What shall be done about Calibar?" said one. "To be sure, Calibar!" said the others, in dismay. Their relations prevailed upon Calibar to be ill for four full days after the escape, which was thus without difficulty effected.

What a mystery is this of the Rastreador! What microscopic

power is developed in the visual organs of these men! How sublime a creature is that which God made in his image and likeness!

THE BAQUEANO, OR PATH-FINDER

Next to the Rastreador comes the Baqueano, a personage of distinction, and one who controls the fate of individuals and of provinces. The Baqueano is a grave and reserved gaucho, who knows every span of twenty thousand square leagues of plain, wood, and mountain! He is the most thorough topographer, the only map which a general consults in directing the movements of his campaign. The Baqueano is always at his side. Modest and mute as a garden-wall, he is in possession of every secret of the campaign; the fate of the army, the issue of a battle, the conquest of a province, all depend upon him. The Baqueano almost always discharges his duty with fidelity, but the general does not place full confidence in him.

Conceive the situation of a commander condemned to be attended by a traitor, from whom he has to obtain the information without which he cannot succeed. A Baqueano finds a little path crossing the road which he is following; he knows to what distant watering-place it leads. If he finds a thousand such paths, some of them even a hundred leagues apart, he is acquainted with each, and knows whence it comes and whither it goes. He knows the hidden fords of a hundred rivers and streams, above or below the ordinary places of crossing. He can point out a convenient path through a hundred distinct and extensive swamps.

In the deepest darkness of the night, surrounded by boundless plains or by forests, while his companions are astray and at a loss, he rides round them inspecting the trees; if there are none, he dismounts and stoops to examine the shrubs, and satisfies himself of his points of compass. He then mounts, and reassures his party by saying, "We are in a straight line from such a place, so many leagues from the houses; we must travel southwards." And he sets out in the direction he has indicated, without uneasiness, without hurrying to confirm his judgment by arriving at the town, and without answering the objections suggested to the others by fear or bewilderment.

If even this is insufficient, or if he finds himself upon the pampa in impenetrable darkness, he pulls up herbs from different places, smells their roots and the earth about them, chews their foliage, and by often repeating this proceeding, assures himself of the neighborhood of some lake or stream, either of salt or of fresh water, of which he avails himself, upon finding it, to set himself exactly right. It is said that General Rosas knows the pasturage of every estate in the south of Buenos Ayres by its taste.

If the Baqueano belongs to the pampa, where no roads exist, and a traveller asks him to show the way straight to a place fifty leagues off, he pauses a moment, reconnoitres the horizon, examines the ground, fixes his eyes upon some point, and gallops off straight as an arrow, until he changes his course for reasons known only to himself, and keeps up his gallop day and night till he arrives at the place named.

The Baqueano also announces the approach of the enemy; that is, that they are within ten leagues; and he also detects the direction in which they are approaching by means of the movements of the ostriches, deer, and guanacos, which fly in certain directions. At shorter distances he notices the clouds of dust, and estimates the number of the hostile force by their density. "They have two thousand men," he says; "five hundred," "two hundred;" and the commander acts upon this assumption, which is almost always infallible. If the condors and crows are wheeling in circles through the air, he can tell whether there are troops hidden thereabouts, or whether a recently abandoned camp, or simply a dead animal is the attractive object. The

Baqueano knows how far one place is from another, the number of days and hours which the journey requires, and besides, some unknown by-way through which the passage may be made in half the time, so as to end in a surprise; and expeditions for the surprise of towns fifty leagues away are thus undertaken, and generally with success, by parties of peasants. This may be thought an exaggeration. No! General Rivera, of the Banda Oriental, is a simple Baqueano, who knows every tree that grows anywhere in the Republic of Uruguay. The Brazilians would not have occupied that country if he had not aided them; nor, but for him, would the Argentines have set it free.

This man, at once general and Baqueano, overpowered Oribe, who was supported by Rosas, after a contest of three years; and at the present day, were he in the field against it, the whole power of Buenos Ayres, with its numerous armies, which are spread all over Uruguay, might gradually fade away by means of a surprise to-day, by a post cut off to-morrow, by some victory which he could turn to his own advantage by his knowledge of some route to the enemy's rear, or by some other unnoticed or trifling circumstance.

General Rivera began his study of the ground in 1804, when making war upon the government as an outlaw; afterwards he waged war upon the outlaws as a government officer; next, upon the king as a patriot; and later upon the patriots as a peasant; upon the Argentines as a Brazilian chieftain; and upon the Brazilians, as an Argentine general; upon Lavalleja, as President; upon President Oribe, as a proscribed chieftain; and, finally, upon Rosas, the ally of Oribe, as a general of Uruguay; in all which positions he has had abundance of time to learn something of the art of the Baqueano.

THE GAUCHO OUTLAW

The example of this type of character, to be found in certain places, is an outlaw, a squatter, a kind of misanthrope. He is Cooper's Hawkeye or Trapper, with all the knowledge of the wilderness possessed by the latter; and with all his aversion to the settlements of the whites, but without his natural morality or his friendly relations with the savages. The name of gaucho outlaw is not applied to him wholly as an uncomplimentary epithet. The law has been for many years in pursuit of him. His name is dreaded—spoken under the breath, but not in hate, and almost respectfully. He is a mysterious personage; his abode is the pampa; his lodgings are the thistle fields; he lives on partridges and hedgehogs, and whenever he is disposed to regale himself upon a tongue, he lassos a cow, throws her without assistance, kills her, takes his favorite morsel, and leaves the rest for the carrion birds. The gaucho outlaw will make his appearance in a place just left by soldiers, will talk in a friendly way with the admiring group of good gauchos around him; provide himself with tobacco, yerba maté, which makes a refreshing beverage, and if he discovers the soldiers, he mounts his horse quietly and directs his steps leisurely to the wilderness, not even deigning to look back. He is seldom pursued; that would be killing horses to no purpose, for the beast of the gaucho outlaw is a bay courser, as noted in his own way as his master. If he ever happens to fall unawares into the hands of the soldiers, he sets upon the densest masses of his assailants, and breaks through them, with the help of a few slashes left by his knife upon the faces or bodies of his opponents; and lying along the ridge of his horse's back to avoid the bullets sent after him, he hastens towards the wilderness, until, having left his pursuers at a convenient distance, he pulls up and travels at his ease. The poets of the vicinity add this new exploit to the biography of the desert hero, and his renown flies through all the vast region around. Sometimes he appears before the scene of a rustic festival with a young woman whom he has carried off, and takes a place in the dance with his partner, goes through the figures of the *cielito*, and disappears, unnoticed. Another day he brings the girl he has seduced, to the house of her offended family, sets her down from his horse's croup, and reckless of the parents' curses by which he is followed, quietly betakes himself to his boundless abode.

This white-skinned savage, at war with society and proscribed by the laws, is no more depraved at heart than the inhabitants of the settlements. The reckless outlaw who attacks a whole troop, does no harm to the traveller. The gaucho outlaw is no bandit, or highwayman; murderous assaults do not suit his temper, as robbery would not suit the character of the *churriador* (sheep-stealer). To be sure, he steals; but this is his profession, his trade, his science. He steals horses. He arrives, for instance, at the camp of a train from the interior; its master offers to buy of him a horse of some unusual color, of a particular shape and quality, with a white star on the shoulder. The gaucho collects his thoughts, considers a moment, and replies, after a short silence: "There is no such horse alive." What thoughts have been passing through the gaucho's mind? In that moment his memory has traversed a thousand estates upon the pampa; has seen and examined every horse in the province, with its marks, color, and special traits, and he has convinced himself that not one of them has a star on its shoulder; some have one on their foreheads, others have white spots on their haunches. Is this power of memory amazing? No! Napoleon knew two hundred thousand soldiers by name, and remembered, when he saw any one of them, all the facts relating to him. Therefore, if nothing impossible is required of him, the gaucho will deliver upon a designated day and spot, just such a horse as has been asked for, and with no less punctuality if he has been paid in advance. His honor is as sensitive upon this point as that of a gambler about his debts.

Sometimes he travels to the country about Cordova or Santa Fé. Then he may be seen crossing the pampa behind a small body of horses; if any one meets him, he follows his course without approaching the new-comer unless he is requested to do so.

THE CANTOR (THE MINSTREL)

And now we have the idealization of this life of resistance, civilization, barbarism, and danger. The gaucho Cantor corresponds to the singer, bard, or troubadour of the Middle Ages, and moves in the same scenes, amidst the struggles of the cities with provincial feudalism, between the life which is passing away and the new life gradually arising. The Cantor goes from one settlement to another "de tapera en galpon," singing the deeds of the heroes of the pampa whom the law persecutes, the lament of the widow whose sons have been taken off by the Indians in a recent raid, the defeat and death of the brave Ranch, the final overthrow of Facundo Quiroga, and the fate of Santos Perez.

The Cantor is performing in his simple way the same labor of recording customs, history, and biography, which was performed by the mediaeval bard, and his verses would hereafter be collected as documents and authorities for the future historian, but that there stands beside him another more cultivated form of society with a knowledge of events superior to that displayed by this less favored chronicler in his artless rhapsodies. Two distinct forms of civilization meet upon a common ground in the Argentine Republic: one, still in its infancy, which, ignorant of that so far above it, goes on repeating the crude efforts of the Middle Ages; the other, disregarding what lies at its feet, while it strives to realize in itself the latest results of European civilization; the nineteenth and twelfth centuries dwell together—one inside the cities, the other without them.

The Cantor has no fixed abode; he lodges where night surprises him; his fortune consists in his verses and in his voice. Wherever the wild mazes of the *cielito* are threaded, wherever there is a glass of wine to drink, the Cantor has his place and his particular part in the festival. The Argentine gaucho only drinks when excited by music and verse,★ and every grocery has its guitar ready for the hands of the Cantor who perceives from afar where the help of his "gay science" is needed, by the group of horses about the door.

The Cantor intersperses his heroic songs with the tale of his own exploits. Unluckily his profession of Argentine bard does not shield him from the law. He can tell of a couple of stabs he has dealt, of one or two *misfortunes* (homicides!) of his, and of some horse or girl he has carried off.

In 1840, a Cantor was sitting on the ground, cross-legged, on the banks of the majestic Paraná, in the midst of a group of gauchos whom he was keeping in eager suspense by the long and animated tale of his labors and adventures. He had already related the abduction of his love, with the difficulties overcome on the occasion; also his *misfortune* and the dispute that led to

★Without wandering from our subject, we may here call to mind the noteworthy resemblance between the Argentines and the Arabs. In Algiers, Oran, Mascara, and the desert encampments, I constantly saw the Arabs collected in coffee-shops—strong drink being forbidden them,—closely crowded about the singer, or more usually two singers, who accompany themselves with guitars in a duet, and recite national songs of a mournful character like our *tristes* before mentioned. The Arabian bridle is of plaited leather thongs, continued into a whip-lash like ours; the bit which we use is that of the Arabs, and many of our customs show the intercourse of our ancestors with the Moors of Andalusia. I have met some Arabs whom I could have sworn I had seen in my own country.

it; and was relating his encounter with the soldiery, and the stabs with which he defended himself, when the noisy advance and the shouts of a body of troops made him aware that this time he was surrounded. The troops had, in fact, closed up in the form of a horseshoe, open towards the Paraná, the steep banks of which rose twenty yards above the water. The Cantor, undismayed by the outcry, was mounted in an instant, and after casting a searching look at the ring of soldiers and their ready pieces, he wheeled his horse towards the river's bank, covered the animal's eyes with his poncho, and drove his spurs into him. A few moments after, the horse, freed from his bit so that he could swim more easily, emerged from the depths of the Paraná, the minstrel holding him by the tail, and looking back to the scene on shore which he had quitted, as composedly as if he had been in an eight-oared boat. Some shots fired by the troops did not hinder him from arriving safe and sound at the first island in sight.

To conclude, the original poetry of the minstrel is clumsy, monotonous, and irregular, when he resigns himself to the inspiration of the moment. It is occupied rather with narration than with the expression of feeling, and is replete with imagery relating to the open country, to the horse, and to the scenes of the wilderness, which makes it metaphorical and grandiose. When he is describing his own exploits or those of some renowned evil-doer, he resembles the Neapolitan improvisatore, his style being unfettered, commonly prosaic, but occasionally rising to the poetic level for some moments, to sink again into dull and scarcely metrical recitation. The Cantor possesses, moreover, a repertory of popular poems in octosyllabic lines variously combined into stanzas of five lines, of ten, or of eight. Among them are many compositions of merit which show some inspiration and feeling.

To these original types might be added many others of equal peculiarity, but they would not, like the former, illustrate the national customs, a knowledge of which is necessary for the right comprehension of our political personages and of the primitive and American nature of the bloody strife which distracts the Argentine Republic. In the course of this narrative the reader will himself discover where are to be met the Track-viewer, Path-finder, Gaucho-outlaw, and Minstrel. He will see in the chieftains whose fame has passed the Argentine frontiers, and even in those who have filled the world with the horror of their names, the vivid reflection of the internal condition, customs, and organization of the country.

CHAPTER III
Association

The gaucho lives on privations, but his luxury is freedom. Proud of an unrestricted independence, his feelings, though wild as his life, are yet noble and good.

—HEAD

LA PULPERIA (THE COUNTRY STORE)

In the first chapter we left the Argentine rustic, at the moment of his arrival at maturity, in the possession of such a character as had resulted from the natural circumstances about him, and from his want of any true society. We have seen that he is a man independent of every want, under no control, with no notion of government, all regular and systematic order being wholly impossible among such people. With these habits of heedlessness and independence he enters on another step of rural life, which, commonplace as it is, is the starting-point of all the great events which we are shortly to describe.

It is to be remembered that I am speaking of the essentially pastoral part of the people, and that I select for consideration only their fundamental characteristics, neglecting the accidental modifications they receive, the partial effects of which will be indicated separately. I am speaking of the combination of landed proprietaries which cover the surface of a province, four leagues, more or less, being occupied by each.

The society of the agricultural districts is also much subdivided and dispersed, but on a smaller scale. One laborer assists another, and the implements of tillage, the numerous tools, stores, and animals employed, the variety of products and the various arts which agriculture calls to its aid, establish necessary

47

relations between the inhabitants of a valley and make it indispensable for them to have a rudiment of a town to serve as a centre. Moreover, the cares and occupations of agriculture require such a number of hands that idleness becomes impossible, and the men of an estate are compelled to remain within its limits. The exact contrary takes place in the singular society we are describing. The bounds of ownership are unmarked; the more numerous the flocks and herds the fewer hands are required; upon the women devolve all the domestic duties and manufactures; the men are left without occupations, pleasures, ideas, or the necessity of application. Home life is wearisome and even repulsive to them. They need, then, factitious society to remedy this radical want of association. Their early acquired habit of riding gives them an additional incentive to leave their houses.

It is the children's business to drive the horses to the corral before the sun has quite risen; and all the men, even the lads, saddle their horses, even when they have no object in view. The horse is an integral part of the Argentine rustic; it is for him what the cravat is to an inhabitant of the city. In 1841, El Chacho, a chieftain of the Llanos, emigrated to Chili. "How are you getting on, friend?" somebody asked him. "How should I be getting on?" returned he, in tones of distress and melancholy. "Bound to Chili, and on foot!" Only an Argentine gaucho can appreciate all the misfortune and distress which these two phrases express.

Here again we have the life of the Arab or Tartar. The following words of Victor Hugo might have been written in the pampas:—

He cannot fight on foot; he and his horse are but one person.
He lives on horseback; he trades, buys, and sells on horseback;
drinks, eats, sleeps, and dreams on horseback.—*Le Rhin*

The men then set forth without exactly knowing where they are going. A turn around the herds, a visit to a breeding-pen or to the haunt of a favorite horse, takes up a small part of the day; the rest is consumed in a rendezvous at a tavern or grocery store. There assemble inhabitants of the neighboring parishes; there are given and received bits of information about animals that have gone astray; the traces of the cattle are described upon the ground; intelligence of the hunting-ground of the tiger or of the place where the tiger's tracks have been seen, is communicated. There, in short, is the Cantor; there the men fraternize while the glass goes round at the expense of those who have the means as well as the disposition to pay for it.

In a life so void of emotion, gambling exercises the enervated mind, and liquor arouses the dormant imagination. This accidental reunion becomes by its daily repetition a society more contracted than that from which each of its individual members came; yet in this assembly, without public aim, without social interest, are first formed the elements of those characters which are to appear later on the political stage. We shall see how. The gaucho esteems skill in horsemanship and physical strength, and especially courage, above all other things, as we have said before. This meeting, this daily club, is a real Olympic circus where each man's merit is tested and assayed.

The gaucho is always armed with the knife inherited from the Spaniard. More fully even than in Spain is here realized that peninsular peculiarity, that cry, characteristic of Saragossa —*war to the knife*. The knife, besides being a weapon, is a tool used for all purposes; without it, life cannot go on. It is like the elephant's trunk, arm, hand, finger, and all. The gaucho boasts of his valor like a trooper, and every little while his knife glitters through the air in circles, upon the least provocation, or with none at all, for the simple purpose of comparing a stranger's prowess with his own; he plays at stabbing as he would play at dice. So deeply and intimately have these pugnacious habits entered the life of the Argentine gaucho that custom has created a code of honor and a fencing system which protect life. The rowdy of other lands takes to his knife for the purpose of killing, and he kills; the Argentine gaucho unsheathes his to fight, and he only wounds. To attempt the life of his adversary he must be very drunk, or his instincts must be really wicked, or his rancor very deep. His aim is only to *mark* his opponent, to give him a slash in the face, to leave an indelible token upon him. The numerous scars to be seen upon these gauchos, accordingly, are seldom deep. A fight is begun, then, for the sake of shining, for the glory of victory, for the love of fame. A close ring is made around the combatants, and excited and eager eyes follow the glitter of the knives which do not cease to move. When blood flows in torrents the spectators feel obliged to stop the fight. If a *misfortune* has resulted, the sympathies are with the survivor; the best horse is available for his escape to a distant place where he is received with respect or pity. If the law overtakes him he often shows fight, and if he rushes through soldiers and escapes, he has from that time a wide-spread renown. Time passes, the judge in place has been succeeded by another, and he may again show himself in the township without further molestation: he has a full discharge.

Homicide is but a misfortune, unless the deed has been so often repeated that the perpetrator has gained the reputation of an assassin. The landed proprietor, Don Juan Manuel Rosas, before being a public man, had made his residence a sort of asylum for homicides without ever extending his protection to robbers; a preference which would easily be explained by his character of gaucho proprietor, if his subsequent conduct had not disclosed affinities with evil which have filled the world with terror.

With respect to equestrian sports, it will suffice to point out one of the many which are practiced, that the reader may judge what daring is required of those who engage in them. A gaucho rides at full speed before his comrades. One of them flings a set of *bolas* at him so as to shackle the horse in the midst of his career. Issuing from the whirlwind of dust raised by his fall, appears the rider at a run, followed by the horse, the latter carried on by the impulse of his interrupted career according to the laws of physics. In this pastime, life is staked, and sometimes lost.

Will it be believed that these displays of valor or skill and boldness in horsemanship are the basis of the great exploits which have filled the Argentine Republic with their name and changed the face of the country? Nothing is more certain, however. I do not mean to assert that assassination and crime have always been a ladder by which men have risen. Thousands of daring men have remained in the position of obscure bandits; but those who owe their position to such deeds are to be counted by larger numbers than hundreds. In all despotic societies, great natural gifts tend to lose themselves in crime; the Roman *genius* which could conquer the world is to-day the terror of the Pontine Marshes, and the Spanish Zumalacarreguis and Minas are to be met by hundreds in Sierra Morena. Man's need of developing his strength, capacity, and ambition, requires him, upon the failure of legitimate means, to frame a world, with its own morality and laws, where he shows complacently that he was born to be a Napoleon or a Caesar.

In this society, then, where mental culture is useless or impossible, where no municipal affairs exist, where, as there is no public, the public good is a meaningless word, the man of unusual gifts, striving to exert his faculties, takes with that design the means and the paths which are at hand. The gaucho will be a malefactor or a military chief, according to the course which things are taking at the moment when he attains celebrity.

Such customs need vigorous methods of repression, and to restrain hardened men, judges still more hardened are required. What I said at the outset, of the captain of the freight-carts, is exactly applicable to the country justice. He wants bravery more than anything else; the terror of his name is more powerful than the punishments he inflicts. The justice is naturally some one of former notoriety recalled to orderly life by old age and his family ties. Of course, the law he administers is altogether arbitrary; his conscience or his passions determine it, and his decrees are final. Sometimes justices officiate during their whole lives, and are remembered with respect. But the consciousness of these methods of administration and the arbitrary nature of the attendant penalties, produce among the people ideas of judicial authority which will have their effects hereafter. The justice secures obedience by his reputation for formidable boldness, by his force of character, his informal decisions, his decree, the announcement "such are my commands," and the forms of punishment which he invents himself. From this disorder, perhaps long since inevitable, it follows that the military commander who reaches distinction during rebellions possesses a sway, undisputed and unquestioned by his followers, equal to the wide and terrible power now only to be found among the nations of Asia. The Argentine chieftain is a Mohammed who might change the prevailing religion, if such were his whim, and contrive another. He has power in all its forms; his injustice is a misfortune for his victim, but no abuse on his part; for he may be unjust—still more, he must be unjust,—for he has been a lawless man all his life.

These remarks are also applicable to the country commandant. This personage is of more importance than the former, and requires in a higher degree the combination of the reputation and antecedents which distinguish him. Far from being lessened, the evil is even aggravated by an additional circumstance. The title of country commandant is conferred by the rulers of the cities; but as the city is destitute of power, influence, and supporters in the country, the administration lays hold of the men it most fears, and confers this office upon them in order to retain their obedience—a well known procedure of all weak governments, which put off the evil of the moment only to allow it to appear later in colossal dimensions. Thus the Papal government has dealings with banditti, to whom it gives offices in Rome, encouraging brigandage by this means, and making its continuance certain; thus did the Sultan grant Mehemet Ali the rank of Pacha of Egypt, having afterwards to purchase the continuance of his own reign by recognizing his vassal's title to an hereditary throne. It is singular that all the chieftains of the Argentine revolutionary movement were country commandants: Lopez and Ibarra, Artigas and Guemes, Facundo and Rosas. This is the constant starting-point of ambition. When Rosas had made himself master of the city, he exterminated all the commandants to whom he owed his elevation, intrusting with this influential position commonplace men, who could only follow the path he had traced. Pajarito, Celarragan, Arbolito, Pancho el ñato, Molina, were among the commandants of whom Rosas cleared the country.

I assign so much importance to these lesser points, because they will serve to explain all our social phenomena, and the revolution which has been taking place in the Argentine Republic. The features of this revolution are distorted because described in words from the political dictionary, which disguise and hide them by the mistaken ideas they call up. In the same way that of the Spaniards gave familiar European names to the new animals they encountered upon landing in America; saluting with the terrible name of lion, which calls up the notion of the magnanimity and strength of the king of beasts, a wretched cat called the puma, which runs at the sight of the dogs, and naming the jaguar of our woods the tiger. Evidence will soon be brought to show the firm and indestructible nature of the foundations upon which I assert the civil war to be based, however unstable and ignoble they may appear. The life of the Argentine country people as I have exhibited it is not a mere accident; it is the order of things, a characteristic, normal, and in my judgment unparalleled system of association, and in itself affords a full explanation of our revolution.

Before 1810, two distinct, rival, and incompatible forms of society, two differing kinds of civilization existed in the Argentine Republic: one being Spanish, European, and cultivated, the other barbarous, American, and almost wholly of native growth. The revolution which occurred in the cities acted only as the cause, the impulse, which set these two distinct forms of national existence face to face, and gave occasion for a contest between them, to be ended, after lasting many years, by the absorption of one into the other.

I have pointed out the normal form of association, or want of association, of the country people, a form worse, a thousand times, than that of the nomad tribe. I have described the artificial associations formed in idleness, and the sources of fame among the gauchos—bravery, daring, violence, and opposition to regular law, to the civil law, that is, of the city. These phenomena of social organization existed in 1810, and still exist, modified in many points, slowly changing in others, and yet untouched in several more. These foci, about which were gathered the brave, ignorant, free, and unemployed peasantry, were found by thousands through the country. The revolution of 1810 carried everywhere commotion and the sound of arms. Public life, previously wanting in this Arabico-Roman society, made its appearance in all the taverns, and the revolutionary movement finally brought about provincial, warlike associations, called *montoneras*, legitimate offspring of the tavern and the field, hostile to the city and to the army of revolutionary patriots. As events succeed each other, we shall see the provincial montoneras headed by their chiefs; the final triumph, in

Facundo Quiroga, of the country over the cities throughout the land; and by their subjugation in spirit, government, and civilization, the final formation of the central consolidated despotic government of the landed proprietor, Don Juan Manuel Rosas, who applied the knife of the gaucho to the culture of Buenos Ayres, and destroyed the work of centuries—of civilization, law, and liberty.

CHAPTER IV
The Revolution of 1810

When the battle opens, the Tartar utters a terrible cry, closes, vanishes, and returns like a flash of lightning.

—VICTOR HUGO

I have been obliged to traverse the whole of the route hitherto pursued, in order to reach the point at which our drama begins. It is needless to consider at length the character, object, and end, of the Revolution of Independence.

They were the same throughout America, and sprang from the same source, namely, the progress of European ideas. South America pursued that course because all other nations were pursuing it. Books, events, and the impulses given by these, induced South America to take part in the movement imparted to France by North American demands for liberty, and to Spain by her own and by French writers. But what my object requires me to notice, is, that the revolution—except in its external symbolic independence of the king—was interesting and intelligible only to the Argentine cities, but foreign and unmeaning to the rural districts. Books, ideas, municipal spirit, courts, laws, statutes, education, all the points of contact and union existing between us and the people of Europe, were to be found in the cities, where there was a basis of organization, incomplete and comparatively evil, perhaps, for the very reason it was incomplete, and had not attained the elevation which it felt itself capable of reaching, but it entered into the revolution with enthusiasm. Outside the cities, the revolution was a problematical affair, and so far as shaking off the king's authority was shaking off judicial authority, it was acceptable. The pastoral districts could only regard the question from this point of view. Liberty, responsibility of power, and all the questions which the revolution was to solve, were foreign to their mode of life and to their needs. But they derived this advantage from the revolution, that it tended to confer an object and an occupation upon the excess of vital force, the presence of which among them has been pointed out, and was to add a broader base of union than that to which throughout the country districts the men daily resorted. These Spartan constitutions, that warlike nature hitherto ill-satisfied by the free use of the dagger, that Roman-like idleness which could only be exchanged for the activity of a battle-field, that utter impatience of judicial control, were all to have at last a fit sphere of action in the world.

Revolutionary movements then began in Buenos Ayres, and the call met with a decided response from all the interior cities. The pastoral districts became unsettled and joined in the movement. Tolerably disciplined armies were raised in Buenos Ayres to be sent to Upper Peru and Montevideo, where the Spanish forces under General Vigodet were stationed. General Rondeau laid siege to Montevideo with a disciplined army, and Artigas, a noted chieftain, took part in the siege with some thousands of gauchos. Artigas had been a formidable outlaw till 1804, when the civil authorities of Buenos Ayres succeeded in bringing him over and inducing him to undertake the duties of country commandant, as a supporter of the same authorities upon whom he had, till then, made war. If the reader has not forgotten the baqueano, and the general requisites of a country commandant, he will readily understand the character and feelings of Artigas. After a time, Artigas and his gauchos withdrew from General Rondeau, and began to make war upon him.

The latter's position was the same as Oribe's when he conducted the siege of Montevideo while taking care of another enemy at his rear. The only difference between the cases is that

Artigas was hostile at once to patriots and royalists. It is not my purpose to determine with precision the causes or pretexts which occasioned this rupture, and I am as little disposed to apply to it any designation from the language of politics, for none such would be appropriate. When a nation engages in a revolution, it is begun by the conflict of two opposing interests, the revolutionary and the conservative; among us the names of patriots and royalists were applied to the corresponding parties. It is natural for the victors, after their triumph, to separate into moderate and extreme factions, one set wishing to carry out all the consequences of the revolution, while their opponents seek to restrain it within certain bounds. It is also characteristic of revolutions for the originally conquered party to renew its organization, and to find a means of success in the dissensions of its conquerors. But when one of the parties called to the aid of a revolution, immediately loses its connection with the others, forms a third entity, and shows hostility indiscriminately to both combatants (royalists and patriots), this detached party is heterogeneous, not having been conscious of existence until that time, the revolution having served to develop it and make it known.

This was the element set in motion by the renowned Artigas. It was a blind tool, but a tool full of life and of instincts hostile to European civilization and to all regular organization; opposed to monarchy as to republicanism, because both came from the city and possessed already order and reverence for authority. This tool was employed by the various parties, principally by that least revolutionary, in the civilized cities, until in the course of time the very men who had summoned it to their aid, yielded to it; and with them fell the city, its ideas, its literature, its colleges, its tribunals, its civilization!

This spontaneous movement of the pastoral districts was so ingenuous in its first manifestations, so full of genius and expression in its spirit and tendencies, that its adoption and baptism by the parties of the cities, with the political names which divided them, makes the sincerity of the latter appear in the most unfavorable light. The force which supported Artigas in Entre Rios, did the same for Lopez in Santa Fé, for Ibarra in Santiago, for Facundo in the Llanos. Its essence was individual action; its exclusive weapon, the horse; its stage, the vast pampas. The Bedouin hordes which in our day disturb the Algerian frontier by their war-cries and depredations, gives an exact idea of the Argentine montonera, which has been made use of by men of sagacity, as well as by noted desperadoes. In Africa, at the present day, there exists the same struggle between civilization and barbarism; the *goom* and the montonera are distinguished by the same characters, the same spirit, the same undisciplined strategy. Immense masses of horsemen wander in each case over the wilderness, offering battle to the disciplined forces of the cities, if they feel themselves the stronger party; dispersing in all directions like clouds of Cossacks, if the fight is even, to unite again and fall unexpectedly upon their sleeping foes, snatch away their horses, and kill their laggards and advanced parties. Ever at hand, but too much scattered to be successfully attacked, impotent in battle, but powerful and invincible in an extensive region, they finally decimate and overpower an organized force by means of skirmishes, surprises, fatigues, and privations.

The montonera, as it appeared under the command of Artigas in the early days of the Republic, already showed that character of brutal ferocity and the promise of a reign of terror, which it was reserved for the immortal bandit, the Buenos Ayres land-owner, to convert into a legislative system applied to a civilized society, and to present to the contemplation of Europe, to the shame and disgrace of America. Rosas invented nothing; his talent was only that of copying his predecessors and combining the brutal instincts of the ignorant masses into a coolly planned system.

The thongs made of Colonel Maciel's skin, and by command of Rosas converted into a pair of manacles, have been actually seen by foreign officials, an outrage not without its precedent, under the rule of Artigas and the other barbarous and Tartaric chiefs of the time. The montonera of Artigas *waistcoated* its enemies; that is, sewed them up in an envelope of raw hide, and left them in the fields in this condition.

The reader may imagine all the horrors of this slow death, and this horrible punishment was repeated in 1836, in the case of a colonel in the army. The infliction of death by cutting the throat with a knife instead of by shooting, is the result of the butcherly instinct which led Rosas to encourage cruelty, to give executions a more barbarous form which he thought would give pleasure to the assassins; in other words, he changed the legal punishments recognized by civil society, for others which he called American, and in the name of which he invited his fellow-Americans to come forward in his defense when the sufferings of Brazil, Paraguay, and Uruguay invoked the aid of the European powers to assist in their liberation from the cannibal, who was even then overrunning them with his sanguinary hordes. It is impossible to maintain the calmness needed to investigate historic truth when we are forced to remember at every step that America and Europe have been so long successfully deluded by a system of assassination and cruelty, scarcely tolerated in the African provinces of Ashantee or Dahomey.

Such is the character presented by the montonera from its first appearance; a singular kind of warfare and civil polity, unprecedented except among the tribes of the Asiatic plains, and not to be confounded with the habits, ideas, and customs of the Argentine cities, which were, like all South American cities, a continuation of European civilization, and especially that of Spain.

The only explanation of the montonera is to be discovered

by the examination of the society from which it proceeded. Artigas, the baqueano and outlaw, at war with the authorities of the city, but bought over as provincial commandant and chief of equestrian bands, presents a type reproduced with little change in each provincial commandant who came to be a partisan leader. Like all civil wars in which deep differences of education, belief, and motives divide the parties engaged in them, the internal warfare of the Argentine Republic was long and obstinate, until one of the elements of the strife was victorious. The Argentine Revolutionary War was twofold: 1st, a civilized warfare of the cities against Spain; 2d, a war against the cities on the part of the country chieftains with the view of shaking off all political subjection and satisfying their hatred of civilization. The cities overcame the Spaniards, and were in their turn overcome by the country districts. This is the explanation of the Argentine Revolution, the first shot of which was fired in 1810, and the last is still to be heard.

I will not enter into all the details of this contest. The struggle was of various duration in different places; some cities yielded at first, others later. The life of Facundo Quiroga will afford us an opportunity of displaying this strife in all its naked deformity. What I have now to notice is that the triumph of these chiefs involved the disappearance of all civil order, even as it existed among the Spaniards. In some places it has totally disappeared; in others only in part, but it is clearly on its way to destruction. The mass of men are incapable of distinctly comparing one epoch with another; the present moment is the only one embraced by their observation; and for this reason no one has yet observed this destruction and decadence of the cities; just as the visible progress of the people of the interior to total barbarism escapes notice. Buenos Ayres has so many of the elements of European civilization that it will end by educating Rosas and repressing his bloody and barbarous instincts. The high position which he occupies, his relations with European governments, the necessity of respecting strangers and of denying through the press the atrocities he has committed, in order to escape universal reprobation, all combine to check his outrages,—a perceptible advantage.

Four cities have already been annihilated by the rule of the partisan supporters of Rosas: Santa Fé, Santiago del Estero, San Luis, and La Rioja. Santa Fé, situated at the junction of the Paraná and another navigable river, the mouth of which is close by the town, is one of the most favored spots of South America, and yet contains less than two thousand souls; San Luis, the capital of a province with a population of fifty thousand, in which it is the only city, contains less than fifteen hundred.

To make the ruin and decadence of civilization and the rapid progress of barbarism perceptible to the reader, I must select two cities—one already annihilated, the other insensibly proceeding towards barbarism—La Rioja and San Juan. La Rioja was formerly a city of some account, but its own sons would fail to recognize it in its present condition. When the revolution of 1810 began, it contained a large number of capitalists, and men of note, who have figured in a distinguished manner in arms, at the bar, on the bench, or in the pulpit. From Rioja came Dr. Castro Barros, deputy to the Congress of Tucuman, and a celebrated divine; General Dávila, who freed Copiapo from the Spanish power in 1817; Gabriel Ocampo, one of the most noted members of the Argentine bar; and a large number of advocates of the families Ocampo, Dávila, and Garcia, at present scattered over the Chilian territory, as well as various priests of much learning, among whom is Dr. Gordillo, actual curate of Huasco.

The ability of a province to produce in a given epoch so many eminent and illustrious men, proves the diffusion of learning among a greater number of individuals, and that it was respected and desired. If such was the case in the early days of the revolution, what an increase of enlightenment, wealth, and population, might we not expect to find now, if a fearful retrogression towards barbarism had not checked the development of that unfortunate people! What Chilian city, however insignificant, is there, in which no progress has been made during a period of ten years, in enlightenment, wealth, and elegance, even if we include among these such as have been destroyed by earthquakes?

Let us now look at the condition of La Rioja, as exhibited by the answers given to one of the many inquiries I have instituted for the purpose of gaining a thorough knowledge of the facts on which I base my theories. These are the statements of a reliable person, who was unacquainted with my object in investigating his memory of matters which must have been fresh in his mind, for it was only four months before that he left Rioja.*

1. What is about the actual amount of the population of Rioja city?

Ans. About fifteen hundred souls. It is said that only fifteen adult males reside in the city.

2. How many persons of note live in it?

Ans. Six or eight in the city.

3. How many lawyers' offices are open there?

Ans. None.

4. How many men wear dress-coats?

Ans. None.

5. How many young men from La Rioja are studying at Cordova or Buenos Ayres?

Ans. I know of only one.

6. How many schools are there, and how many children attend them?

Ans. None.

*Dr. Don Manuel Ignacio Castro Barros, canon of the Cordova Cathedral.

7. Are there any public charitable institutions?

Ans. None, nor any means for the simplest instruction. The only Franciscan ecclesiastic of the place has given instruction to some children.

8. How many of the churches are in ruins?

Ans. Five; the Matriz is the only one at all serviceable.

9. Are new houses building?

Ans. Not one, nor are people making any of the needed repairs.

10. Are the existing houses going to ruins?

Ans. Almost all, owing to the frequency with which the streets are flooded.

11. How many priests in orders are there?

Ans. Only two young men in the city: one is a secular curate, the other an ecclesiastic of Catamarca. There are four others in the province.

12. Are there any fortunes of fifty thousand dollars? and how many of twenty thousand?

Ans. None; all the people are extremely poor.

13. Has the population increased or diminished?

Ans. It has diminished by more than one half.

14. Is there any feeling of terror prevalent among the people?

Ans. A very strong one; there is a fear of uttering even harmless words.

15. Is the money coined of full value?

Ans. That of the province is debased.

These facts speak with all their sad and fearful severity. The only example of so rapid a decline towards barbarism is presented by the history of the Mohammedan conquests of Greece. And this happens in America, and in the nineteenth century, and is the work of but twenty years!

What is true of La Rioja is equally so of Santa Fé, San Luis, and Santiago del Estero, which have become skeletons of cities, decrepit and devastated, mere apologies for towns. In San Luis there has been but one priest for ten years past, and for the same period it has contained no school, nor any person who wears a dress-coat. But let us judge by San Juan the fate of the cities which have escaped destruction, but in which barbarism is insensibly increasing.

San Juan is an exclusively agricultural and commercial province. Its want of open country has long kept it free from the rule of the provincial chieftains. Whatever party was in power, its governor and officials were taken from the educated part of its population until 1833, when Facundo Quiroga placed a man of the lower class in possession of the government. This person, unable to avoid the influence of the civilized usages, went over to the party of culture and yielded to their dictations, until he was overthrown by Brizuela, chief of La Rioja. Brizuela was succeeded by General Benavides, whose power has lasted nine years, and has come to seem rather his own property than a magistracy held for a term. San Juan has grown in population,—owing to the progress of agriculture there, and to the emigrants driven by hunger and wretchedness from La Rioja and San Luis,—and its buildings have sensibly increased in number; facts which prove the natural wealth of the region, and the progress that might be made under a government which cared to foster education and culture, the sole methods of elevating a nation.

The despotism of Benavides is mild and pacific, so that men's minds are kept quiet and calm. He is the only subordinate of Rosas who has not reveled in blood; but this does not lessen the tendency to barbarism inherent in the present system.

All the courts are held by men destitute of the slightest knowledge of law, worthless in every sense. There is no military man who has served in regular armies outside the Republic.* Is it credible that such an inferior position is naturally that of a city of the interior? No, the past proves the contrary. Twenty years ago San Juan was one of the most civilized towns of the interior; and what must be the decline and prostration of a South American city which has to look back twenty years for its time of prosperity!

In 1831 two hundred heads of families, youths, educated men, advocates, soldiers, and other of its citizens, emigrated to Chili, Copiapo, Coquimbo, Valparaiso; and other parts of that Republic are still full of these noble victims of proscription, among whom are capitalists, intelligent miners, merchants, farmers, lawyers, and physicians. As at the Babylonian dispersion, none of them have yet been able to return to see the promised land. A second set of emigrants left the city in 1840, never to return.

San Juan had been, before these days, rich enough in distinguished men to give to the celebrated Congress of Tucuman a President of the capacity and rank of Dr. Laprida, who was afterwards assassinated by the Aldaos; a prior to the Recoleta Dominica of Chili, in the person of the distinguished sage and patriot Oro, afterwards Bishop of San Juan. An illustrious patriot, Don Ignacio de la Rosa, who, in conjunction with San Martin, prepared the expedition to aid Chili, and who scattered

---

*From 1845, when this book was written, to the present date, a salutary reaction occurred in the province of San Juan. It now contains one male and one female academy, and the Honorable House of Representatives has just proclaimed primary education for both sexes a public institution of the province. More than twenty youths are studying in Buenos Ayres, Cordova, and Chili, for the professions of law or medicine. Music and drawing have become quite frequent accomplishments for both sexes, and the artisans and other grades of society dress by preference in civilized costume, which is a sign of a satisfactory direction of the public mind to the improvement of its condition.

through his country the seeds of the *equality of classes* promised by the Revolution, was also a citizen of San Juan; as were a minister of the government of Rivadavia, Dr. Carril; a minister of the Argentine Legation, Don Domingo Oro, whose diplomatic talents are yet insufficiently appreciated; a deputy to the Congress of 1826, the enlightened priest Vera; a deputy to the convention of Santa Fé, in the presbyter Oro, an orator of note; one to that of Cordova, Don Rudecindo Rojo, as eminent for his talents and genius for industrial pursuits as for his great learning; and, among others, General Rojo, a soldier in the army, who saved two provinces by suppressing conspiracies, which he did solely by his quiet determination of character, and of whom General Paz, a competent judge of such matters, said, that he bade fair to be one of the first generals of the Republic. San Juan then possessed a theatre and a permanent company of actors.

There are still in existence the remains of six or seven private libraries, which comprised the most valuable books of the eighteenth century, and translations of the best Greek and Latin works. I had no other instruction up to 1836 than that afforded me by these rich, though partially destroyed libraries. San Juan had so many illustrious men in 1825 that the House of Representatives contained six noted orators. Let the wretched peasants who now* disgrace the House of Representatives of San Juan, within which have been heard such eloquent speeches and such elevated sentiments, turn from the record of those times and flee abashed at the profanation of that august sanctuary by their diatribes!

The judicial chairs and the administrative offices were then occupied by educated men, and a sufficient number remained to plead the causes of others.

The elegance of manners, the refinement of customs, the

*1845.

cultivation of literature, the great commercial interests, the public spirit which animated the people,—all announced to foreigners the existence of a society of culture advancing rapidly to the attainment of a distinguished rank, and justified the following estimate of San Juan given to America and Europe through the London press:—

They are showing the strongest inclination to advance in civilization, and this city is regarded at present as only second to Buenos Ayres in the progress of social reform. Various institutions lately established in Buenos Ayres have been adopted at San Juan on a scale proportionate to its size, and the people have made extraordinary progress in ecclesiastical reform, incorporating all the monastic orders with the secular clergy, and suppressing the convents of the latter.

But the state of primary education will give the best idea of the culture of the period we are considering. No portion of the Argentine Republic has been more distinguished by its anxiety for the diffusion of knowledge than San Juan, nor have more complete results been obtained elsewhere. The government, not satisfied with the capacity of the men of the province for the fulfillment of so important a duty, sent in 1815 for a person uniting competent learning and high morals from Buenos Ayres. Some gentlemen of the name of Rodriguez accordingly came to San Juan. These were three brothers worthy of ranking with the first families of the country, with whom they became connected, such was their merit, and such were the many excellent qualities they possessed. My present profession as superintendent of primary education, and my study of such subjects, enable me to say that if ever any parallel to the celebrated Dutch schools described by M. Cousin, occurred in Spanish America, it was in the school of San Juan. The moral and religious instruction was perhaps superior to the elementary teaching given there; and to this cause I attribute the small number of crimes committed in San Juan, and the moderate conduct of Benavides himself, who like most of the present citizens of San Juan, was educated in that famous school, where the pupils were indoctrinated into the precepts of morality with special care.

If these pages reach the hands of Don Ignacio and Don Roque Rodriguez, I trust they will accept this feeble homage, due, as I believe, to the eminent service done to the culture and morality of a whole city, in connection with their late brother, Don José.★

Such is the history of the Argentine cities. They can all claim past glory, civilization, and distinction. For the present they are borne down to the level of barbarism, and this barbarism of the interior has succeeded in penetrating even to the streets of Buenos Ayres.

From 1810 to 1840 the provinces which contained such civilized cities, were yet sufficiently barbarous to destroy by their propensities the colossal work of the Revolution of Independence! Now that nothing is left of what men, enlightenment, and institutions they once held, what will become of them? Ignorance and its consequence, poverty, are waiting like carrion birds for the last gasp of the cities of the interior to devour their prey, and to convert them into fields and pastures. Buenos Ayres may again become what it was; for there European civilization has such strength that it must maintain itself in spite of the brutality of the government. But what can the provinces

★A detailed account of the system and organization of this public educational establishment will be found in *Popular Education*, a special work devoted to that subject, and the fruit of my journey to Europe and the United States, undertaken by order of the Chilian government.

depend upon? Two centuries will not suffice for their restoration to the path they have abandoned, if the present generation shall educate their children in the barbarism which they have reached. Are we now asked for what we are contending? We are contending for the restoration of their former life, and the promise of improvement to the cities.

CHAPTER V

Life of Juan Facundo Quiroga

Moreover these traits belong to the original character of the human race. The man of nature who has not yet learned to restrain or disguise his passions, displays them in all their energy, and gives himself up to their impetuosity.

—ALÉX. *History of the Ottoman Empire*

HIS INFANCY AND YOUTH

Between the cities of San Luis and San Juan, lies an extensive desert, called the Travesia, a word which signifies *want of water*. The aspect of that waste is mostly gloomy and unpromising, and the traveller coming from the east does not fail to provide his *chifles* with a sufficient quantity of water at the last cistern which he passes as he approaches it. This Travesia once witnessed the following strange scene. The consequences of some of the encounters with knives so common among our gauchos had driven one of them in haste from the city of San Luis and forced him to escape to the Travesia on foot, and with his riding gear on his shoulder, in order to avoid the pursuit of the law. Two comrades were to join him as soon as they could steal horses for all three. Hunger and thirst were not the only dangers which at that time awaited him in the desert; a tiger that had already tasted human flesh had been following the track of those who crossed it for a year, and more than eight persons had already been the victims of this preference. In these regions, where man must contend with this animal for dominion over nature, the former sometimes falls a victim, upon which the tiger begins to acquire a preference for the taste of human flesh, and when it has once devoted itself to this novel form of chase, the pursuit of mankind, it gets the name of *man-*

eater. The provincial justice nearest the scene of his depredations
calls out the huntsmen of his district, who join, under his authority and guidance, in the pursuit of the beast, which seldom
escapes the consequences of its outlawry.

When our fugitive had proceeded some six leagues, he
thought he heard the distant roar of the animal, and a shudder
ran through him. The roar of the tiger resembles the screech
of the hog, but is prolonged, sharp, and piercing, and even
when there is no occasion for fear, causes an involuntary tremor
of the nerves as if the flesh shuddered consciously at the menace
of death. The roaring was heard clearer and nearer. The tiger
was already upon the trail of the man, who saw no refuge but
a small carob-tree at a great distance. He had to quicken his
pace, and finally to run, for the roars behind him began to
follow each other more rapidly, and each was clearer and more
ringing than the last. At length, flinging his riding gear to one
side of the path, the gaucho turned to the tree which he had
noticed, and in spite of the weakness of its trunk, happily quite
a tall one, he succeeded in clambering to its top, and keeping
himself half concealed among its boughs which oscillated violently. Thence he could see the swift approach of the tiger,
sniffing the soil and roaring more frequently in proportion to
its increasing perception of the nearness of its prey. Passing
beyond the spot where our traveller had left the path, it lost
the track, and becoming enraged, rapidly circled about until it
discovered the riding gear, which it dashed to fragments by a
single blow. Still more furious from this failure, it resumed its
search for the trail, and at last found out the direction in which
it led. It soon discerned its prey, under whose weight the slight
tree was swaying like a reed upon the summit of which a bird
has alighted. The tiger now sprang forward, and in the twin-
kling of an eye, its monstrous fore-paws were resting on the
slender trunk two yards from the ground, and were imparting
to the tree a convulsive trembling calculated to act upon the

nerves of the gaucho, whose position was far from secure. The beast exerted its strength in an ineffectual leap; it circled around the tree, measuring the elevation with eyes reddened by the thirst for blood, and at length, roaring with rage, it crouched down, beating the ground frantically with its tail, its eyes fixed on its prey, its parched mouth half open. This horrible scene had lasted for nearly two mortal hours; the gaucho's constrained attitude, and the fearful fascination exercised over him by the fixed and bloodthirsty stare of the tiger, which irresistibly attracted and retained his own glances, had begun to diminish his strength, and he already perceived that the moment was at hand when his exhausted body would fall into the capacious mouth of his pursuer. But at this moment the distant sound of the feet of horses on a rapid gallop gave him hope of rescue. His friends had indeed seen the tiger's foot-prints, and were hastening on, though without hope of saving him. The scattered fragments of the saddle directed them to the scene of action, and it was the work of a moment for them to reach it, to uncoil their lassoes, and to fling them over the tiger, now blinded by rage. The beast, drawn in opposite directions by the two lassos, could not evade the swift stabs by which its destined victim took his revenge for his prolonged torments. "On that occasion I knew what it was to be afraid," was the expression of Don Juan Facundo Quiroga, as he related this incident to a group of officers.

He too was called "the tiger of the Llanos," a title which did not ill befit him. There are, in fact, as is proved by phrenology and comparative anatomy, relations between external forms and moral qualities, between the countenance of a man and that of some animal whose disposition resembles his own. Facundo, as he was long called in the interior,—or, General Don Facundo Quiroga, as he afterwards became, when society had received him into its bosom and victory had crowned him with laurels,—was a stoutly built man of low stature, whose short neck and broad shoulders supported a well-shaped head, covered with a profusion of black and closely curling hair. His somewhat oval face was half buried in this mass of hair and an equally thick black, curly beard, rising to his cheek-bones, which by their prominence evinced a firm and tenacious will. His black and fiery eyes, shadowed by thick eyebrows, occasioned an involuntary sense of terror in those on whom they chanced to fall, for Facundo's glance was never direct, whether from habit or intention. With the design of making himself always formidable, he always kept his head bent down, to look at one from under his eyebrows, like the Ali Pacha of Monovoisin. The image of Quiroga is recalled to me by the Cain represented by the famous Ravel troupe, setting aside the artistic and statuesque attitudes, which do not correspond to his. To conclude, his features were regular, and the pale olive of his complexion harmonized well with the dense shadows which surrounded it.

The formation of his head showed, notwithstanding this shaggy covering, the peculiar organization of a man born to rule. Quiroga possessed those natural qualities which converted the student of Brienne into the genius of France, and the obscure Mameluke who fought with the French at the Pyramids, into the Viceroy of Egypt. Such natures develop according to the society in which they originate, and are either noble leaders who hold the highest place in history, ever forwarding the progress of civilization, or the cruel and vicious tyrants who become the scourges of their race and time.

Facundo Quiroga was the son of an inhabitant of San Juan, who had settled in the Llanos of La Rioja, and there had acquired a fortune in pastoral pursuits. In 1779, Facundo was sent to his father's native province to receive the limited education, consisting only of the arts of reading and writing, which he could acquire in its schools. After a man has come to employ the hundred trumpets of fame with the noise of his deeds, curiosity or the spirit of investigation is carried to such an extent as to scent out the insignificant history of the child, in order to connect it with the biography of the hero; and it is not seldom that the rudiments of the traits characteristic of the historical personage are met amid fables invented by flattery. The young Alcibiades is said to have lain down at full length upon the pavement of the street where he was playing, in order to insist that the driver of an approaching vehicle should yield the way to avoid running over him. Napoleon is reported to have ruled over his fellow-students, and to have entrenched himself in his study to resist an apprehended insult. Many anecdotes are now in circulation relating to Facundo, many of which reveal his true nature. In the house where he lodged, he could never be induced to take his seat at the family table; in school he was haughty, reserved, and unsocial; he never joined the other boys except to head their rebellious proceedings or to beat them. The master, tired of contending with so untamable a disposition, on one occasion provided himself with a new and stiff strap, and said to the frightened boys, as he showed it to them, "This is to be made supple upon Facundo." Facundo, then eleven years old, heard this threat, and the next day he tested its value. Without having learned his lesson, he asked the head-master to hear it himself, because, as he said, the assistant was unfriendly to him. The master complied with the request. Facundo made one mistake, then two, three, and four; upon which the master used his strap upon him. Facundo, who had calculated everything, down to the weakness of the chair in which the master was seated, gave him a buffet, upset him on his back, and, taking to the street in the confusion created by this scene, hid himself among some wild vines where they could not get him out for three days. Was not such a boy the embryo chieftain who would afterwards defy society at large?

In early manhood his character took a more decided cast,

constantly becoming more gloomy, imperious, and wild. From the age of fifteen years he was irresistibly controlled by the passion for gambling, as is often the case with such natures, which need strong excitement to awaken their dormant energies. This made him notorious in the city, and intolerable in the house which afforded him its hospitality; and finally under this influence, by a shot fired at one George Peña, he shed the first rill of blood which went to make up the wide torrent that marked his way through life.

On his becoming an adult, the thread of his life disappears in an intricate labyrinth of bouts and broils among the people of the surrounding region. Sometimes lying hid, always pursued, he passed his time in gambling, working as a common laborer, domineering over everybody around him, and distributing his stabs among them.

On the Godoy farm in San Juan are shown to this day mud-walls of Quiroga's treading; there are others in Fiambola, in La Rioja, made by him. He himself pointed out others in Mendoza, in the very place where one afternoon he had twenty-six of the officers who surrendered at Chacon dragged from their houses and shot to avenge Villifañe. He also showed some monuments of his wandering life of labor in the country districts of Buenos Ayes. What motives induced this man, brought up in a respectable family, son of a man of means and creditable life, to descend to a hireling's position, and moreover to select the dullest and most brutish kind of work, needing only bodily strength and endurance? Was it because the labor of building these mud-walls is recompensed with double wages, and that he was in haste to get together a little money?

The most connected account of this obscure and roaming part of his life that I can procure is as follows:

Towards 1806, he went to Chili with a consignment of grain on his parent's account. This he gambled away, as well as the animals, which had brought it, and the family slaves who had accompanied him.

He often took to San Juan and Mendoza droves of the stock on his father's estate, and these always shared the same fate; for with Facundo, gambling was a fierce and burning passion which aroused the deepest instincts of his nature. These successive gains and losses of his must have worn out his father's generosity, for at last he broke off all amicable relations with his family.

When he had become the terror of the Republic, he was once asked by one of his parasites, "What was the largest bet you ever made in your life, General?" "Seventy dollars," replied Quiroga, carelessly, and yet he had just won two hundred dollars at one stake. He afterwards explained that once when a young man, having only seventy dollars, he had lost them all at one throw. But this fact has its characteristic history. Facundo had been at work for a year as a laborer upon the farm of a lady, situated in the Plumerillo, and had made himself conspicuous by his punctuality in going to work, and by the influence and authority which he exercised over the other laborers. When they wanted a holiday to get drunk in, they used to apply to Facundo, who informed the lady, and gave her his word, which was always fulfilled, to have all the men at work the next day. On this account the laborers called him *the father*. At the end of a year of steady work, Facundo asked for his wages, which amounted to seventy dollars, and mounted his horse without knowing where he was bound, but seeing a collection of people at a grocery store, he alighted, and reaching over the group around the card-dealer, bet his seventy dollars on one card. He lost them, and remounting, went on his way, careless in what direction, until after a little time a justice, Toledo by name, who happened to be passing, stopped him to ask for his passport. Facundo rode up as if about to give it to him, pretended to be feeling for something in his pocket, and stretched the justice on the ground with a stab. Was he taking his revenge upon the judge for his recent loss at play? or was it his purpose to satisfy the irritation against civil authority natural to a gaucho outlaw, and increase, by this new deed, the splendor of his rising fame? Both are true explanations. This mode of revenging himself for misfortunes upon whatever first offered itself, had many examples in his life. When he was addressed as General, and had colonels at his orders, he had two hundred lashes given one of them in his house at San Juan, for having, as he said, cheated at play. He ordered two hundred lashes to be given to a young man for having allowed himself a jest at a time when jests were not to his taste; and two hundred lashes was the penalty inflicted on a woman in Mendoza for having said to him as he passed, "Farewell, General," when he was going off in a rage at not having succeeded in intimidating a neighbor of his, who was as peaceable and judicious as Facundo was rash and gaucho-like.

Facundo reappears later in Buenos Ayres, where he was enrolled in 1810 as a recruit in the regiment of Arribeños, which was commanded by General Ocampo, a native of his own province, and afterwards president of Charcas. The glorious career of arms opened before him with the first rays of the sun of May; and doubtless, endowed with such capacity as his, and with his destructive and sanguinary instincts, Facundo, could he have been disciplined to submit to civil authority and ennobled in the sublimity of the object of the strife, might some day have returned from Peru, Chili, or Bolivia, as a General of the Argentine Republic, like so many other brave gauchos who began their careers in the humble position of a private soldier. But Quiroga's rebellious spirit could not endure the yoke of discipline, the order of the barrack, or the delay of promotion. He felt his destiny to be to rule, to rise at a single leap, to create for himself, without assistance, and in spite of a hostile and civilized society, a career of his own, combining bravery and crime, government and disorganization. He was subsequently recruited into the army of the Andes, and enrolled in the Mounted Grenadiers. A lieutenant named Garcia took him for an assistant, and very soon desertion left a vacant place in those glorious files. Quiroga, like Rosas, like all the vipers that have thriven under the shade of their country's laurels, made himself notorious in after-life by his hatred for the soldiers of Independence, among whom both the men above named made horrible slaughter.

Facundo, after deserting from Buenos Ayres, set out for the interior with three comrades. A squad of soldiery overtook him; he faced the pursuers and engaged in a real battle with them, which remained undecided for awhile, until, after having killed four or five men, he was at liberty to continue his journey, constantly cutting his way through detachments of troops which here and there opposed his progress, until he arrived at San Luis. He was, at a later day, to traverse the same route with a handful of men, to disperse armies instead of detachments, and proceed to the famous citadel of Tucuman to blot out the last remains of Republicanism and civil order.

Facundo now reappears in the Llanos, at his father's house. At this period occurred an event which is well attested. Yet one of the writers whose manuscripts I am using, replies to an inquiry about the matter, "that to the extent of his knowledge Quiroga never attempted forcibly to deprive his parents of money," and I could wish to adopt this statement, irreconcilable as it is with unvarying tradition and general consent. The contrary is shocking to relate. It is said that on his father's refusal to give him a sum of money which he had demanded, he watched for the time when both parents were taking an afternoon nap to fasten the door of the room they occupied, and to set fire to the straw roof, which was the usual covering of the buildings of the Llanos!★

But what is certain in the matter is that his father once requested the governor of La Rioja to arrest him in order to check his excesses, and that Facundo, before taking flight from the Llanos, went to the city of La Rioja, where that official was to be found at the time, and coming upon him by surprise, gave him a blow, saying as he did so, "You have sent, sir, to have me arrested. There, have me arrested now!" On which he mounted his horse and set off for the open country at a gallop. At the end of a year he again showed himself at his father's house, threw himself at the feet of the old man whom he had used so ill, and succeeded amid the sobs of both, and the son's assurances of his reform in reply to the father's recriminations, in reëstablishing peace, although on a very uncertain basis.

But no change occurred in his character and disorderly habits; races, gambling parties, and expeditions into the country were the occasions of new acts of violence, stabbings, and assaults on his part, until he at length made himself intolerable to all, and rendered his own position very unsafe. Then a great thought which he announced without shame, got hold of his mind. The deserter from the Arribeños regiment, the mounted grenadier who refused to make himself immortal at Chacabuco or Maipù, determined to join the montonera of Ramirez, the offshoot from that led by Artigas, whose renown for crime and hatred for the cities on which it was making war, had reached the Llanos, and held the provincial government in dread. Facundo set forth to join those buccaneers of the pampa. But perhaps the knowledge of his character, and of the importance

---

★The author afterwards learned that Facundo related this story to a company of ladies, and one of his own early acquaintances testified to his having given his father a blow on one occasion.

of the aid which he would give to the destroyers, alarmed his fellow provincials, for they informed the authorities of San Luis, through which he was to pass, of his infernal design. Dupuis, then (1818) governor, arrested him, and for sometime he remained unnoticed among the criminals confined in the prison. This prison of San Luis, however, was to be the first step in his ascent to the elevation which he subsequently attained. San Martin had sent to San Luis a great number of Spanish officers of all ranks from among the prisoners taken in Chili. Irritated by their humiliations and sufferings, or thinking it possible that the Spanish forces might be assembled again, this party of prisoners rose one day and opened the doors of the cells of the common criminals, to obtain their aid in a general escape. Facundo was one of these criminals, and as soon as he found himself free from prison, he seized an iron bar of his fetters, split the skull of the very Spaniard who had released him, and passing through the group of insurgents, left a wide path strewn with the dead. Some say that the weapon he employed was a bayonet, and that only three men were killed by it. Quiroga, however, always talked of the iron bar of the fetters, and of fourteen dead men. This may be one of the fictions with which the poetic imagination of the people adorns the types of brute force they so much admire; perhaps the tale of the iron bar is an Argentine version of the jaw-bone of Samson, the Hebrew Hercules. But Facundo looked upon it as a crown of glory, in accordance with his idea of excellence, and whether by bar or bayonet, he succeeded, aided by other soldiers and prisoners whom his example encouraged, in suppressing the insurrection and reconciling society to himself by this act of bravery, and placing himself under his country's protection. Thus his name spread everywhere, ennobled and cleansed, though with blood, from the stains which had tarnished it.

Facundo returned to La Rioja covered with glory, his country's creditor; and with testimonials of his conduct, to show in

the Llanos, among gauchos, the new titles which justified the
terror his name began to inspire; for there is something imposing, something which subjugates and controls others in the
man who is rewarded for the assassination of fourteen men at
one time.

Something still remains to be noticed of the previous character and temper of this pillar of the Confederation. An illiterate
man, one of Quiroga's companions in childhood and youth,
who has supplied me with many of the above facts, sends me
the following curious statements in a manuscript describing
Quiroga's early years: "His public career was not preceded by
the practice of theft; he never committed robbery even in his
most pressing necessities. He was not only fond of fighting, but
would pay for an opportunity, or for a chance to insult the
most renowned champion in any company. He had a great
aversion to respectable men. He never drank. He was very
reserved from his youth, and desired to inspire others with awe
as well as with fear, for which purpose he gave his confidants
to understand that he had the gift of prophecy, in short was a
soothsayer. He treated all connected with him as slaves. *He never
went to confession, prayed, or heard mass;* I saw him once at mass
after he became a general. He said of himself that he believed
in nothing." The frankness with which these words are written,
prove their truth.

And here ends the private life of Quiroga, in which I have
omitted a long series of deeds which only show his evil nature,
his bad education, and his fierce and bloody instincts. The facts
stated appear to me to sum up the whole public life of Quiroga.
I see in them the great man, the man of genius, in spite of
himself and unknown to himself; a Caesar, Tamerlane, or Mohammed. The fault is not his that thus he was born. In order
to contend with, rule, and control the power of the city, and
the judicial authority, he is willing to descend to anything. If
he is offered a place in the army, he disdains it, because his

impatience cannot wait for promotion. Such a position demands submission, and places fetters upon individual independence; the soldier's coat oppresses his body, and military tactics
control his steps, all of which are insufferable! His equestrian
life, a life of danger and of strong excitements, has steeled his
spirit and hardened his heart. He feels an unconquerable and
instinctive hatred for the laws which have pursued him, for the
judges who have condemned him, and for the whole society
and organism from which he has felt himself withdrawn from
his childhood, and which regards him with suspicion and contempt. With these remarks is connected by imperceptible links
the motto of this chapter, "He is the natural man, as yet unused
either to repress or disguise his passions; he does not restrain
their energy, but gives free rein to their impetuosity. This is
the character of the human race." And thus it appears in the
rural districts of the Argentine Republic. Facundo is a type of
primitive barbarism. He recognized no form of subjection. His
rage was that of a wild beast. The locks of his crisp black hair,
which fell in meshes over his brow and eyes, resembled the
snakes of Medusa's head. Anger made his voice hoarse, and
turned his glances into dragons. In a fit of passion he kicked
out the brains of a man with whom he had quarreled at play.
He tore off both the ears of a woman he had lived with, and
had promised to marry, upon her asking him for thirty dollars
for the celebration of the wedding; and laid open his son John's
head with an axe, because he could not make him hold his
tongue. He violently beat a beautiful young lady at Tucuman,
whom he had failed either to seduce or to subdue, and exhibited in all his actions a low and brutal yet not a stupid nature,
or one wholly without lofty aims. Incapable of commanding
noble admiration, he delighted in exciting fear; and this pleasure was exclusive and dominant with him to the arranging all
his actions so as to produce terror in those around him, whether
it was society in general, the victim on his way to execution,

or his own wife and children. Wanting ability to manage the machinery of civil government, he substituted terror for patriotism and self-sacrifice. Destitute of learning, he surrounded himself with mysteries, and pretended to a foreknowledge of events which gave him prestige and reputation among the commonalty, supporting his claims by an air of impenetrability, by natural sagacity, an uncommon power of observation, and the advantage he derived from vulgar credulity.

The repertory of anecdotes relating to Quiroga, and with which the popular memory is replete, is inexhaustible; his sayings, his expedients, bear the stamp of an originality which gives them a certain Eastern aspect, a certain tint of Solomonic wisdom in the conception of the vulgar. Indeed, how does Solomon's advice for discovering the true mother of the disputed child differ from Facundo's method of detecting a thief in the following instances:—

An article had been stolen from a band, and all endeavors to discover the thief had proved fruitless. Quiroga drew up the troops and gave orders for the cutting of as many small wands of equal length as there were soldiers; then, having had these wands distributed one to each man, he said in a confident voice, "The man whose wand will be longer than the others to-morrow morning is the thief." Next day the troops was again paraded, and Quiroga proceeded to inspect the wands. There was one whose wand was, not *longer* but *shorter* than the others. "Wretch!" cried Facundo, in a voice which overpowered the man with dismay, "it is thou!" And so it was; the culprit's confusion was proof of the fact. The expedient was a simple one; the credulous gaucho, fearing that his wand would really grow, had cut off a piece of it. But to avail one's self of such means, a man must be superior in intellect to those about him, and must at least have some knowledge of human nature.

Some portions of a soldier's accoutrements having been stolen and all inquiries having failed to detect the thief, Quiroga had the troops paraded and marched past him as he stood with crossed arms and a fixed, piercing, and terrible gaze. He had previously said, "I know the man," with an air of assurance not to be questioned. The review began; many men had passed, and Quiroga still remained motionless, like the statue of Jupiter Tonans or the God of the Last Judgment. All at once he descended upon one man, and said in a curt and dry voice, "Where is the saddle?" "Yonder, sir," replied the other, pointing to a thicket. "Ho! four fusileers!" cried Quiroga. What revelation was this? that of terror and guilt made to a man of sagacity.

On another occasion, when a gaucho was answering to charges of theft which had been brought against him, Facundo interrupted him with the words, "This rogue has begun to lie. Ho, there! a hundred lashes!" When the criminal had been taken away, Quiroga said to some one present, "Look you, my master, when a gaucho moves his foot while talking, it is a sign he is telling lies." The lashes extorted from the gaucho the confession that he had stolen a yoke of oxen.

At another time he was in need of a man of resolution and boldness to whom he could intrust a dangerous mission. When a man was brought to him for this purpose, Quiroga was writing; he raised his head after the man's presence had been repeatedly announced, looked at him and returned to his writing with the remark, "Pooh! that is a wretched creature. I want a brave man and a venturesome one!" It turned out to be true that the fellow was actually good for nothing.

Hundreds of such stories of Facundo's life, which show the man of superior ability, served effectually to give him a mysterious fame among the vulgar, who even attribute superior powers to him.

CHAPTER VI
La Rioja

The sides of the mountain enlarge and assume an aspect at once more grand and more barren. By little and little, the scanty vegetation languishes and dies; and mosses disappear, and a red burning hue succeeds.
—ROUSSÉE'S *Palestine*

THE COUNTRY COMMANDANT

In a document dating as far back as 1560, I have seen recorded the name of Mendoza of the valley of La Rioja. But La Rioja proper is an Argentine province lying north of San Juan, from which it is separated by several strips of desert, although these are broken by some inhabited valleys. Its western portion is intersected in parallel lines by spurs branching off from the Andes and including in their valleys los Pueblos and Little Chili, as it was called by the Chilian miners, who frequented the rich and renowned mines of Famatina.

Further to the east stretches a sandy, barren, and sunscorched plain, at the northern extremity of which, and near a mountain covered to its summit with rank and lofty vegetation, lies the skeleton of La Rioja, a lonely city with no suburbs, and withered away, as it were, like Jerusalem at the foot of the Mount of Olives. This sandy plain is bounded, far towards the south, by the Colorados, mountains of hardened clay, whose regular outlines take the most picturesque and fantastic forms; sometimes resembling a smooth wall with projecting bastions; sometimes suggesting to the eye massive towers and the battlements of ruined castles. Lastly, in the southeast and surrounded by extensive wastes, lie the Llanos, a broken and hilly region, in spite of its name, forming an oasis of pasturage which formerly maintained thousands of flocks.

The general aspect of the country is desolate, its climate torrid, its soil parched and destitute of running streams. Reservoirs called *represas* are constructed by the peasantry to collect rain-water for the supply of their animals. I have always been disposed to think that the general aspect of Palestine resembles that of La Rioja, in the reddish or ochreous tints of the soil, the dryness of some regions and their cisterns; also the orange-trees, vines, and fig-trees bearing exquisite and enormous fruits, which are raised along the course of some turbid and confined Jordan. There is a strange combination of mountain and plain, fruitfulness and aridity, parched and bristling heights, and hills covered with dark green forests as lofty as the cedars of Lebanon.

What chiefly brings these reminiscences of the East before my imagination is the truly patriarchal appearance of the country people of La Rioja. Thanks to caprices of fashion, there is now nothing unusual in seeing men with full beards, according to the immemorial practice of Eastern nations; but yet this fact would not wholly prevent the surprise naturally occasioned by the sight of a Spanish-speaking population among whom full beards, frequently descending to the chest, are, and always have been worn; a population of melancholy, silent, sedate, and crafty demeanor; of Arabic appearance, riding upon asses, and sometimes clothed in goat-skins, like the hermit of En-gedi. There are places where the people live exclusively on wild honey and the fruit of the carob-tree, as St. John did on locusts in the desert. The Llanista himself is alone unconscious of being the most unfortunate, wretched, and barbarous of mortals, and thanks to this ignorance, he lives contentedly and happily when hunger does not trouble him.

I have already said that there are in Rioja some reddish

mountains which bear at a distance a resemblance to towers and feudal castles in ruins; and still other mediaeval characteristics are mingled with the Oriental resemblances above referred to, for in Rioja there has been a contest of a century between two hostile families, whose enmity, rank, and celebrity find an accurate parallel among the Ursini, Colonnas, and Medici of Italian feuds. The whole history of the civilized inhabitants of La Rioja is that of the contentions of the Ocampos and Dávilas. These families, alike ancient, rich, and noble, long strove with each other for supremacy, and, even long before the Revolution of Independence, had divided the population into parties like those of the Guelphs and Ghibellines. A great number of the members of these two families have distinguished themselves in arms, at the bar, and in industrial pursuits; for the Dávilas and the Ocampos were ever attempting to surpass each other by every method of acquiring power recognized by civilization. The extinction of this hereditary animosity was often an object of the policy of the patriots of Buenos Ayres. The two families were induced by the logic of Lautaro to unite an Ocampo with a lady of the Dávila family in order to promote a reconciliation. All know that such was the Italian practice; but on this occasion the Romeo and Juliet were more fortunate. Towards 1817 the government of Buenos Ayres, also with the view of ending the hostility of these families, sent the province a governor from without, Barnachea by name, who fell ere long under the influence of the Dávila party, dependent upon the support of Don Prudencio Quiroga, a man much beloved by the inhabitants of the Llanos where he lived; he had been summoned to the city and appointed Treasurer and Alcalde. The rural districts were just beginning, although in a legitimate and noble manner, in Don Prudencio Quiroga, Facundo's father, to come into play as a political element among the civil parties. The Llanos I have stated, consist of a hilly oasis of pasture land in the midst of an extensive desert (travesia);

their inhabitants, exclusively shepherds, lead that patriarchal and primitive life which its isolation preserves in all its purity and hostility to the cities. Hospitality is in that region a duty of general obligation. The laborer defends his master from all kinds of danger, even at the risk of his own life. These customs will of themselves furnish a partial explanation of the phenomena we are to witness.

After the event that occurred in his favor at San Luis, Facundo made his appearance on the Llanos invested with the prestige of his recent exploit, and fortified with a recommendation from the government. The parties dividing La Rioja were not slow to solicit the adhesion of a man regarded by all with the respect and dread always felt for deeds of unusual daring. The Ocampos, who came into power in 1820, gave him the title of Sergeant Major of the Militia of the Llanos, with the influence and authority of Commandant.

The beginning of his public career starts from this moment. The pastoral and barbaric element of La Rioja, the same with that third force which appears with Artigas at the siege of Montevideo, is now to present itself at La Rioja with Quiroga, upon whom one of the parties of the *city* had called for support. The moment of such an action is a solemn and critical one in the history of all the pastoral states of the Argentine Republic; in each there comes a day when a man of audacity is made country commandant either because he is already dreaded, or because foreign aid is needed. Such a man is a Grecian horse like that which the Trojans made haste to bring into the city.

At this time occurred at San Juan the unfortunate insurrection of the first regiment of the Andes, which had returned from Chili for reorganization. Francisco Aldao and Corro, foiled in the objects of the rebellion, undertook a calamitous retreat towards the north to join Güemes, a partisan chieftain of Salta. General Ocampo, Governor of La Rioja, took measures to bar their passage, and for that purpose called out all the forces of the province and made ready for a battle. Facundo was at hand with his Llanistas [men of the plains]. The action began, and a few minutes were enough to show that the First Regiment had, by rebellion, lost none of their ancient lustre on fields of battle. Corro and Aldao moved upon the city, and their scattered antagonists betook themselves for reorganization to the Llanos, where they could await the arrival of the troops from San Juan and Mendoza who were in pursuit of the fugitives. Facundo meanwhile, abandoning the point of reunion, fell upon the rear-guard of the victors, skirmishing with and harassing them, and killing or capturing their stragglers. Facundo was the only man endowed with a life of his own, waiting for no orders, wholly influenced by the motive power within himself. He had felt himself called to action, and waited for no impulse from without. Yet more; he spoke scornfully of the government and of the General, and declared his intention of overthrowing it and acting henceforward as his judgment might dictate. It is said that a council of the chief officers of the army urged upon General Ocampo his arrest, trial, and execution; but the General declined, perhaps less from moderation than from a feeling that Quiroga was now less a subordinate officer than a formidable ally.

A definite agreement between Aldao and the government decided that the former should return to San Luis, it not being his wish to follow Corro, and the government engaging to provide means for his passage through its territory by a route across the Llanos. Facundo was charged with the performance of this part of the stipulation, and returned with Aldao to the Llanos. Quiroga by this time was conscious of his power; and when he turned his back on La Rioja, he might have taken leave of it with the saying, "Woe to thee, O city! Verily I say unto thee that yet a little while, and there shall not be left of thee one stone upon another."

Aldao, upon his arrival at the Llanos, offered Quiroga, with whose discontent he had become acquainted, a hundred drilled soldiers, to enable him to make himself master of La Rioja, in exchange for his aid in future enterprises. Quiroga eagerly assented, set out for the city, took it, captured the officers of the government, sent them confessors, and orders to prepare themselves for death. What object had he in this revolution? None. Feeling himself powerful and stretching out his arms, he overthrew the city. Is it his fault?

Old Chilian patriots doubtless still remember the prowess of Sergeant Araya of the Mounted Grenadiers; for among those veterans the halo of glory frequently rested upon the common soldier. The priest Menéses has informed me that, after the rout of Cancha Rayada, Sergeant Araya and seven grenadiers went to Mendoza. It was heart-breaking to the patriots to see the bravest soldiers of their army passing and repassing the Andes while Las Heras still had forces at his command to face the Spaniards. The detention of Sergeant Araya was projected; but a difficulty presented itself. Who was to approach him? A detachment of seventy militia-men was at hand; but all the soldiers knew that the fugitive was Sergeant Araya, and they would have been a thousand times more ready to attack the Spaniards than this lion of the grenadiers.

Upon this, Don José Maria Menéses, alone and unarmed, followed and overtook Araya, and, intercepting him on his way, reminded him of his past glories and of the disgrace of an objectless flight. Araya was not deaf to this appeal, and yielded unresistingly to the entreaties and commands of the good neighbor. He then became enthusiastic, hastened to stop other squads of grenadiers who had preceded him in flight, and his diligence and reputation enabled him to join the army again with seventy comrades in arms, who cleared their laurels at Maipú of the momentary stain which had rested on them.

This Sergeant Araya and a man named Lorca, also known in Chili by his bravery, commanded the force placed by Aldao

under Facundo's orders. The prisoners at La Rioja who were
under sentence of death, among them Dr. Don Gabriel
Ocampo, a former minister of government, entreated Lorca to
protect them by his intercession. Facundo, feeling yet insecure
in his momentary elevation, consented to grant their lives; but
this limit set to his power made him aware that he must have
full control of this veteran force, in order to avoid future opposition.

Returning to the Llanos, he came to an understanding with
Araya, and in pursuance of their agreement, they fell upon the
rest of Aldao's force by surprise, and Facundo then found himself at the head of four hundred regulars, from whose ranks
were afterwards drawn the officers of his first armies.

Remembering that Don Nicholas Dávila was in exile at
Tucuman, he summoned him to take charge of the annoying
details of the government of La Rioja, himself retaining the real
supremacy, which followed him to the Llanos. The breach between him and men like the Ocampos and Dávilas was too
wide, and the change from their government to his, too sudden, to be effected at a blow; the spirit of the city was still too
powerful for that of the country to control openly; a Doctor
of Laws was still thought to make a better government official
than any laborer. But all this was afterwards changed.

Dávila undertook the government under Facundo, and for
the time all occasion for trouble seemed over. The possessions
and estates of the Dávilas were situated near Chilecito, and
there, consequently, in the kinsmen and friends of the family,
was concentrated the physical and moral force likely to sustain
the new governor. As the population of Chilecito increased
with the profitable working of the mines, and as large fortunes
had been amassed there, the government established a provincial bank in this small town, to which it transferred its residence, either to carry out the undertaking or to withdraw itself
from the Llanos and the disagreeable subjection in which Qui-

roga was disposed to keep that region. Before long, Dávila proceeded from these purely defensive measures to more decided
action. Availing himself of Facundo's temporary absence at San
Juan, he laid plans with Captain Araya to have him arrested on
his return. Facundo learned what awaited him, and, secretly entering the Llanos, had Araya assassinated. The government whose
authority had been thus contemptuously defied, summoned him
to answer to the charge of assassination. Ridiculous parody! But
there was no other means of appealing to arms and of kindling
civil war between the government and Quiroga, between the
city and the Llanos. Facundo, in his turn, sent commissioners to
the Representative Assembly, to request the deposition of Dávila. The Assembly had urgently called upon the governor to
invade the Llanos and with the support of all the citizens, to
disarm Quiroga. The members had a local interest in the matter,
which was the transfer of the bank to the city of La Rioja; but
as Dávila persisted in residing at Chilecito, the Assembly yielded
to Facundo's solicitations and declared Dávila deposed.

Governor Dávila had assembled many of Aldao's soldiers under the command of Don Miguel Dávila. He had a good supply
of military equipments, many adherents desirous of preserving
the province from the rule of the chieftain who was strengthening himself in the Llanos, and also several regular officers to
lead his troops. Preparations for war were begun, then, with
equal zeal, in Chilecito and in the Llanos. Rumors of these
unhappy events reached San Juan and Mendoza, the government of which sent a commission to attempt to make an ar-
rangement between the belligerents, who, by that time, were
on the point of actual conflict. Corbalan, the same now serving
in Rosas' ordnance corps, visited Quiroga's camp to attempt
the mediation for which he had been sent, and which the chieftain accepted; he next went to the opposing camp, where he
met the same cordial reception; and finally returned to the
camp of Quiroga to arrange the exact terms of agreement, but

Quiroga, leaving him there, marched hastily against his enemy, whose forces he easily routed and dispersed, owing to the negligence into which the deluded envoy's assurances had caused them to fall. Don Miguel Dávila, collecting some of his men, resolutely attacked Quiroga, and succeeded in wounding him in one thigh before being himself disabled by a shot in the wrist; he was afterwards surrounded and killed by Quiroga's soldiers. A fact very characteristic of the gaucho spirit is connected with this incident. A soldier takes pleasure in showing his wounds; the gaucho hides such as he has received in close combat, and avoids having their existence known, because they attest a want of skill on his part. Facundo, faithful to these notions of honor, never mentioned the wound which Dávila had given him.

Here ends the history of the Ocampos and Dávilas, and with it that of La Rioja. What follows is the history of Quiroga.

That day of evil omen corresponds to April of 1835 in the history of Buenos Ayres—when its country commandant, its desert hero, made himself master of the city.

I ought not to omit, since it is to Quiroga's honor, a curious fact which (1823) occurred at this time. The feeblest gleam of light is not to be disregarded in the blackness of that night.

Facundo, upon his triumphant entry into La Rioja, stopped the ringing of the bells, and after sending a message of condolence to the widow of the slain General, directed his ashes to be honored with a stately funeral. He appointed for governor one Blanco, a Spaniard of low rank, and with him began the new order of affairs which was to realize the best ideal of government, as conceived by Facundo Quiroga; for, in his long career among the various cities which he conquered, he never took upon himself the charge of organizing governments; he always left that task to others.

The moment of the grasp of power over the destinies of a commonwealth by a vigorous hand is ever an important one and deserves attention. Old institutions are strengthened, or give place to others, newer and more productive of good results, or better adapted to prevailing ideas. From such a focus often diverge the threads which, as time weaves them together, change the web of history.

It is otherwise when the prevailing force is one foreign to civilization,—when an Attila obtains possession of Rome, or a Tamerlane traverses the plains of Asia; old forms remain, but the hand of philosophy would afterwards vainly remove them with the view of finding beneath them plants which had gained vigor from the human blood given them for nourishment. Facundo, a man imbued with the genius of barbarism, gets control of his country; the traditions of government disappear, established forms deteriorate, the law is a plaything in vile hands; and nothing is maintained, nothing established, amid the destruction thus accomplished by the trampling feet of horses. Freedom from restraint, occupation, and care, is the supreme good of the gaucho. If La Rioja had contained statues, as it contained doctors, they would have had horses tied to them, but they would have served no other purpose.

Facundo wanted to have means at his command, and, as he was incapable of creating a revenue system, he resorted to the ordinary proceeding of dull or weak governments; but in this case the monopoly bears the stamp of South American pastoral life, spoliation, and violence. The tithes of La Rioja were, at this time farmed out at ten thousand piastres a year; this was the average rate. Facundo made his appearance at the board, and his presence overawed the shepherds. "I offer two thousand piastres a year," said he, "and one more than the best bid." The committee repeated the proposal three times; no one made a bid; all present left, one by one, reading in Quiroga's sinister glance that it was the last one he would allow. The next year he contented himself with sending to the board the following note:—

"I give two thousand dollars and one more than the best bid.
                                            Facundo Quiroga

The third year the ceremony of adjudication was omitted, and in 1831, Quiroga again sent to La Rioja the sum of two thousand dollars, his estimate for the tithes.

But to make his tithes bring in a hundred for one, another step was required, and, after the second year, Facundo refused to receive the tribute of animals otherwise than by giving his mark among the proprietors, so that they might brand with it the animals set apart for the tithe and keep them on the place until he called for them. The creatures multiplied, their number was constantly augmented by new tithes, and, after ten years, it might be reckoned that half the stock of a whole pastoral province belonged to the commanding general of the forces, and bore his mark.

It was the immemorial custom in La Rioja that the *estrays*, or the animals that were not marked at a certain age, should become the lawful property of the treasury, which sent its agents to collect these gleanings, and derived no contemptible revenue from them, but the annoyance to the proprietors was intolerable. Facundo demanded the adjudication to himself of these animals, to meet the expenses he had incurred for the invasion of the city; expenses which were reducible to the summons of irregular forces, who assembled, mounted on horses of their own, and lived constantly on what came in their way. Already the proprietor of herds which brought him six thousand bullocks a year, he sent his agents to supply the city markets, and woe to any competitor who should appear! This business of supplying meat for the markets was one which he carried on wherever he ruled, in San Juan, Mendoza, or Tucuman; and he was always careful to secure the monopoly of it by proclamation or simple notification. It is with shame and disgust that I mention these disgraceful transactions, but the truth must be told.

The general's first order, after a bloody battle which had laid a city open to him, was that no one should supply the markets with meat! In Tucuman he learned that a resident of the place was killing cattle in his house, in spite of this order. The general of the army of the Andes, the conqueror of the Citadel, thought the investigation of so dreadful a crime should be entrusted only to himself. He went in person, and knocked lustily at the door of the house, which refused to yield, and which the inmates, taken by surprise, did not open. A kick from the illustrious general broke it in, and exposed to his view a dead ox, whose hide was in process of removal by the master of the house, who also fell dead in his turn at the terrible sight of the offended general!*

*In consequence of the present law, the government of the province has obtained the assent of His Excellency General Don Juan Facundo Quiroga, to the following stipulations, agreeably to his note of September 14, 1833.

1. That he will make good to the Most Excellent Government of Buenos Ayres the sum invested by it in the said property.

2. That he will supply the province without incumbrance to the revenue, with five thousand pesos, to meet the difficulty of filling its contingent; three thousand pesos in cash and the remainder in the produce of live stock: for the payment of which only the members of the trade of butchering shall be responsible.

3. That he is to have the exclusive right of supplying the markets, selling to the public at the rate of five reals the arroba of meat, which now costs six, and is of bad quality; and to the state at three reals without raising the current price of the article.

4. That his cattle are to be slaughtered gratis, from the 18th of the present month to the 10th of January inclusive, and to have pasture at the public expense for two reals a month for every head he shall provide from the 1st of October next.

Ruiz.—Vicento Atienzo
Official Register of the Province of San Juan

San Juan, September 13, 1833

I do not intentionally dwell upon these things. How many I omit! How many misdeeds I pass over in silence which are fully proved and known to all! But I am writing the history of government by barbarians, and I am forced to state its methods.

Mehemet Ali, who became master of Egypt by means identical with those of Facundo, delivers himself up to a rapacity unexampled even in Turkey; he establishes monopolies in every occupation and turns them to his own profit; but Mehemet Ali, though he springs from a barbarous nation, rises above his condition so far as to wish to acquire European civilization for himself and for the people he oppresses. Facundo, on the contrary, not only rejects all recognized civilization, but destroys and disorganizes. Facundo, who does not govern, because any government implies labor for others' good, gives himself up to the instincts of an immoderate and unscrupulous avarice. Selfishness is the foundation of almost all the great characters of history; selfishness is the chief spring of all great deeds. Quiroga had this political gift in an eminent degree and made everything around him contribute to his advantage; wealth, power, authority, all centred in him; whatever he could not acquire,—polish, learning, true respectability,—he hated and persecuted in all those who possessed them.

His hostility to the respectable classes and to the refinement of the cities was every day more perceptible, and the governor of La Rioja, whom he had himself appointed, finally was forced, by daily annoyances, to resign his place. One day, Quiroga, feeling inclined to pleasantry, was amusing himself with a young man as a cat sports with a frightened mouse; he liked to play at killing; the terror of the victim was so ludicrous, that the executioner was highly diverted, and laughed immoderately, contrary to his habit. He must have sympathy in his mirth, and he at once ordered the *general** to be beat through-

*A certain call to arms.

out the city of Rioja, which called out the citizens under arms. Facundo, who had given the summons for diversion's sake, drew up the inhabitants in the principal square at eleven o'clock at night, dismissed the populace and retained only the well-to-do householders and the young men who still had some appearance of culture. All night he kept them marching and countermarching, halting, forming line, marching by front or by flank. It was like a drill-sergeant teaching recruits, and the sergeant's stick travelled over the heads of the stupid, and the chests of those who were out of line; "What would you have? this is the way to teach!" Morning came, and the pallor, weariness, and exhaustion of the recruits showed what a night they had passed. Their instructor finally sent them to rest, and extended his generosity to the purchase and distribution of pastry, each recipient made in haste to eat his share, for that was part of the sport.

Lessons of such a kind are not lost upon cities, and the skillful politician who has raised similar proceedings to a system in Buenos Ayres, has refined upon them and made them wonderfully effective. For example: during the periods between 1835 and 1840 almost the whole population of Buenos Ayres has passed through the prisons. Sometimes a hundred and fifty citizens would be imprisoned for two or three months, to be then replaced by two hundred who would be kept, perhaps half the year. Wherefore? What had they done? What had they said? Idiots! Do you not see that this is good discipline for the city? Do you not remember the saying of Rosas to Quiroga, that no republic could be established because the people were not prepared for it! This is his way of teaching the city how to obey; he will finish his work, and in 1844, he will be able to show the world a people with but one thought, one opinion, one voice, and that a boundless enthusiasm for the person and will of Rosas! Then, indeed, they will be ready for a republic!

But we will return to La Rioja. A feverish excitement on

the subject of investments in the mines of the new States of Spanish America had arisen in England; powerful companies were proposing to draw profit from those of Mexico and Peru; and Rivadavia, who was then residing in London, urged speculators to invest their capital in the Argentine Republic. The mines of Famatina offered an opening for a great enterprise. At the same time, speculators from Buenos Ayres obtained the exclusive right to work these mines, meaning to sell it for an enormous sum to the English companies. These two speculations, one started in England and the other in Buenos Ayres, conflicted with each other, and were irreconcilable. Finally, a bargain was made with another English house, which was to supply funds, and in fact, sent out English superintendents and miners. Later, a speculation was got up to establish a bank at La Rioja, which was to be sold at a high price to the national government when it should be organized. On being solicited, Facundo took a large number of shares, making payment with the Jesuits' College, which had been assigned to him, on his demand, in payment of his salary as general. A party of Buenos Ayres stockholders came to La Rioja to carry out the project, and soon asked to be presented to Quiroga, whose name had begun to exercise everywhere a mysterious and terrific power. Facundo received them in his lodgings, in very fine silk stockings, ill-made pantaloons, and a common linen poncho.

The grotesque appearance of this figure was not provocative of any smiles from the elegant citizens of Buenos Ayres. They were too sagacious not to read the riddle. The man before them meant to humiliate his polished guests, and show them what account he made of their European dresses.

The administrative system established in his province was finally completed by exorbitant duties on the exportation of cattle which did not belong to him. But in addition to these direct methods of acquiring wealth, he had one which embraced his whole public career,—gambling! He had a rage for play as some men have for strong drink, and others for tobacco. His mind, though a powerful one, had not the capacity of embracing a large sphere of ideas, and stood in need of this factitious occupation, in which a passion of the soul is in constant exercise, as it is crossed, appeased, provoked, excited, and kept upon the rack. I have always thought that the passion for gambling was some useful faculty that organized society has perverted or left in inaction. The will, self-control, and steadfastness which it requires, are the same which advance the fortunes of the enterprising merchant, the banker, and the conqueror who plays for empires with battles. Facundo had habitually gambled since his childhood; play had been the only pleasure, the only relaxation of his life. But what an agreeable partner he must be who controls the terrors and the lives of the whole party! No one can conceive such a state of things without having had it before his eyes for twenty years. Facundo played unfairly, say his enemies. I do not believe the charge, for cheating at play was unnecessary in his case, and he had been known to pursue to the death, others who were guilty of it. But he played with unlimited means; he never let any one carry from the table the money he used for stakes; the game could not be stopped till he chose; he would play forty hours or more at a time; he feared no one, and if his fellow gamblers annoyed him, he could have them whipped or shot at pleasure. This was the secret of his good luck. Few men ever won much money from him, although, at some periods of the game, heaps of coin lost by him lay upon the table; the game would go on; for the winner did not dare to rise, and in the end he would have nothing but the glory of reckoning that his winnings, afterwards lost, had once been so large.

Gambling, then, was to Quiroga a system of plunder as well as a favorite amusement. No one in La Rioja received money from him, no one possessed any, without being at once invited to a game, or, in other words, to leave his funds in the chieftain's hands. Most of the tradesmen of La Rioja failed and vanished, their money having taken up its quarters in the general's purse; and it was not for want of lessons in prudence from him. A young man had won four thousand dollars from Facundo, and Facundo declined to play longer. His opponent thought that a snare was in readiness for him, and that his life was in danger. Facundo repeated that he had finished playing; the stupid fellow insisted on another game, and Facundo, complying with the demand, won the four thousand dollars from the other, who then received two hundred lashes for his uncivil pertinacity.

I am weary of reading the accounts of infamous acts in which all the manuscripts I am consulting agree. I suppress them out of respect to my vanity as an author, and to the literary pretensions of my work. By saying more I should make my pictures appear too highly colored, coarse, and repulsive.

This terminates one period of the life of the country commandant after he had abolished and suppressed the city. Hitherto Facundo was what Rosas was in his own domain, although not so far degraded before reaching power, either by gambling or by the brutal gratification of various passions. But he is to enter upon a new sphere, and we are soon to follow him over the whole Republic and seek him on battle fields.

What consequences to La Rioja were occasioned by the destruction of all civil order? Reasonings and discussions are here out of place. A visit to the scene of these occurrences will be sufficient to answer the query. The Llanos of La Rioja are now deserted; their population has emigrated to San Juan; the cisterns are dry which once gave drink to thousands of flocks. Those Llanos which fed those flocks twenty years ago, are now the home of the tiger who has reconquered his former empire, and of a few families of beggars who live upon the fruit of the carob-tree. This is the retribution the Llanos have suffered for the evils which they let loose upon the Republic. "Woe to ye, Bethsaida and Chorazin! Verily I say unto you, that the lot of Sodom and Gomorrah was more tolerable than that which was reserved for you!"

CHAPTER VII

Social Life

Society in the Middle Ages was composed of the wrecks of a thousand other societies. All the forms of liberty and servitude were found in it; the monarchical liberty of the king, the individual liberty of the priest, the privileged liberty of kings, the representative liberty of the nation, Roman slavery, barbarian serfage, and the servitude of escheatage (aubane).

—CHATEAUBRIAND

Facundo is now in possession of La Rioja, its umpire and absolute master; no other voice is heard there, no other interest than his exists there. As there is no literature, there are no opposing opinions. La Rioja is a military machine which will move as it is moved. Thus far, however, Facundo has done nothing new; Dr. Francia, Ibarra, Lopez, and Bustos, had done the same; and Güemes and Araos had attempted it in the North; that is, to destroy all existing rights for the purpose of strengthening their own. But beyond La Rioja lay an agitated world of ideas and of contradictory interests, whence came to Quiroga's residence in the Llanos the distant sounds of the controversies of the press and of political parties. Again his rise to power was necessarily attended by the spread of the clamor resulting from his overthrow of the edifice of civilization, and by his becoming an object of attention to the neighboring commonwealths. His name had passed the frontiers of La Rioja; Rivadavia was inviting him to assist in the organization of the Republic; Bustos and Lopez wished him to oppose it; the government of San Juan complacently reckoned him among its friends, and strangers came to the Llanos to pay him their respects and to ask support in behalf of one party or another.

At that time the Argentine Republic presented an animated

and interesting picture. All interests, all ideas, all passions, met together to create agitation and tumult. Here, was a chief who would have nought to do with the rest of the Republic; there, a community whose only desire was to emerge from its isolation; yonder, a government engaged in bringing Europe over to America; elsewhere, another to which the very name of civilization was odious; the Holy Tribunal of the Inquisition was reviving in some places; in others, liberty of conscience was proclaimed the first of human rights; the cry of one party was for confederation; of others for a central government; while each different combination was backed by strong and unconquerable passions. I must clear up the chaos a little, to show the rôle which it fell to Quiroga to enact, and the great work he was to bring to pass. In order to depict the provincial commandant who took possession of the city and annulled its constitution, I have found it necessary to describe the face of nature in the Argentine Republic, with the habits induced and the forms of character developed by it. And to describe Quiroga extending his power beyond his own province and proclaiming a principle, an idea, and carrying it everywhere at the point of the bayonet, I must likewise sketch the geographical distributions of the ideas and interests which were agitated in the cities. With this object, it is requisite for me to examine two cities under the sway of opposite ideas. These cities are Cordova and Buenos Ayres, as they existed in 1825, and previously.

CORDOVA

Cordova, though somewhat in the grave old Spanish style, is the most charming city in South America in its first aspect. It is situated in a hollow formed in an elevated region called the Altos. So closely are its symmetrical buildings crowded together for want of space, that it may be said to be folded back upon itself. The sky is remarkably clear, the winter season dry and bracing, the summers hot and stormy. Towards the east it has a promenade of singular beauty, the capricious outlines of which strike the eye with magical effect. It consists of a square pond surrounded by a very broad walk, shaded by ancient willow-trees of colossal size. Each side is of the length of a *cuadra*,* and the inclosure is of wrought iron grating, with enormous doors in the centre of each of the four sides, so that the promenade is an enchanted prison, within which its inmates circulate around a beautiful temple of Greek architecture. In the chief square stands the magnificent cathedral, of Gothic construction, with its immense dome carved in arabesques, the only model of mediaeval architecture, so far as I know, existing in South America. Another square is occupied by the church and convent of the Society of Jesus, in the presbytery of which is a trap-door communicating with excavations which extend to some distance below the city, which are at present but imperfectly explored; dungeons have also been discovered where the Society buried its criminals alive. If any one wishes to become acquainted with monuments of the Middle Ages, and to examine into the power and the constitution of that celebrated religious order above referred to, Cordova is the place where one of its greatest central establishments was situated.

In every square of that compact city stands a superb convent, a monastery, or a house for unprofessional nuns, or for the performance of specific religious exercises. In former times every family included a priest, a monk, a nun, or a chorister; the poorer classes contenting themselves with having among them a hermit, a lay brother, a sacristan, or an acolyte.

Each convent or monastery possessed a set of adjoining outbuildings, where lived and multiplied eight hundred slaves of

*Eighty-five yards in Montevideo, one hundred and twenty-seven in Buenos Ayres.

the Order, negroes, zamboes, mulattoes, and quadroons, with blue eyes, fair and waving hair, limbs as polished as marble, genuine Circassians adorned with every grace, but showing their African origin by their teeth, serving for bait to the passions of man, all for the greater honor and profit of the convent to which these houris belonged.*

Here is also the celebrated University of Cordova, founded as long ago as the year 1613, and in whose gloomy cloisters eight generations of medicine and divinity, both branches of law, illustrious writers, commentators, and scholars have passed their youth. Let us hear the description given by the celebrated Dean Funes of the course of instruction and the spirit of this famous university, which has for two centuries provided a great part of South America with theologians and doctors. "The course of theology lasted for five years and a half. Theology had come to share in the corruption of philosophy. The Aristotelian philosophy applied to theology had resulted in a mixture of the profane with the spiritual. Mere human reasonings, deceptive subtleties and sophisms, frivolous and misplaced inquiries—such were the conditions under which the ruling taste of these schools had been formed." If you would look a little deeper into the spirit of liberty likely to be the result of such teaching, listen a little longer to Dean Funes: "This university was originated and established wholly by Jesuits, who founded it in their college of the city of Cordova, called Maximo." Very distinguished advocates have proceeded from this institution, but no man of letters who has not also been educated at Buenos Ayres with modern books.

This learned city has never yet had a public theatre, nor become acquainted with the opera. It is still without journals, and typography is a branch of industry which has failed to take root in it. The spirit of Cordova up to 1829 was monastic and

*A similar order of things exists to this day in the city of Havana.

scholastic; the conversation of its society always turned on pro-
cessions, the saints' days, university examinations, taking the
veil, and reception of the doctor's "tassels."

How far these circumstances tended to influence the temper
of a population occupied with such ideas for two centuries,
cannot be determined; but some influence they must have had,
as is plain at a glance. The inhabitant of Cordova does not look
beyond his own horizon; that horizon is four blocks distant
from his own. When he takes his afternoon stroll, instead of
going and returning through a spacious avenue of poplars as
long as the Paseo of Santiago, which expands and animates the
mind, he follows an artificial lake of motionless and lifeless water, in the centre of which stands a structure of magnificent
proportions, immovable and stationary. The city is a cloister
surrounded by ravines; the promenade is a cloister with iron
grates; every square of houses has a cloister of nuns or friars;
the colleges are cloisters; the jurisprudence taught there, the
theology, all the mediaeval scholastic learning of the place, is a
mental cloister within which the intellect is walled up and fortified against every departure from text and commentary. Cordova knows not that aught besides Cordova exists on earth; it
has, indeed, heard that there is such a place as Buenos Ayres,
but if it believes this, which it does not always, it asks: "Has it
a university? but it must be an affair of yesterday. How many
convents has it? Has it such a promenade as this? If not, it
amounts to nothing."

"Whose work on jurisprudence do you study?" inquired the
grave Doctor Gijena, of a young man from Buenos Ayres.

"Bentham's."

"Whose, sir, do you say? Little Bentham's?"* indicating
with his finger the size of the duodecimo in which Bentham's
work is published. . . . "That wretched little Bentham's! There

---

*Benthancito, the termination expressing derision.

is more sense in one of my writings than in all those wind-bags. What a university, and what contemptible doctors!"

"And you," said the other, "whose book do you study? What!"

"Cardinal Lucques."

"What say you, sir? seventeen folio volumes?"

It is a fact that as a traveller approaches Cordova, he looks along the horizon without discovering the sanctimonious and mysterious city, the city which wears the doctor's cap and tassels. At last his guide says, "Look there, it is down there among the bushes." And in reality, as he fixes his gaze upon the ground at a short distance in advance, there appear one, two, three, ten crosses, followed by domes and towers, belonging to the many churches which adorn this Pompeii of mediaeval Spain.

To conclude, the mechanics shared the spirit of the upper classes: a master-shoemaker put on the airs of a doctor in shoe-making, and would level a Latin aphorism at a man as he gravely took his measure; the *ergo* of the scholar might be heard in the kitchens, and every dispute between a couple of porters took the sound and shape of philosophical demonstrations. We may add, that throughout the revolution, Cordova was the asylum of all fugitive Spaniards. What impression would the revolution of 1810 be likely to make upon a population educated by Jesuits, and secluded thus by nature, by teaching, and by art?

Had revolutionary ideas, such as are found in Rousseau, Mably, and Voltaire, happened to spread over the pampas and descend into this Spanish catacomb,—if we may so speak,—what response would they have been likely to find from those brains disciplined by the Aristotelian system to reject all new ideas, those intellects which, like their own promenade, had an immovable idea in their centre, unapproachable through a stagnant lake?

Toward 1816 the illustrious and liberal Dean Funes succeeded in introducing into the ancient university of the city the studies previously so much contemned: mathematics, living languages, public law, physics, drawing, and music. From that time the youth of Cordova began to direct their ideas into new channels which, ere long, led them to consequences of which we will speak hereafter. At present, I am describing the old traditional spirit of the place, which was the dominant one.

The Revolution of 1810 found the ears of Cordova closed to it at the very time when all the provinces were at once responding to the cry of "To arms! Liberty!" It was in Cordova that Liniers began to raise armies to put down the revolution in Buenos Ayres. It was to Cordova that the Junta sent one of its members and its troops to decapitate Spain. It was Cordova, which, offended by this outrage, and looking for vengeance and reparation, wrote, with the learned hand of the University, and in the idiom of the breviary and the commentators, that celebrated acrostic* which pointed out to those who passed the spot the tomb of the first royalists who were sacrificed upon the altars of the state.

In 1820, a force stationed in Arequete revolted, and General Bustos, its leader, abandoning the banners of his country, established himself quietly at Cordova, which congratulated itself for having thus robbed the nation of one of its armies. Bustos created an irresponsible colonial government, introduced court

*C	L	A	M	O	R
o	i	l	o	r	o
n	n	l	r	e	d
c	i	e	e	l	r
h	e	n	n	l	i
a	r	d	o	a	g
	s	e		n	u
				a	e
					z

etiquette and the perennial torpor of Spain, and thus prepared, Cordova entered upon the year 1828, when the question before the country was the organization of the Republic and the establishment of the revolutionary system with all its consequences.*

*On going over the pages of this first historical essay, the author regrets certain defects which cannot be expunged without recasting the whole work, for it would thus be impossible to preserve the thread of the ideas. The heat of the early years of exile, the impossibility of verifying details in such circumstances, and the prejudices of party feeling, have left some indelible traces. The description of Cordova is stained with this capital vice, and the author would willingly expunge it, if it did not contain a certain malicious exaggeration which make striking the contrast of the modern spirit which characterized Buenos Ayres in 1825.

But the author owes to the friendly frankness of Dr. Alsina, corrections upon this and several other points, which as a point of honor as well as an excuse, he submits to the examination of the reader, thus making every possible reparation for error without destroying the spirit of the original text.

"I seem to see," he says in these notes, "a capital defect in this book, that of exaggeration, independent of a certain vivacity, if not in the ideas, in their allocution. If you do not propose to write a romance or an epic, but a veritable history, political, social, and military, your rule must be not to depart from rigid historical exactness, and exaggeration is inconsistent with this. You show a *penchant* for systems, and in social science, systems do not constitute the best means of arriving at the truth. When the mind is occupied with a previous idea, and proposes to make that triumph in its demonstration of it, it exposes itself to original errors without being aware of it. Then instead of proceeding analytically, instead of examining each fact in itself, to see what can be deduced from it, and from these collected deductions and observations, to bring out a general deduction or result, instead of proceeding thus, a writer uses synthesis, that is to say, he poses a certain leading idea, reviews whatever facts present themselves, not to examine them philosophically and in detail, but to make them prove his favorite idea, and to construct by their means the edifice of his system. The natural result of this is, that when he meets with a fact which supports his idea, he exaggerates and amplifies it, and when he finds another which does not square well with his system, or which contradicts it, he presents only one aspect of it, disfigures it, or interprets it in his own way; hence forced analogies and applications, inexact or partial judg-

ments of men or events, and the generalizations with which a writer deduces
a rule or a doctrine from an individual, and often accidental fact, perhaps
insignificant in itself. All this is a necessity of systems. It is necessary to sacrifice
a great deal to them. You propose to show the *active* struggle between civilization and barbarism, a struggle where germs began to move toward development long years ago, and which during years blindly excited the struggle
between country and city, in which by a necessary law and almost by fatality,
the latter triumphed, and ought to have triumphed. I think there may be
truth at the bottom of this idea, although it has not any in my humble
opinion.

"You treat with undeserved harshness that poor city of Cordova. You do
not cite facts that justify your general assertion, made so strongly and severely.
To recall the crime of Bustos in 1820 would be inopportune, that crime
proves something else, but not that. That Liniers and other distinguished men,
almost all Spaniards, acted like Spaniards in 1810, is not astonishing, and their
recontre at Cordova should not be imputed to a love of royalty in the people
any more than the appearance of that kind of acrostic which you copy, and
which might have been the work of an individual, should be imputed to the
same thing. These proofs go out of the limits of the circumspection of history
to justify an accusation so positive and so general. There were families of the
Spanish party there as in all the provinces, without excluding that of Buenos
Ayres, and this was natural. After it was delivered from Liniers and his asso-
ciates, what fact reveals the opposition or dissent of Cordova to the revolution? What does Cordova do less than any other of the provinces where the
Spanish armies did not go? What more have the others done than Cordova?
It received with decision the first patriotic army, and contributed what it
could to it. From 1810 it furnished many soldiers; from 1810 it furnished
many men and young men who became excellent officers; it gave Valey, who
died gloriously at Desaguadero; also Leevá, Bustos, Julian, and José Maria Paz,
J. G. Echevarria, who died for liberty in 1831, as you say further on; it gave
my client Colonel Rojas, who made his *debut* at Dehesa, and others whose
names I do not now remember. Cordova sent its deputies to the first Junta,
and has since sent them to all the national bodies. In what other way would
you have a province take part in the revolution? In what manner *have* others
taken part in it?

                                                              "Alsina"

BUENOS AYRES

Let us now turn our attention to Buenos Ayres. Its first struggle was with the aborigines by whom it was swept from the face of the earth. It recovered itself more than once, until in 1620 it figured in the Spanish dominions sufficiently to be erected into a district governed by a Captain-general, and to be separated from Paraguay, under whose government it had previously existed. In 1777, Buenos Ayres had already become very conspicuous, so much so, indeed, that it was necessary to remould the administrative geography of the colonies, and to make Buenos Ayres the chief section. A viceroyal government was expressly created for it.

In 1806, the attention of English speculators was turned to South America, and especially attracted to Buenos Ayres by its river, and its probable future. In 1810, Buenos Ayres was filled with partisans of the revolution, bitterly hostile to anything originating in Spain or any part of Europe. A germ of progress, then, was still alive west of the La Plata. The Spanish colonies cared nothing for commerce or navigation. The Rio de la Plata was of small importance to them. The Spanish disdained it and its banks. As time went on, the river proved to have deposited its sediment of wealth upon those banks, but very little of Spanish spirit or Spanish modes of government. Commercial activity had brought thither the spirit and the general ideas of Europe; the vessels which frequented the waters of the port brought books from all quarters, and news of all the political events of the world. It is to be observed that Spain had no other commercial city upon the Atlantic coast. The war with England hastened the emancipation of men's minds and awakened among them a sense of their own importance as a state. Buenos Ayres was like a child, which, having conquered a giant, fondly deems itself a hero, and is ready to undertake greater adventures. The *Social Contract* flew from hand to hand. Mably and

Raynal were the oracles of the press; Robespierre and the Convention the approved models. Buenos Ayres thought itself a continuation of Europe, and if it did not frankly confess that its spirit and tendencies were French and North American, it denied its Spanish origin on the ground that the Spanish Government had patronized it only after it was full grown. The revolution brought with it armies and glory, triumphs and reverses, revolts and seditions. But Buenos Ayres, amidst all these fluctuations, displayed the revolutionary energy with which it is endowed. Bolivar was everything; Venezuela was but the pedestal for that colossal figure. Buenos Ayres was a whole city of revolutionists—Belgrano, Rondeau, San Martin, Alyear; and the hundred generals in command of its armies were its instruments; its arms, not its head nor its trunk. It cannot be said in the Argentine Republic that such a general was the liberator of the country; but only that the Assembly, Directory, Congress, or government of such or such a period, sent a given general to do this thing or that. Communication with all the European nations was ever, even from the outset, more complete here than in any other part of Spanish America; and now, in ten years' time (but only, be it understood, in Buenos Ayres), there comes to pass a radical replacement of the Spanish by the European spirit. We have only to take a list of the residents in and about Buenos Ayres to see how many natives of the country bear English, French, German, or Italian surnames. The organization of society, in accordance with the new ideas with which it was impregnated, began in 1820; and the movement continued until Rivadavia was placed at the head of the government. Hitherto Rodriguez and Las Heras had been laying the usual foundations of free governments. Amnesty laws, individual security, respect for property, the responsibility of civil authority, equilibrium of powers, public education, everything, in fine, was in peaceful course of establishment when Rivadavia came from Europe, brought Europe as it were, but Europe was yet undervalued. Buenos Ayres—and that means, of course, the Argentine Republic—was to realize what republican France could not realize, what the English aristocracy did not even wish for, what despotic Europe wanted still less. This was not an illusion of Rivadavia's; it was the general thought of the city, its spirit, and its tendency.

Parties were divided, not by ideas essentially opposed to each other, but by the greater or less extent of their aims. And how else could it have been with a people which in only fourteen years had given England a lesson, overrun half the continent, equipped ten armies, fought a hundred pitched battles, been everywhere victorious, taken part in all events, set at nought all traditions, tested all theories, ventured upon everything and succeeded in everything; which was still vigorous, growing rich, progressing in civilization? What was to ensue, when the basis of government, the political creeds received from Europe, were vitiated by errors, absurd and deceptive theories, and unsound principles? for the native politicians who were as yet without any definite knowledge of political organization, could not be expected to know more than the great men of Europe. I desire to call attention to the significance of this fact. The study of constitutions, races, and creeds, in short, history, has now diffused a certain amount of practical knowledge which warns us against the glitter of theories based upon *a priori* conceptions; but previous to 1820, nothing of that had transpired in the European world. France was roused into insurrection by the paradoxes of the Social Contract; Buenos Ayres was similarly roused; Montesquieu designated three powers, and immediately we had three; Benjamin Constant and Bentham annulled power; here they declared it originally null; Say and Smith preached free-trade; "commercial liberty," we repeated; Buenos Ayres confessed and believed all that the learned world of Europe believed and confessed. Not till after the revolution of 1830 in France, and its incomplete results, did the Social

Sciences take a new direction and illusions begin to be dispelled. From that time European books began to come to us, which demonstrated that Voltaire had not much reason, and that Rousseau was a sophist, and Mably and Raynal anarchists; that there were no three powers, nor any Social Contract, etc. From that time we learned something of races, of tendencies, of national habits, of historical antecedents. Tocqueville revealed to us for the first time the secret of North America; Sismondi laid bare the emptiness of constitutions; Thierry, Michelet, and Guizot, gave us the spirit of history; the revolution of 1830, all the hollowness of the constitutionalism of Benjamin Constant; the Spanish revolution, all that is incomplete and behindhand in our own race. Of what then were Rivadavia and Buenos Ayres accused? Of not knowing more than the European savants who were their guides? On the other side, how was it possible not to embrace with ardor the general ideas of a people who had contributed so much and so well to make the revolution general? How bridle the imaginations of the inhabitants of an illimitable plain bordered by a river whose opposite bank could not be seen—a step from Europe, not knowing even its own traditions, indeed without having them in reality; a new, suddenly improvised people, which from the very cradle had heard itself called great?

Thus elevated, and hitherto flattered by fortune, Buenos Ayres set about making a constitution for itself and the Republic, just as it had undertaken to liberate itself and all South America: that is, eagerly, uncompromisingly, and without regard to obstacles. Rivadavia was the personification of this poetical, utopian spirit which prevailed. He therefore continued the work of Las Heras upon the large scale necessary for a great American State—a republic. He brought over from Europe men of learning for the press and for the professor's chair, colonies for the deserts, ships for the rivers, freedom for all creeds, credit and the national bank to encourage trade, and all the great social theories of the day for the formation of his government. In a word, he brought a second Europe, which was to be established in America, and to accomplish in ten years what elsewhere had required centuries. Nor was this project altogether chimerical; all his administrative creations still exist, except those which the barbarism of Rosas found in its way. Freedom of conscience, advocated by the chief clergy of Buenos Ayres, has not been repressed; the European population is scattered on farms throughout the country, and takes arms of its own accord to resist the only obstacle in the way of the wealth offered by the soil. The rivers only need to be freed from governmental restrictions to become navigable, and the national bank, then firmly established, has saved the people from the poverty to which the tyrant would have brought them. And, above all, however fanciful and impracticable that great system of government may have been, it was at least easy and endurable for the people; and, notwithstanding the assertions of misinformed men, Rivadavia never shed a drop of blood, nor destroyed the property of any one; but voluntarily descended from the Presidency to poverty and exile. Rosas, by whom he was so calumniated, might easily have been drowned in the blood of his own victims; and the forty millions of dollars from the national treasury, with the fifty millions from private fortunes which were consumed in ten years of the long war provoked by his brutalities, would have been employed by the "*fool*—the *dreamer*—Rivadavia," in building canals, cities, and useful public buildings. Then let this man, who died for his country, have the glory of representing the highest aspirations of European civilization, and leave to his adversaries that of displaying South American barbarism in its most odious light. For Rosas and Rivadavia are the two extremes of the Argentine Republic, connecting it with savages through the pampas, and with Europe through the River La Plata.

I am not making the eulogy, but the apotheosis of Rivadavia

and his party, which has ceased to exist as a political element
of the Argentine Republic, though Rosas persists in calling his
present enemies *"Unitarios."* The old union party, like that of
the Girondists, disbanded many years ago; but with all its im-
possibilities and fanciful illusions it had much that was noble
and great to which the succeeding generation should do justice.
Many of those men are still among us, though no longer as an
organized party; they are the remains of the Argentine Republic, as noble and as venerable as those of Napoleon's empire.
These Unitarios of the year 1825 form a distinct class of men,
recognized by their manners, tone of voice, and opinions. A
Unitario would be known among a thousand by his stately
bearing, his somewhat haughty manner of speaking, and his
positive gestures; on the eve of a battle he will pause to discuss
a question logically, or to establish some new legal formality;
for legal formulas are the outward worship which he offers to
his idols—the Constitution and individual rights. His religion
is the future of the Republic, whose image, sublime and colossal, is ever before him, covered with the mantle of its past
glory. Never was there a generation so enterprising, so gifted
with reasoning and deductive powers, and so wanting in practical common sense. A Unitario will not believe in the evident
success of his enemies. He has such faith in the greatness of his
cause, that neither exile, nor poverty, nor lapse of years can
weaken his enthusiasm; and in calmness of mind and in energy
of soul he is infinitely superior to the present generation. These
men also excel us in ceremonious politeness and refinement of
manner; for conventionalities are more and more disregarded
among us as democracy progresses, and it is now difficult to
realize the culture and refinement of society in Buenos Ayres
before 1828. Europeans who went there found themselves, as
it were, still in Europe, in the saloons of Paris; nothing was
wanting, not even the insolence of the Parisian *élegant*, which

was well imitated by the same class of young men in Buenos Ayres.

I have been particular in mentioning these little things in order to give an idea of the period when the Republic was in the process of formation, and of its different elements struggling for precedence. On one side Cordova, Spanish in education, in literature, and in religion, conservative and strongly opposed to all innovations; and on the other, Buenos Ayres, revolutionary by nature, ready for any change and progress.

These were the types of the two parties that divided every city; and I doubt if there is another such phenomenon in America; that is, two parties, conservative and revolutionary, retrograde and progressive, each represented by a city having its own peculiar form of civilization, and receiving opinions from entirely different sources: Cordova, from Spain, the Councils, the Commentators, the Digest; Buenos Ayres, from Bentham, Rousseau, Montesquieu, and French literature in general.

To these elements of antagonism must be added another not less important, namely, the want of any national bond after the provinces became independent of Spain. When government authority is removed from one centre to another, time is necessary for its firm establishment.

The "Republican" recently declared that "government is no more than a compact between the governors and the governed." Evidently there are still many Unitarios among us! *Government is in reality founded upon the unpremeditated consent which a nation gives to a permanent fact.* Where there is deliberation, there is no authority. This transition state is called a confederation. Out of each revolution and consequent change of government, different nations derive their ideas and modes of confederation.

I will explain myself. When Ferdinand VII was driven from Spain, government—*that permanent fact*—ceased to exist; and

Spain was formed into provincial assemblies which denied the authority of those who governed in the name of the king. This was the *Spanish Confederation*. When the news reached America, the South American provinces revolted from Spain, and being divided into sections, formed the *South American Confederation*. From Buenos Ayres came at the end of the contest, four states,—Bolivia, Paraguay, Banda Oriental, and the Argentine Republic; these formed the *Confederation of the Viceroyalty*. Finally, the Argentine Republic was divided, not as formerly into districts, but according to its cities, and so became a *confederation of cities*.

It is not that the word confederation signifies separation, but that when separation has already taken place, it expresses the union of the different parts. The Argentine Republic was at this social crisis, and many persons of note in the cities believed that, for mere convenience, or whenever an individual or a community felt no respect for the nominal government, a new confederation might be formed. Here then was another apple of discord in the Republic, and the two parties, after having been called "Royalists" and "Patriots," "Congresistas" and "Executivistas," "Conservatives," and "Liberals," now bore the names of "Federales" and "Unitarios."* Perhaps, to finish the list, I should give the name bestowed upon the latter party by Don Juan Manuel Rosas, that is, *"salvajes inmundos Unitarios."*

But the Argentine Republic is so situated geographically, that it is destined to a consolidation, whatever Rosas may say to the contrary. Its continuous plain, its rivers confined to one outlet, and therefore to one port, force it inevitably to be *"one and indivisible."* Rivadavia, who well understood the necessities of the country, advised the provinces to unite under a common

---

Federales, those who held to a confederation of the old provinces, or a union of states. *Unitarios*, those who advocated a consolidated central government.

constitution, and to make a national port of Buenos Ayres. Aguero, his supporter in Congress, said to the citizens of Buenos Ayres, "Let us voluntarily give to the provinces what, sooner or later, they will claim by force." The prophecy failed in one respect; the provinces did not claim the port of Buenos Ayres by force of arms, but by force of the barbarism which they sent upon her in Facundo and Rosas. Buenos Ayres feels all the effects of the barbarism, while the port has been of no use to the provinces.

I have been obliged to explain all these antecedents in order to continue the life of Juan Facundo Quiroga; for, though it seems ridiculous to say it, Facundo was the rival of Rivadavia. Everything disconnected with these men was of little importance, and left no impression. There were in the Republic two parties: one in Buenos Ayres, supported by the Liberals in the provinces; the other originating in the provinces and supported by the provincial commanders who had obtained possession of cities. One of these powers was civilized, constitutional, European; the other barbarous, arbitrary, South American.

These two parties had reached their full development, and only needed a word to begin the contest; one, as the revolutionary party, was already called "Unitario," the opposite party assumed the name of "Federal," without well understanding it.

But that barbarian party or power was scattered throughout the Republic, in the provinces, and in the Indian territories, and a strong arm was needed to establish it firmly in a compact form, and Quiroga offered his for the work.

Though the Argentine gaucho has some qualities common to all shepherds, he has strong local attachments. Whether he belongs in Buenos Ayres, Santa Fé, Cordova, or the Llanos, all his aspirations are confined to his own province; and he is an enemy or a stranger to all the others. These provinces are like different tribes ready to make war upon one another. Lopez, as governor of Santa Fé, cared nothing for what was passing around him, except occasionally when obliged to drive out troublesome intruders from his territory. But as these provinces had points of contact, nothing could prevent them from finally joining in a common interest, thus bringing about that consolidation which they had so struggled against.

As I have already said, Quiroga's wandering life in youth gave rise to his future ambition; for, though a gaucho, he was troubled with no local attachment. He was born in Rioja, but educated in San Juan, and lived afterwards both in Mendoza and Buenos Ayres. He was acquainted with the whole Republic, and his ambition had no narrow limits. Master of Rioja, he delighted to present himself clothed with authority in that town, where he had learned to read; in another city, which was the scene of his boyish *escapadas*; and in another still, where he had distinguished himself by his prison exploit. If it was for his interest to leave a province, he was not detained by his affections; and, unlike Lopez or Ibarra, who only cared to defend their own possessions, he was fond of attacking his neighbor's territory and taking it into his own hands.

CHAPTER VIII
Experiments

How long are the days now? for to-morrow I wish to gallop ten leagues over a field sown with corpses.

—SHAKESPEARE

The political condition of the Republic was such as we have described in 1825, when the governor of Buenos Ayres* invited the provinces to unite in a congress and assume the form of a general government. This idea was everywhere favorably received, either because every military commander expected to be made governor of his own province, or because the glory of Buenos Ayres dazzled all eyes. The governor of Buenos Ayres has been blamed for proposing this question, the solution of which was to be so unfortunate for himself and for the civilization of the country.

Facundo, in behalf of La Rioja, eagerly accepted the invitation, perhaps on account of the sympathy which all highly gifted minds have for good plans!

In 1825 the Republic prepared for the Brazilian war by calling upon each province to raise a regiment for the army. Colonel Madrid went to Tucuman for this purpose, and impatient to obtain the reluctant recruits and other necessaries for his company, did not hesitate to set aside the slow authorities and to take things into his own hands in order to expedite the necessary decrees. This act of subversion placed the governor of Buenos Ayres in a very delicate position; for there was already some distrust among the governments, arising from provincial jealousies, and the coming of Colonel Madrid from

*Rivadavia.

Buenos Ayres, and his interference with provincial authorities, were regarded as acts instigated by the governor himself.

To remove this suspicion, Facundo was sent to Tucuman for the purpose of reëstablishing the local authorities. Madrid explained to the governor the real motive—certainly a very insufficient one—which had actuated him, and professed sincere devotion to the cause. But it was too late, Facundo was already on his way, and he could only prepare to resist him. Madrid had at his disposal a company which was passing through Salta; but not wishing to aggravate the charges already made against him, contented himself with fifty guns and as many swords; enough, as he thought, to meet the invading force.

This Colonel Madrid belonged to a class of men essentially Argentine by birth and spirit. At the age of fourteen he began to fight the Spaniards, and the stories of his romantic valor are numerous and often incredible. He was said to have been in a hundred and fifty encounters, his sword always bearing marks of much service; the very smell of powder and neighing of the horses so excited him, that cavalry, artillery, infantry, everything that came in his way, fell before his mad energy. Besides his love of fighting, he had the gift of the Argentine *cantor*, and animated his soldiers with war-songs, such as have already been described. Unfortunately, he was not a well-balanced general, such as Napoleon liked; his bravery predominated over the other qualities desirable in a general in the proportion of a hundred to one,—a fact well proved by the event at Tucuman. Though able to call in a sufficient force, he persisted in giving battle with only a handful of men, accompanied by Colonel Diasvelez, who was not less brave than himself. Facundo had with him two hundred of infantry and his own Red Cavalry; Madrid had fifty foot-soldiers and a few squadrons of militia. At the beginning of the contest, Facundo and his cavalry were routed, and he himself did not return to the field of battle until all was over. Meanwhile the body of infantry stood firm; Madrid ordered his men to charge upon them, but not being obeyed, he actually rushed upon them alone. He was thrown from his horse, but, recovering himself, charged about him, slaying on the right, on the left, and before him, until horse and horsemen fell pierced with balls and bayonets, and victory was decided in favor of the infantry.

Facundo now came back to recover his black flag which had been lost, and found his victory gained, and Madrid dead, actually dead. His equipments were there,—sword, horse, and all,—but his body could not be recognized among the stripped and mutilated corpses that lay upon the field. Colonel Diasvelez, who was a prisoner, said that his ally had a bayonet wound in his leg, and no body was found with such a wound.

Madrid had dragged himself under some bushes where his aid found him raving deliriously about the battle; and at the sound of approaching footsteps, he cried, "I do not surrender!" Never until then had Colonel Madrid surrendered.

This was the famous fight at Tala, the first exploit of Quiroga beyond the limits of his province. He had conquered "the bravest of the brave," and kept his sword as a trophy of the victory. Will he stop there? But let us see the force which sustained itself against the colonel of the 13th regiment, who overthrew a government to equip his company. Facundo raised at Tala a flag which was not Argentine, but of his own invention; namely, a black ground with a skull and cross-bones in the centre. This was the flag which he had lost early in the engagement, and which he intended to recover, as he said to his routed soldiers, even at the mouth of hell. Terror, death, hell, were represented on the banner and in the proclamations of this general of the Llanos.

And there was still another revelation of the Arab-Tartar spirit of that power which was to destroy the cities. The Argentine colors are blue and white; the clear sky of a fair day, and the bright light of the disk of the sun: "peace and justice for all." In our hatred of tyranny and violence, we reject on our national flag warlike devices. Two hands, as a sign of union, support the Phrygian cap of Liberty. "The United Cities" says this symbol, "will sustain their acquired liberty." The sun begins to illumine the background of this device, while the darkness of night is disappearing. The armies of the Republic, which were to spread over the whole country to enforce the coming of that promised light, wear a uniform of dark blue. But now, in the very heart of the Republic, the color red appears on the national banners, in the dress of the soldiers, and in the cockade which every native Argentine must wear under pain of death. Let us look up the significance of the color red. I have before me a picture of all the national flags of the world. In civilized Europe there is but one in which this color prevails, notwithstanding the barbaric origin of its banners. The *red* ones are: Algiers, a *red* flag with skull and cross-bones; Tunis, a *red* flag; Mongolia, the same; Turkey, a *red* flag with a crescent; Morocco; Japan, *red* with the exterminating knife; Siam has the same.

I remember that travellers in the interior of Africa provide themselves with *red* cloth for the negro princes. "The king of Elve," say the brothers Lander, "wore a Spanish coat of *red* cloth and pantaloons of the same color."

I remember that the presents sent by the government of Chili to the caciques of Aranco, were *red* cloaks and coats, because savages liked this color especially.

The royal robes of the barbarian kings of Europe were always *red*. The royal edict of Genoa declared that the senators must wear a red toga, and especially in pronouncing judgment on criminals, that they might inspire the prisoners with terror.

Until within the last century it was the custom in all the countries of Europe for the executioner to be dressed in *red*.

The armies of Rosas wore a red uniform; his likeness is stamped on a red ribbon.

What remarkable connection is there between these facts? Is it chance that Algiers, Tunis, Japan, Turkey, Siam, the Africans, the savages, the Roman Neros, the barbarian kings, the hangmen, and Rosas, should be clothed in a color now proscribed by Christian and civilized communities? No, it is because red is the symbol of violence, blood, and barbarism. If not, why this antagonism?

The Argentine revolution of independence was symbolized by two blue stripes and one white one; signifying, *justice, peace, justice.*

The amendment made by Facundo and approved by Rosas, was a red band, signifying *terror, blood, barbarism.*

In all ages this significance has been given to the color purple or red; study the history of those nations who have hoisted this color, and you will always find a Rosas and a Facundo—terror, barbarism, and blood always prevailing. In Morocco, the emperor has the singular prerogative of killing criminals with his own hand. Each phase of civilization is expressed in its garments, and every style of apparel is indicative of an entire system of ideas. Why do we wear beards at the present day? Because of the researches recently made in mediaeval history; the direction given to romantic literature is reflected in the fashions of the day. And why are these constantly changing? Because of the freedom of thought in Europe; let thought be stationary, enslaved, and the costume will remain unchanged. Thus in Asia, where men live under such governments as that of Rosas, the same style of dress has been worn since the time of Abraham.

And still further; every form of civilization has had its style of apparel, and every revolution of institutions has produced a change of costume. The Roman civilization had one style of dress; the Middle Ages another; the frock-coat was not worn in Europe until after the revival of letters. It is ever the most civilized nation that imposes its fashions on the rest of the world. All Christian nations now wear the coat, and when the Sultan of Turkey, Abdul-Medjid, desired to introduce European civilization into his dominions, he laid aside the turban and caftan for the frock-coat, pantaloons, and cravat.

The Argentine people know the violent opposition to civilized costume made by both Rosas and Facundo. One night, in the year 1840, a couple of *mazorqueros*★ were dodging around the streets of Buenos Ayres in pursuit of a man who wore a coat, and at last he was seized by the throat, when he exclaimed, "I am Simon Pereira!" "Pardon, sir," said the men, "but you expose yourself by wearing this coat." "That is just why I wear it; who else wears a coat? I do it to be known at a distance."

This Simon was the purveyor and agent of Rosas. But to finish the illustration of the spirit of the civil war by its symbols, I must refer to the history of the *"red ribbon"* of quite extensive notoriety.

In 1820, Rosas appeared in Buenos Ayres with his *Colorados de las Conchas.*† Twenty years afterwards, he colored the whole city with red; houses, doors, paper-hangings, tapestry, etc.; but finally he consecrated the color to official purposes, and made it a test of loyalty to the state.

The history of the red ribbon is rather singular. At first it was adopted only by party enthusiasts; then it was ordered that every one should wear it as a *proof of unanimity of opinion*. If there was no intentional disobedience, but in changing the dress the badge was forgotten, the police came to the assistance of memory. *Mazorqueros* were stationed in all the streets, and par-

---

★*Mazorqueros*, agents of Rosas, employed in cases of secret vengeance.
†A company of provincial militia, dressed in red.

ticularly at the doors of the churches, and when the ladies came out, slashes with a cowhide were distributed without mercy. There were yet stricter regulations. If the ribbon was carelessly tied: "Stripes! the fellow must be a Unitario." If the ribbon was too short: "Stripes for the Unitario!" And if a man did not wear it at all, he was put to death for contempt of the laws. The care of the governor for the public education did not stop here. It was not enough to be a Federal and to wear the red ribbon; the likeness of the illustrious Restaurador must be stamped upon it, with the motto, "Death to the dirty savages, Unitarios," and it must be worn near the heart in token of deep love. It might be thought that the work of debasing a cultivated people and destroying all personal dignity, was now ended. But they were not yet sufficiently disciplined. One morning a ridiculous figure painted on paper, with a streamer of red ribbon half a yard long, appeared at the corner of a street in Buenos Ayres. The first person who saw it rushed back, terrified, and gave the alarm. Immediately every one hurried to the shops and soon appeared wearing half a yard of ribbon. A few days after, a slight alteration in the ribbon or the painted figure was followed by the same result. If any ladies happened to forget the red knots prescribed for them instead of the ribbon, the police would most likely furnish them one gratis—of melted tar! Thus was uniformity of opinion secured, and not a person was to be found who was not a Federal, or did not imagine himself one. It frequently happened that some one coming out of his house found the end of the street swept, and in less than a half hour the whole street was swept, the impression having become general that there was a police order to that effect.

One day a grocer put out a small flag to attract customers; the example was followed from house to house, from street to street, until banners floated over the whole city; and the officials thought that some great news had come, unknown to them.

And this was the people who once forced eleven thousand English to surrender in the streets, and who afterward sent five armies against the Spaniards!

The fact is, that terror is a mental disease which attacks a people like cholera, small-pox, or scarlet fever. Every one is liable to the contagion, and when the inoculation has been going on for ten years, it is doubtful if even the vaccinated escape. Do not laugh then at the sight of so much degradation. Remember that you are Spaniards, and that the Inquisition educated Spain! We bear this disease in our blood.

Let us now resume the thread of our history. Facundo entered Tucuman in triumph, where he passed several days without committing any remarkable acts of violence, and without imposing taxes; for the constitutional course of Rivadavia had given the people an amount of knowledge which could not at once be ignored. Facundo then returned to Rioja, inimical to the Presidency, though not knowing what motive to give for this opposition, for he could not have explained it to himself.

"I am not a Federal," he always said, "I am not such a fool." "Do you know," he said once, to Don Dalmacio Velez, "why I went to war? For this," showing, as he spoke, an ounce of gold. This was not true.

At other times he said, "Carril, governor of San Juan, treated me very badly in paying no attention to my recommendation of Carita, and for this I put myself in opposition to the Congress." This also was false. His enemies said, that he owned many shares in the bank, and proposed to sell them to the national government for three hundred thousand dollars. Rivadavia rejected this proposition as a scandalous theft, and from that time Facundo enlisted him among his enemies. This was true as a fact, but it was not his motive. It was believed that he yielded to the suggestions of Bustos and Ibarra in joining the opposition party; but there is a document which proves the contrary. In a letter which he wrote in 1832 to General Madrid, he said, "When I was invited by those two low fellows, Bustos and Ibarra, I did not consider them capable of making a successful opposition to that despot, President Don Bernadino Rivadavia, and refused to join them; but having been informed by Colonel Manuel del Castillo, aide-de-camp of Bustos, that you were engaged in this affair, and much interested in it, I did not hesitate a moment in deciding to join unconditionally; counting upon your sword alone for success. . . . What was my misfortune," etc.

So he considered it a fool's part to be a Federal! Was it necessary then to be as ignorant as a country commandant to know what form of government was most suitable for the Republic? Was the least educated man most capable of judging of difficult political questions? Were such thinkers as Lopez, Ibarra, and Facundo, with their great historical, social, geographical, philosophical, and legal information to solve the problem of the proper organization for a state? Ah! let us lay aside the vain words that have deceived so many. Facundo turned against the government by which he was sent to Tucuman, for the same reason that he turned against Aldao who sent him to Rioja. He found himself with the power and the will for action; and, impelled by a blind, vague instinct, he obeyed it. He was commander of a company, *a gaucho-outlaw*, an enemy of civil justice, of civil order, of educated men, of savants, of the frock-coat, in a word, of the city. He was ordained for the destruction of these by Providence, and must needs fulfill his mission.

At this time a singular question arose to complicate affairs. In Buenos Ayres, the seaport and residence of sixteen thousand foreigners, the governor granted these foreigners liberty of conscience; and the higher clergy approved of and sustained this law. Convents of different orders had been already suppressed, and the priests provided for. In Buenos Ayres this matter gave no trouble, for all were agreed upon necessity of toleration.

The question of liberty of conscience is in South America a question of political economy, for it implies European emigration and population. This was so fully recognized in Buenos Ayres that even Rosas did not dare to revoke the law of freedom; and that thing must be impossible, indeed, which Rosas would not attempt.

In the provinces, however, this was a question of religion, of salvation, and of eternal damnation. Imagine how it would be considered in Cordova! In Cordova, an inquisition was established. In San Juan, there was a *Catholic* insurrection, so called to distinguish its party from the Liberalistas, their enemies. This revolution having been suppressed in San Juan, they found one day that Facundo was at the gates of the city with a black flag, bearing a red cross, and the device "RELIGION OR DEATH!"

As the reader will remember, I have quoted from a manuscript that Facundo never went to confession, nor heard mass, nor prayed, and that he himself said he believed in nothing. And yet party spirit led a celebrated preacher to call him *one sent by God*, to induce many to follow his banner. When the eyes of this same priest were opened, and he withdrew from the wicked crusade which he had preached, Facundo said he was only sorry that he did not have him at hand to give him six hundred lashes.

On his arrival at San Juan, the chief men of the city, the magistrates who had not fled, and the priests grateful for this divine aid, went out to meet him, forming two long files in the streets. Facundo passed through without looking at them. They followed at a distance, mortified, and exchanging glances in their common humiliation, until they reached a clover pasture, which this shepherd-general, this modern *hicso*, chose for his quarters, and preferred to the fine edifices of the city. A negress, who had nursed him in his infancy, came to see her boy Facundo. He seated her by his side and conversed affectionately with her, while the priests and dignitaries of the city stood unaccosted, the chief not even deigning to dismiss them.

The Catholics must have been somewhat doubtful of the importance and divinity of the aid which came to them in such an unexpected form. A few days after, learning that the Curé of the Conception was in favor of free worship, Facundo caused him to be arrested, thrown into prison, and sentenced to death. My Chilian readers must know that there were in San Juan at this time, priests, curés, and monks, who believed in freedom of conscience, and belonged to the party of the President. Among others the presbyter Centeno, well-known in Santiago, together with six others, was very zealous in the ecclesiastical reform. But something must be done in the cause of religion, to justify the device of the flag. With this laudable aim, Facundo wrote to a priest of his party, asking his advice about the resolution he had formed to shoot all the city authorities for not having decreed the restitution of the secular revenues of the clergy.

The good priest, who had not foreseen the consequences of arming crime in the name of God, felt some scruple about such a mode of reparation, and advised that the officials should be commanded to make the necessary decrees.

Was there any real question of religion in the Argentine Republic? I should deny it utterly if I did not know that the more barbarous and irreligious a people is, the more liable it is to prejudice and fanaticism. But the masses did not move of their own accord, and it is plain that those who adopted this device, Facundo, Lopez, Bustos, etc., were completely indifferent. The religious wars of the fifteenth century in Europe were maintained on both sides by sincere believers, fanatical and devoted even to martyrdom, without political aims, and without ambition. The Puritans read the Bible at the moment of going into battle, prayed, and observed fasts and penances. The spirit of a party is evidently sincere, when after triumph it accomplishes all and even more than it promised before the contest. When this result is wanting, there is a deception in terms. When the so-called Catholic party had triumphed in the Argentine Republic, what did it do for religion or the interests of the priesthood?

As far as I know, it only drove out the Jesuits, beheaded four respectable priests in Santos Lugares, after having flayed their heads and hands, and carried in procession the host and the portrait of Rosas side by side, under a canopy. Did the Liberal party ever commit such horrible profanations?

But enough of this. While at San Juan, Facundo occupied his time in gambling; leaving to the authorities the care of providing him with the sums necessary to defray the expenses incurred in the defense of religion. All the time that he remained there he lived in a tent on the clover field, ostentatiously dressed in the *chiripá*, an intentional insult to a city where most of the inhabitants used English saddles, and where the barbarous dress and habits of the gauchos were especially disliked, San Juan being an exclusively agricultural province.

One more campaign against General Madrid at Tucuman, completed the *début* of this new emir of shepherds. General Madrid had resumed the government of Tucuman, sustained by the whole province, and Facundo thought it his duty to dislodge him. There was a new expedition, a new battle, and a new victory. I omit the details with the exception of one characteristic anecdote. Madrid had in the battle of Rincon one hundred and ten infantry; and when the combat ended, there were sixty dead, while of the remaining fifty all except one were wounded. On the following day Madrid declared himself again ready for battle, but Quiroga sent one of his aides to say that the action would begin by shooting the fifty prisoners already kneeling to receive their fate. Madrid abandoned all further attempt at resistance.

In these three expeditions, in which Facundo tested his

power, there was no unusual effusion of blood and but few outrages. It is true that in Tucuman he seized upon some flocks and hides, and imposed heavy taxes upon them, but as yet there was no cowhiding of the citizens, no outrages upon the women; there were the evils of conquest, but none of its horrors. The pastoral system had not yet developed that brutality and entire absence of restraint which afterwards characterized it.

What part had the legitimate governor of Rioja in these expeditions? The government only existed nominally; all the real power was in the hands of the "Provincial Commander." Blanco resigned the office, overwhelmed with humiliations; and Aguero assumed the government. One day, however, Quiroga rode up to his door and said to him, "Sir, I came to inform you that I have encamped with my escort two miles from here." It is hardly necessary to say that Aguero resigned. A new governor was now to be chosen, and at the petition of the people, Quiroga condescended to nominate Galvan, who accepted the office, but was assaulted the same night by a troop of soldiers, and fled. Quiroga enjoyed the adventure excessively. It is well to mention that the assembly of representatives was composed of men who did not know how to read.

Facundo needed money for his first expedition to Tucuman, and demanded of the treasurer of the bank eight thousand dollars on account of his shares for which he had never paid. In Tucuman, he demanded twenty-five thousand dollars to pay his soldiers, who received none of it; and some time after sent a bill of eighteen thousand dollars to Dorrego to pay the cost of the expedition made by order of the governor of Buenos Ayres. Dorrego did not hesitate to satisfy so just a demand. This sum was shared with Moral, the governor of Rioja, who had suggested the idea. Six years after, in Mendoza, he gave this same Moral seven hundred lashes for his ingratitude. While Blanco was governor, there was a dispute about a game of cards, and Facundo, seizing his opposer by the hair, shook him until his neck was broken. The body was buried, and the man declared to have died a *natural death*.

When about to leave Tucuman, he sent a party of soldiers to the house of one Sarate, who was shot at his own door and left for his widow to bury; the victim was a man of property and a peaceable citizen, but well known for his bravery and contempt of Quiroga. On his return from the expedition, Facundo happened to meet with Gutierrez, ex-governor of Catamarca, whom he persuaded to go and live at Rioja. There they were quite intimate for some time, but seeing Gutierrez surrounded one day by some gaucho friends, Facundo had him arrested and sentenced to death, to the terror of all Rioja, for Gutierrez was much respected, and had gained the affections of every one. The presbyter, Dr. Colina, and several other clergymen of high standing, petitioned that the miserable man might at least have time to arrange his affairs and confess his sins. "I see," answered Facundo, "that he has many partisans here. Ho! there! Take these men to prison and let them be shot instead of Gutierrez." They attempted to flee, and two escaped; one lost his life, and the others were imprisoned; but Facundo laughed loudly when he heard the adventure, and ordered them to be set at liberty. Such scenes as this were frequent between the priests and their aid *"sent by God."*

In San Juan he had a negro dressed up as a priest, and made him walk through the streets. In Cordova, he refused to receive any one except Dr. Castro Barros, with whom he had an account to arrange. In Mendoza, he walked to the place of execution by the side of a priest whom he had condemned to death; he did the same with the curé of Alguia and the prior of Tucuman. It is true that in these cases he did not go so far as to have the sentence actually executed, but it was a great terror and humiliation to the clergymen; yet in spite of all this, the old people and bigots still offered prayers to heaven for the success of his arms.

But the story of Gutierrez is not quite ended yet. Fifteen days later he received a sentence of exile, and an escort was to conduct him beyond the boundaries. The party having encamped for the night, a fire was made to cook supper, and while Gutierrez was stooping to blow the scarcely lighted sticks, the chief official struck him on the head with a staff, and blows from others followed, until his brains were literally knocked out.

These were some of the events which took place in Facundo's first attempt at union in the Republic, for these were but attempts; the time had not yet come for the alliance of the pastoral powers by which the Republic was to be reorganized. Rosas was already famous in the province of Buenos Ayres, though he bore no titles as yet; nevertheless he was busy in his own cause. The constitution proposed by Congress was rejected wherever the provincial commanders had any influence. When the government deputy presented himself in Santiago del Estero, in his official dress, Ibarra received him in shirt-sleeves and *chiripá*. Rivadavia resigned the presidency because the provinces were opposed to him,—"but barbarism will soon be down upon us," he added, after his farewell. He did well to resign. Rivadavia's mission was to present before us the constitutionalism of Benjamin Constant with all its empty words, its deceptions, and absurdities. Rivadavia did not know that when the civilization and liberty of a people are in question, a ruler has great responsibilities both to God and future generations; and that there is neither charity nor compassion in abandoning a nation for thirty years to the devastation of the first ruthless sword that offers. Communities in their infancy are like children who foresee nothing and understand nothing, and need men of knowledge and foresight to guide them.

CHAPTER IX
Civil War—Tablada, a city

There is a fourth element coming; they are the barbarians, new hordes who come to throw themselves upon the old society with complete freshness of manners, soul and spirit, and who have as yet done nothing, but are ready to receive everything with the aptitude of the most suave and naïve ignorance.

—CHERMINIER

The presidency had fallen amid the hissings and rejoicings of its enemies. Dorrego, the able leader of the opposition in Buenos Ayres, was the friend of the governors of the interior, who were his abettors and supporters in the Provincial Congress in which he was triumphant. Victory was no longer with the Republic in its foreign wars; and, though its arms had met with no disasters in Brazil, the necessity for peace was everywhere felt. The opposition of the provincial leaders had weakened the army by destroying regiments, or refusing to furnish recruits. An apparent tranquillity reigned in the interior, but the earth trembled; strange rumors were afloat. The newspapers of Buenos Ayres were filled with gloomy prophecies. Threats came alike from the government and the opposition. The administration of Dorrego began to show a want of strength, because the party of the *city*, called Federal, which had established it, had not the power to sustain itself with honor after the fall of the presidency. The new administration, far from resolving any of the questions which divided the Republic, showed, on the contrary, all the weakness of Federalism. Dorrego was essentially Buenos Ayrean in his sympathies, and had little regard for the fate of the provinces. He had promised the provincial leaders and communities to do all he could to favor the interests of the former and to insure the rights of the latter; but, having once obtained the government, he said to his immediate friends, "What is it to us if the petty tyrants carry things with a high hand? What are the four thousand dollars' salary to Lopez, or the eighteen thousand to Quiroga, to us who control the seaport, and a custom-house that brings us in a million and a half, which that stupid Rivadavia wished to convert into national revenue?" Let us not forget that the motto of egotism is always "Each for himself." Dorrego and his party did not foresee that the provinces would come some day to punish Buenos Ayres for having refused them its civilizing influence; and that, because of the indifference to their ignorance and barbarism, this very ignorance and barbarism would penetrate into the streets of Buenos Ayres and take up its quarters even in the fort.

But Dorrego might have seen it, if he or his party had had better eyes. Here were the provinces at the gates of the city, only waiting an occasion to invade it. From the time of the fall of the presidency the decrees of the civil authorities could not be enforced beyond the suburbs of the city. Dorrego had employed, as an instrument of opposition, this outside resistance; and, when his party triumphed, he bestowed upon his ally beyond the walls the title of commander-in-chief of the provinces. What logic of the sword is it that makes the rank of commander-in-chief of the provinces a necessary step in the elevation of a military leader? Where this rank does not exist, as was then the case in Buenos Ayres, it is created expressly; as if, before letting the wolf into the fold, it was necessary to expose him to general observation.

Dorrego afterwards found that the provincial commander, who had caused the presidency to totter, and had contributed so powerfully to overthrow it, was a lever perpetually applied to the government; and that when Rivadavia had fallen, and Dorrego was in his place, the lever still continued its action.

Dorrego and Rosas were face to face, each watching and threatening the other. Dorrego's friends recall his favorite phrase,—"The gaucho-rogue! Let him be as troublesome as he pleases; and when he is least expecting it, I will shoot him." This was just what the Ocampos said when they first felt Quiroga's heavy arm upon them.

Indifferent to the people of the interior, not in high favor with the Federal party of the city, and already in antagonism with the provincial power which he had called to his aid, Dorrego, who had obtained the government through parliamentary opposition, now tried to win the Unitarios, whom he had conquered; but parties have neither charity nor foresight. The Unitarios laughed in their sleeves, and said among themselves, "He totters, let him fall." The Unitarios did not understand that with Dorrego would fall those who might have interposed between them and the provinces; or that the monster whom they feared was not seeking Dorrego, but the *city*, the civil institutions, of which they themselves were the exponents.

Things were in this condition when peace was concluded with Brazil, and the first division of the army, commanded by Lavalle, was disbanded. Dorrego knew well the spirit of these veterans of the War of Independence, who, covered with wounds, and grown gray in the service, had obtained only the rank of colonels, majors, or captains; two or three, perhaps, becoming generals; while in the interior of the Republic, without ever having passed the frontiers, were dozens of leaders, who, in four years, had been raised from the rank of gaucho-outlaws to that of commanders; from commanders to generals, and from generals to absolute masters of provinces. Need we look for any other motive for the implacable hatred of the veterans for these men? What had they to anticipate, now that the new order of things had taken from them the hope of entering the capital of Brazil as conquerors?

On the 1st of December, two companies of regulars were

drawn up in Victoria Square. Governor Dorrego had fled to the country, and the Unitarios filled the air with shouts of triumph. A few days afterwards, seven hundred cuirassiers, commanded by general officers, went out through Peru Street towards the pampas to meet several thousand gauchos and Indians, together with a few soldiers, commanded by Dorrego. For a moment the field of Navarro was covered with the dead, and the following day an officer, now in the service of Chili, brought in Dorrego as prisoner. An hour later, the body of Dorrego lay pierced with balls. The officer who had ordered his execution announced it to the city in the following terms:—

I have the honor of informing the deputy-governor that Colonel Manuel Dorrego has just been shot by my order, in front of the regiments which compose this division. History will judge impartially whether Señor Dorrego should have lived or died; or whether in sacrificing him for the peace of a city, brought to grief by him, I could have had any other motive than that of the public good. Let the people of Buenos Ayres be persuaded that the death of Colonel Dorrego is the greatest sacrifice that I could make for them.

I salute, Señor, the minister with all due consideration.

Juan Lavalle

Was Lavalle wrong? It is needless to add another affirmative in support of those who, after seeing the consequences, assumed the easy task of criticizing his motives. If an evil exists, it is in things not in persons. When Caesar was assassinated, he relived more terrible than ever in Octavius. Lavalle did not then know that in killing the body he could not kill the spirit; and that political personages take their character and existence from the ideas, interests, and ends of the party they represent. If Lavalle had shot Rosas instead of Dorrego, perhaps he would have saved the world from a great scandal, humanity from a great opprobrium, and the Republic from much blood and many tears; but, even if Rosas had been shot, the provinces would still have had representatives; and there would have been only the change of one historical picture for another. But what people pretend to ignore to-day, is, that—notwithstanding the purely personal responsibility of the deed, as far as Lavalle is concerned—the death of Dorrego was a necessary consequence of the prevailing ideas of the time; and that by this act the soldier who was brave enough to defy history, only accomplished the avowed wish of the citizens. What had interfered with the proclamation of the Constitution of 1826 but the hostility of Ibarra, Lopez, Bustos, Quiroga, Ortiz, and the Aldaos, each of whom ruled a province, and some of whom influenced the others? Now, what would appear so reasonable at that time, and to those men who reasoned *à priori*, as to get rid of what they considered the only obstacle to the desired organization of the Republic?

These political errors which belonged to the time rather than to the men, are yet worthy of consideration, for upon them depend the explanation of many social phenomena. Lavalle in shooting Dorrego, just as he would have shot Bustos, Lopez, Facundo, and others of that class, only fulfilled the requirements of his time and party. Even in 1834 there were still men in France who believed that if they could get rid of Louis Philippe, the French Republic would revive in all the greatness and glory of the past! Perhaps also the death of Dorrego was one of those fated events which form the nucleus of history, without which it would be incomplete and unmeaning. Civil war had been long threatening the Republic. Rivadavia had foreseen it with all its horrors; Facundo had unconsciously kept his hordes on the slopes of the Andes in waiting for this event; and Rosas' private life had been a ten years' preparation towards the same end. Dorrego was in the way of all parties: of the Unitarios, for they despised him; of the provincial leaders, for he had proved useless to them; and in that of Rosas, because he was impatient of keeping under the shadow of the city parties, and eager to obtain the government, or in other words, to become what he was not, and could never be, that is, a Federal, in the strict sense of the term. He represented the third social element, which from Artigas to Facundo had been eager to show itself without disguise, and to measure its strength with that of European civilization. If Dorrego had not died, it does not follow that the craving thirst of Facundo would have been quieted, or that Rosas would have failed to represent the provinces in the struggle which had begun long before 1820. No, Lavalle only lighted the match which was to fire the mine long ago prepared by both Unitarios and Federals.

From this moment there was nothing for the timid but to stop their ears and shut their eyes. All others everywhere rushed to arms; the tread of horsemen was heard over the pampas, and the cannon's black mouth was seen at the gates of the cities.

We must now leave Buenos Ayres to see what is passing in the other provinces. It must be mentioned, by the way, that Lopez, having been beaten in several encounters, sued in vain for reasonable terms of peace; and that Rosas had serious thoughts of going over to the side of Brazil. Lavalle refused to share in any of the transactions, and was soon put down; here was the true Unitario disdain of the gaucho, and faith in the final triumph of the "city." If Lavalle had adopted another line of conduct and kept the seaport in the hands of the citizens, might not the cruel Pampas Government have been prevented?

Facundo was in his element. A campaign was about to begin; expresses rushed to and fro; the feudal system of independence was to become a confederation of war. Everything was put in requisition for the coming campaign, and it was found unnecessary to go to the banks of the La Plata for a good battle-field. General Paz, with eight hundred veterans, had gone to Cordova, fought and conquered Bustos, and taken possession of the city, which was but a step from the Llanos, and within reach of the cries from the "montoneras" of the Sierra Cordova.

Facundo hastened his preparations; he longed for a personal encounter with a one-armed general who could not manage a lance or flourish a sword. What could Paz hope for in an encounter with the conqueror of Colonel Madrid? Facundo was to be joined by Don Felix Aldao, a friar general from Mendoza, with a regiment of trained auxiliaries equipped entirely in red; and without waiting for a force of seven hundred regulars from San Juan, he set out for Cordova with four thousand men, eager to measure arms with the cuirassiers of the second division and their officers.

The battle of Tablada is so well known that details are unnecessary. It has been brilliantly described in the "Revue des deux Mondes"; but there is one fact worth remembering. Facundo attacked the city with all his army, and was repulsed for a day and night by one hundred young clerks, thirty mechanics, and seven sick soldiers, from behind slight breastworks defended by only four pieces of artillery. And it was only when he announced his intention of burning the beautiful city, that they consented to surrender the place. Knowing that Paz was approaching, he left his infantry as useless, and went out to meet him with a cavalry force at least three times as large as the army of his opponent; then came hard fighting, and the cavalry charged again and again, but in vain. That mass of horsemen, though surrounding the eight hundred veterans, were driven back every moment, and compelled to return to the charge. The lance of Quiroga forcing back his own retreating men, caused as much terror in the rear of his army as the guns and swords of the enemy in front. But all was in vain; it was like the raging billows of the sea beating against a rough, motionless rock; sometimes, indeed, it is engulfed by the angry waves, but its black summit presently reappears firm and unshaken. Of the eight hundred auxiliaries only sixty survived, and of the six hundred red cavalry, not a third were living; the numerous other companies lost all discipline, and fled in every direction. Facundo retreated to the city, and the next day lay with his guns and infantry like a tiger in ambush; but all was soon over, and fifteen hundred dead bodies proved how obstinate the contest had been on both sides.

The battles of Tablada and Cordova were trials of strength between the provincial and city forces under their great leaders, Facundo and Paz, worthy representatives of the two powers which were struggling for dominion in the Republic. Facundo, ignorant, barbarous, for the greater part of his life an outlaw, and famous only for his acts of desperation; brave to rashness, endowed with herculean strength, always upon his horse, which he managed skillfully through terror and violence, knowing no other power than that of brute force, had no faith but in his horse, and depended for success upon bravery, the lance, and the terrible charges of his cavalry. In all the Argentine Republic there was not a more perfect specimen of the *"gaucho malo."*

Paz, on the contrary, was a true son of the city, and representative of the power of civilization. Lavalle, Madrid, and others like them, were native Argentines; cavalry officers, as brilliant as Murat, perhaps, but the cuirass and epaulets could not hide the gaucho nature. But Paz was a European soldier, and only believed in bravery as subordinate to tactics, strategy, and discipline. He hardly knew how to ride, and having only one hand, could not use a lance. A very large army was unwieldy and troublesome to him; what he liked, was a small number of soldiers thoroughly disciplined. A regiment of his training was sure to be perfect of its kind, and could he have selected his own battle-fields, the fate of the Republic would have been secure. He was in spirit a European soldier, even to the arms he used; he was an artillery officer, and therefore mathematical and scientific. A battle was a problem which he could solve by equations, and foretell the unknown quantity— that is, the victory. General Paz was not a genius, but an able officer, who employed science where others made use of brute force; in a word, he was the representative of European civilization, which was in a fair way to die out in our country. Unfortunate General Paz! Honor be to thee in thy repeated disasters! With thee are the household gods of the Republic! Destiny has not yet decided between thee and Rosas, between the cities and the pampas, between the blue stripe and the red ribbon! Thou hast the only quality of mind that in the end conquers brute force,—the quality in which lay the power of the old martyrs! Thou hast faith. Faith has saved thee, and in thee is the only hope of the Republic.

There is certainly a destiny about this man. He alone, in the ill-advised revolution of the first of December, was able to justify it by victory. Taken at last from the head of his army by the irresistible power of the gaucho, he was kept ten years in prison, Rosas, even, not daring to kill him, as if a guardian angel watched over his life. He escaped almost miraculously one stormy night, and through the rough waters of the La Plata, reached the eastern bank. Repulsed at one place, and disappointed at another, he at last obtained command of the few remaining forces of a province which had seen three armies successively destroyed. From such remnants he again gathered with much care and patience means of resistance, and when the armies of Rosas had triumphed everywhere, and carried terror throughout the Republic, the one-armed general called aloud from the marshes of Caguazu, "The Republic still lives!" Afterwards, despoiled of his laurels by those he had served, and ignominiously taken from the head of his army, he sought refuge among his enemies in Entre Rios, where the very elements seemed to protect him, and even the gauchos of the forest Montiel did not have it in their hearts to kill the one-armed man who harmed no one. At last he reached Montevideo, and learned that Ribera had been defeated, probably because he was not there to take the enemy in his own snares. The whole city was in consternation, and hurried to the poor lodging of the fugitive to beg for advice and comfort. "If I can only have twenty days, they will not take the city," was the only answer, given, not with enthusiasm, but with mathematical certainty. Oribe gave Paz all he asked for, and three years have passed since that day of terror at Montevideo. When he had secured the place well, and accustomed the garrison to fight daily as a matter of course, he went to Brazil and remained longer than was agreeable to his friends, and when Rosas was hoping to hear of him in the hands of the imperial police, he learned that he was at Corrientes training six thousand men; that he had formed an alliance with Paraguay, and also that Brazil had invited France and England to take part in the contest; so that the question between the provinces and the cities had now become a struggle between the one-armed, scientific Paz and the gaucho barbarian Rosas; between the Pampas on one side and Paraguay, Uruguay, Brazil, England, and France on the other.

It was especially to the honor of General Paz that even the enemies he had fought with neither hated nor feared him personally. The "Gaceta" of Rosas, so prodigal of its calumniations, never succeeded in abusing him thoroughly, a proof that he inspired his very detractors with respect. Many of the followers of Rosas in their hearts admired Paz, and the old Federals never forgot that he had always protected them from the fury of the old Unitarios. Who knows if Providence, which holds in its hand the fate of nations, has not preserved this man through many dangers to aid in the reconstruction of the Republic under laws which permit liberty without license, and do not need to be enforced by violence. Paz is a provincial by birth, a guarantee that he would never sacrifice the provinces to Buenos Ayres and the port, as Rosas has done to obtain millions while he impoverishes the people of the interior; just what the Federals had accused the Congress of 1826 of wishing to do.

The conquest of Tablada was the beginning of a new era for the city of Cordova, which, until then, according to the message of General Paz to the provincial representatives, "had occupied the lowest place among the Argentine cities, constantly opposing effort towards the construction of a constitution for the nation, or for its own province, either under the rule of Federals or Unitarios."

However, Cordova, like all the Argentine cities, contained its liberal element, but kept under until then by an absolute and conservative government like that of Bustos. From the moment that Paz entered the city, this element appeared openly, and showed how much it had strengthened during nine years of that Spanish government.

I have before described Cordova as antagonistic in spirit to Buenos Ayres; there is one circumstance in favor of its future development. The inhabitants have the greatest possible respect for learning, an effect produced by the university of two centuries standing. The love of learning presupposes a certain degree of civilization, so that notwithstanding the conservative nature and direction of the studies, there must be in Cordova a large number in favor of progressive culture and intelligence. This respect for learning extends even to the lower classes of society, and this explains why the masses embraced the revolution with an ardor which ten years have not abated, and which has furnished many victims for the vengeance of the Mazorqueros.

Paz brought with him an interpreter who should explain his ideas and objects to the common people—Barcala, the negro colonel, who had so gloriously distinguished himself in Brazil, and was on an equality with the chief officers of the army:

Barcala the freedman, who had devoted himself to the task of interesting the working classes in a revolution which regarded neither color nor class in rewarding true merit. This Barcala was, as far as possible, to make the change of ideas and aims popular among the citizens; and he succeeded beyond the most sanguine expectations. The middle classes of Cordova were from that time in favor of civil order and progressive civilization.

The young men of Cordova were distinguished in the war for their disinterested devotion to the cause; many fell on the field of battle, or under the knife of the assassin, and still more were condemned to the pains of exile. In the battles of San Juan, the bodies of Cordovian "doctors" lay piled in the streets, obstructing the artillery that they were carrying against the enemy.

On the other hand, the clergy, who had encouraged the opposition to Congress and the constitution, had had time to measure the abyss to which civilization would be brought by such defenders of the faith as Facundo, Lopez, etc., and did not hesitate to declare in favor of General Paz.

Thus the "doctors" and young men, the clergy as well as the masses, were now of one opinion, and ready to uphold the principles implied in the new order of things; and Paz could at once begin to reorganize the province and to establish friendly relations with others. A treaty was confirmed with Lopez of Santa Fé, who was induced, by Don Domingo de Oro★ to join Paz.† Salta and Tucuman had already submitted, and only the western provinces remained hostile.

★Domingo de Oro was a noble patriot, who opposed Rosas at the cost of everything that makes life dear.
†General Paz, late Vice-President of the Argentine Republic, died of cholera within this year.

CHAPTER X
Civil War

What has become of Facundo in the mean time? At Tablada he had lost everything,—arms, officers, men, reputation; everything except rage and valor. Moral, governor of Rioja, taken aback by the news of this unlooked-for disaster, availed himself of a slight excuse for leaving the city, and from Sañogasta sent Quiroga a despatch offering him what assistance the province could afford. Before the expedition the friendship between this nominal governor and the all-powerful commander had somewhat cooled. Quiroga thought he had not had the full number of armed men that he considered due him from the result of the census, in addition to the troops already in the province, and which had come from Tucuman, San Juan, Catamarca, etc. And another circumstance strengthened the suspicions with which Quiroga regarded the governor. Sañogasta was the manorial residence of the Dorias Dávilas, the enemies of the commander; and the governor, foreseeing what the suspicions of Facundo would deduce from the date of the despatch, dated it from Uanchin, a place about four leagues distant. But Quiroga knew that Moral was in Sañogasta, and all his doubts were confirmed. Fontanel and Barcena, two of Facundo's odious instruments, were sent out with a party to scour the country for the purpose of impressing as many men as they could find, but the inhabitants took care to escape, so that they were not very successful in their day's hunt, and returned with only eleven persons who were shot upon the spot. Don Inocencio Moral, an uncle of the governor, with his two sons, one only fourteen years of age, were among the victims of that day. There was also among them a Don Mariano Pasos, who had once before incurred the anger of Quiroga. When he was starting on one of his previous expeditions, this man, seeing the disorderly troops, had said to a fellow-merchant, "What men for fighting!" Quiroga, hearing it, had the two criticizers brought before him; one was tied to a post and received two hundred lashes, while the other stood by awaiting his share. The latter, however, was spared when his turn came, and afterwards became the governor of Rioja and a great friend of Quiroga.

Meanwhile, Governor Moral, knowing what he might expect, fled from the province, but he was eventually caught, and received seven hundred lashes for his ingratitude, for it was he who had shared the eighteen thousand dollars extorted from Dorrego.

That Barcena before mentioned was ordered to assassinate the commissioner of the English mining company; and I heard from himself the details of this atrocious murder, which he committed in his own house, desiring his wife and children to stand out of the way of the balls and sword-cuts.

Barcena accompanied Oribe in his expedition to Cordova; and during a ball given in honor of the triumph over Lavalle, threw the bloody heads of three young men into the hall where their families were dancing. This Barcena was the leader of the band of Mazorqueros which went with the army sent to Cordova in persecution of Lavalle, a regularly organized band, each Mazorquero wearing at his side a knife with a blade curved like a small cimeter, which was invented by Rosas himself for the purpose of beheading men dexterously.

What motive could Quiroga have had for these atrocities? He is said to have told Oro at Mendoza that his only object was to inspire terror. And again, during the continual assassinations of wretched peasants, on his way to the head-quarters at Atiles, one of the Villafañes said to him in a tone of fear and compassion, "Is it not enough, General?" "Don't be a fool," Quiroga answered; "how else can I establish my power!" This

was his one method,—terror with the citizen, that he might
fly and leave his fortune; terror with the gaucho, to make him
support a cause in which he had no personal interest. With him
terror took the place of administrative power, enthusiasm, tactics, everything. And it cannot be denied that terror, as a means
of government, produces much larger results than patriotism or
liberty. Russia has made use of it from the time of Ivan, and
has conquered the most barbarous nations; the bandits of the
forest obey the chief, wielding this power which controls the
fiercest natures. It is true that it degrades men, impoverishes
them, and takes from them all elasticity of mind, but it extorts
more from a state in one day than it would have given in ten
years; and what does the rest matter to the Czar of Russia, the
bandit chief, or the Argentine commander?

Facundo ordered all the inhabitants of Rioja to emigrate to
the Llanos under pain of death, and the order was literally
obeyed. It is hard to find a motive for this useless emigration.
Quiroga was not apt to fear, yet he might have feared at the
moment; for the Unitarios were raising an army in Mendoza
to take possession of the government; Tucuman and Salta were
on the north; and on the east, Cordova, Tablada, and General
Paz; he was, therefore, pretty well surrounded, and a general
hunt might very well have brought the Tiger of the Llanos at
bay. These terrorists do have their moments of fear: Rosas cried
like a child when he heard of the rebellion at Chascomus, and
eleven huge trunks were packed with his effects ready to fly an
hour before news came of the victory of Alvarez. But woe
to the people when such moments have passed! Then follow
September massacres, and pyramids of human heads arise in the
squares!

Notwithstanding the order of Facundo, two persons remained in Rioja—a young girl and a priest. The story of Severa
Villafañe is a pitiful romance; a fairy tale in which the loveliest
princess is a wandering fugitive, sometimes disguised as a shep-

herdess, sometimes begging a morsel of bread, or for protection from a frightful giant,—a cruel Bluebeard. Severa had the misfortune to excite the lust of the tyrant, and made superhuman efforts to escape his persecution. It was not only virtue resisting seduction, but the unconquerable repugnance of a delicate woman who detests those coarse types of brute force. A beautiful woman will sometimes barter something of her honor for something of the glory which surrounds a celebrated man; not for the glory which depends on the debasement of others for its brilliancy, but the glory which was the cause of Madame de Maintenon's frailty, or the literary glory to which Madame Roland and other such women are said to have sacrificed their reputations. For whole years Severa resisted. At one time she came near being poisoned by her tiger; at another, Quiroga, in a fit of desperation, tried to poison himself with opium. Once she escaped with difficulty from the hands of some of his creatures, and again she was surprised by Quiroga in her own court-yard, where he seized her by the arm, beat her with his fist until she was covered with blood, then threw her upon the ground and kicked in her skull with the heel of his boot. And was there no one to protect this poor girl, no relatives, no friends! One might well think so; yet she belonged to the first families of Rioja; General Villafañe was her uncle, she had brothers who witnessed the outrages; and there was a curé who shut the doors against her when she sought a refuge in the sanctuary. Finally, Severa fled to Catamarca and went into a convent; two years afterwards, when Facundo was passing through that place, he forced his way into the convent, and ordered the nuns into his presence; at the sight of him one nun uttered a cry and fell senseless upon the floor—it was Severa.

But we must return to the encampment at Atiles, where an army was preparing for the purpose of recovering the reputation lost at Tablada. Two Unitarios of San Juan had fallen into the hands of the tyrant: a young Chilian by the name of Castro y Calvo, and Alexandro Carril. Quiroga asked the latter how much he would give for his life.

"Twenty-five thousand dollars," he answered, trembling.

"And you, sir," asked Quiroga, of the other, "how much will you give?"

"I can only give four thousand," said Castro. "I am only a merchant and have no property."

They sent to San Juan for the money, and behold thirty thousand dollars collected for the war at a very small cost. While waiting for the money, Facundo lodged them under a carob-tree, and employed them in making cartridges, paying them two reals a day for their work.

The governor of San Juan, hearing of the efforts made by the family of Carril to collect this ransom, took advantage of the knowledge. As governor of the city he could not exactly shoot his own citizens, though an independent Federal, and neither did he have the power to extort money from the Unitarios. But he ordered all the political prisoners in the gaols to be sent to the camp at Atiles to join the army. The mothers and wives understood what fate they were to expect, and first one, and then another and another, succeeded in scraping together the sums necessary to keep back their sons and husbands from the den of the Tiger. Thus Quiroga governed in San Juan merely by the terror of his name.

When the brothers Aldao were all powerful in Mendoza, and had not left in Rioja one man, old or young, married or single, who was able to carry arms, Facundo transported his head-quarters to San Juan, where there were still many wealthy Unitarios. There he soon ordered six hundred lashes to a citizen noted for his influence, talent, and wealth, and walked himself by the side of the cart which carried his expiring victim through the streets; for Facundo was very careful about this part of his administration; and not at all like Rosas, who, from his private room where he was taking his *maté*, sent Mazorqueros to execute the atrocities afterward charged upon the *federal enthusiasm* of the people. Not thinking this example sufficient, Facundo seized upon an old man, whom he accused—or scarcely troubled himself to accuse—of having served as a guide to some fugitives, and had him shot without permitting him to speak a word; for this heaven-sent defender of the faith cared very little whether his victims confessed or not.

Public opinion being thus prepared, there were no sacrifices the city of San Juan was not ready to make for the defense of the Confederation; contributions were given in without remonstrance, and arms appeared as if by magic. The Aldaos triumphed in the incapacity of the Unitarios to violate the treaty of Pilar, and then Quiroga left for Mendoza. There no additional terror was needed, for the daily executions ordered by the monk Aldao had paralyzed the city; but Facundo thought it necessary to justify the terror carried everywhere by his name. Some young men of San Juan had been made prisoners, and these, at least, belonged to him. He asked one of them how many guns he could furnish by the end of four days; the young man answered that if he might have time to send to Chili for them, he would do all he could. Quiroga repeated, "How many can you furnish now?"

"None," was the answer; and the next moment his body was taken away to be buried, six others soon following. The same question was put orally or in writing to the prisoners from Mendoza, and the answers were more or less satisfactory. Among these was a General Alvarado, who was brought before Facundo.

"Sit down, General," he said. "How soon can you deliver six thousand dollars for your ransom?"

"Sir, I cannot bring it at all; I have no money."

"But you have friends who would not let you be shot," said Quiroga.

"No, sir; I have none. I was only passing through the province when I was induced by the public wish to take charge of the government."

"Where would you like to go?" continued Quiroga, after a moment of silence.

"Wherever you may order, sir."

"What do you think of San Juan?"

"Just as you please, sir."

"How much money do you need?"

"None, I thank you, sir."

Facundo went to a desk and opening a bag of gold, said, "Take what you need, General."

"Thanks, sir, nothing."

An hour later the carriage of General Alvarado was at his door with his baggage in it, and also General Villafañe, who conducted him to San Juan, and on his arrival there, gave him a hundred ounces of gold from General Quiroga, begging him not to refuse it.

This would seem to prove that Quiroga's heart was not entirely dead to noble impressions. Alvarado was an old soldier, a grave and prudent general, who had given him no trouble. He afterward said of him,—"That Alvarado is a good soldier, but he doesn't understand our warfare."

At San Juan they brought before him a Frenchman named Barreau, who had written about him as only a Frenchman can write. Facundo asked him if he was the author of the abusive articles, and was answered in the affirmative.

"Then what do you expect?"

"Death, sir," said the man; but Quiroga threw him a purse, saying, "There, take that, and go somewhere else to be hung."

At Tucuman, Quiroga one day lay stretched on a bench, when an Andalusian came up and asked for the General.

"He is in there," said Quiroga; "what do you want with him?"

"I have come to pay the four hundred dollars' contribution he has charged upon me,—the fellow gets his living easy."

"Do you know the General, friend?"

"No, and I don't want to know him, the rogue!"

"Come in and take a drink," said Quiroga, but at that moment an aide came up, and began: "General—."

"General!" cried the man, opening his eyes, "so you are the General! Ah, General," he continued, falling on his knees, "I am a poor devil,—you wouldn't be the ruin of me,—the money is all ready, General,—come, don't be angry, now!"

Facundo burst into a loud laugh, told the man to make himself easy, and giving him back the contribution, only took two hundred of it as a loan, which he afterwards faithfully repaid. Two years after this, a paralyzed beggar called out to him in the streets of Buenos Ayres,—

"Good-bye, General, I am the Andalusian of Tucuman, and I'm paralyzed." Facundo gave him six dollars.

These things prove the theory, which the modern drama has exhibited with so much brilliancy, namely, that in the darkest characters of history there will always be found a ray of light, however totally it seems sometimes to vanish.

But let us resume the course of public events. After the solemn inauguration of terror in Mendoza, Facundo retired to Retamo, whither the Aldao brothers had carried a contribution of a hundred thousand dollars extorted from the Unitarios. There they gambled day and night, playing for enormous stakes, until Facundo had won the hundred thousand dollars.

A year passed in preparations for the war, and at the end of 1830 a new and formidable army, composed of divisions recruited in Rioja, San Juan, Mendoza, and San Luis, marched against Cordova. General Paz, desirous of avoiding bloodshed, though sure of winning new laurels should an engagement take place, sent Major Pawnero, an officer of prudence, energy, and sagacity, to meet Quiroga with proposals of peace, and even of alliance. It might be thought that Quiroga would be disposed to accept any reasonable opportunity for adjustment; but the intervention of the Buenos Ayres commission, which had no other object than to prevent any adjustment, and his own pride and presumption on finding himself at the head of a more powerful and better disciplined army than the first, made him reject the peace proposals of the more modest General Paz. Facundo had this time arranged something like a plan for the campaign. Communications established in the Sierra de Cordova had excited the pastoral population to rebellion; General Villafañe approached on the north with the division from Catamarca, while Facundo came up from the south. It was not very difficult for General Paz to see through the designs of Quiroga, and to disappoint them. One night the army disappeared from the immediate neighborhood of Cordova, no one knew where; it had been seen by many persons, but in different places at the same time. If there has ever been in America anything like the complicated strategy of Bonaparte's campaigns in Italy, it was when Paz made forty companies cross the Sierra de Cordova and take a position where they would inevitably intercept all fugitives from a regular battle. The Montonera, paralyzed, surrounded on all sides, fell into the net which had been spread for it. It is not necessary to give the particulars of that memorable battle. General Paz, in his despatch, gave the number of his loss as seventy, for appearance sake, but in fact, he had only lost twelve men in a contest with eight thousand men, and twenty pieces of artillery. A simple maneuvre had defeated the valiant Quiroga; and the army which had cost so many tears and horrors of all kinds, only served to show Facundo's bad management, and to give to Paz several thousand useless prisoners.

CHAPTER XI

Social War

A horse, a horse! my kingdom for a horse.
—SHAKESPEARE

CHACON

Facundo, the gaucho outlaw of the Llanos, did not return to the country this time, but went directly to Buenos Ayres, and it was this unexpected step that prevented him from falling into the hands of his pursuers. He saw that he could do nothing more in the provinces, and for this once he could not even stop to harass the peasantry on his way, for his conquerors were ready to come to their defense from all directions.

Important advantages were secured by this battle of Oncativo or Laguna Larga. Cordova, Mendoza, San Juan, San Luis, La Rioja, Catamarca, Tucuman, Salta, and Jujui, were now free from the rule of the country commandants. The unity of the Republic, which Rivadavia had hoped to bring about through parliamentary means, seemed now about to be effected by means of arms, at least in this portion of it; and General Paz called a congress of deputies from these provinces to consider what form of constitution would be desirable. Lavalle had been less fortunate in Buenos Ayres, and Rosas, who was destined to play such a terrible part in Argentine history, had already begun to influence public affairs, and to rule the city. The Republic was now, therefore, divided into two parts: one in the interior, which desired Buenos Ayres for the capital of the union; the other in Buenos Ayres, which made a pretense of not wishing this city to be the capital, that it might separate itself from European civilization and civil order.

Another fact had been disclosed by this battle, namely, that the Montonera had lost its primitive strength, and that civilized armies could compete with it successfully. It is a significant fact in Argentine history, that, as time passes, the pastoral bands lose their early vigor. Facundo was already obliged to spur them on with terror, and they were but a dull, disorderly set, opposed to troops disciplined and guided by rules of strategy and art. In Buenos Ayres, however, the result was different. Lavalle, notwithstanding his bravery, which had been sufficiently proved at Puente Marquez, and his large number of regular troops, yielded at the end of the campaign, shut up as he was in the city by thousands of gauchos collected by Rosas and Lopez. By a treaty which was to all purpose a capitulation, he gave up his authority, and Rosas entered Buenos Ayres. I believe that only through an unfortunate mistake of his, Lavalle lost the victory. He had been famous for the success of his cavalry charges; at the defeat of Toreta or Moquegua, I do not remember which, Lavalle made forty charges during the day to protect the retreating army, and I doubt if the cavalry of Murat ever did as much. But unfortunately, Lavalle, remembering in 1839 that the Montenera had conquered him in 1830, abandoned his military education and adopted the Montonera system. He equipped four thousand horse, and went into the streets of Buenos Ayres at the same time that Rosas who had conquered him in 1830, gave up his cavalry, in spite of native instincts, and finished the campaign with infantry and artillery. They exchanged parts: the gaucho assumed the military uniform, and the soldier the poncho; the former triumphed, the latter died pierced by a ball from the Montonera. A hard lesson! If Lavalle had made the campaign of 1840 according to military rules, we should now, on the banks of the Plata, be preparing for steam navigation on the rivers, and distributing farms to European emigrants. Paz was the first citizen general who triumphed over the pastoral or provincial element; because he brought to bear against it all the resources of European military art, directed by a mathematical head.

The labors of Paz in Cordova had been to such purpose that after two years Facundo found it impossible to reëstablish his influence in the provinces; it was only the civilized, the refined city of Buenos Ayres that offered an asylum for his barbarism.

The journals of Cordova at that time gave the European news, the sessions of the French assembly; the likenesses of Casimir Perier, Lamartine, Chateaubriand, served as models in the school of design. Such was the interest of Cordova in European affairs. And at this very time the "Mercantile Gazette" was assuming the semi-barbarous tone that henceforth characterized the Argentine press.

Facundo fled to Buenos Ayres, not without shooting two of his own officers for trying to maintain order among his followers. He never belied his theory of terror,—it was his talisman, his palladium. He would sacrifice everything rather than this weapon.

On arriving at the city, he presented himself at the court of Rosas; there he happened to meet General Guido, the most courteous and ceremonious of the generals who have made their way in the world by compliments in the antechamber; he offered one of his very best to Quiroga, who replied surlily, "Am I a dog, for you to laugh at? You people here sent a nice set of doctors (Cavia and Cernadas) to get me into trouble with General Paz. Paz beat me according to rule." He often regretted not having listened to the proposals of Major Pawnero.

Facundo soon merged in the crowd of the great city, and was only occasionally heard of at the gaming-table. General Mancilla once threatened to throw a candlestick at his head, saying, "Do you think you are still in the provinces?" His gaucho dress at first attracted much attention—the poncho, and the long beard which he had sworn never to cut until he had wiped out the disgrace of the defeat at Tablada; but after a little while he was scarcely noticed.

A great expedition against Cordova was then in preparation, and six thousand men from Buenos Ayres and Santa Fé had enlisted for the enterprise. Lopez was the commander-in-chief, with Balcarce, Enrique Martinez, and other officers under him. Facundo undertook a desperate attack upon Rioja or Mendoza. He received for the purpose two hundred criminals from the prisons, collecting in addition sixty men in the city, and with this company began his march.

At Pavon, Rosas was collecting his red cavalry; Lopez of Santa Fé was also there, and Facundo stopped to wait for the other leaders. Here, therefore, were the three famous provincial leaders met together on the pampas: Lopez, the pupil and successor of Artigas; Facundo, the barbarian of the interior; and Rosas, the bloodhound, who had been in training, but was now about to begin the hunt on his own account. The old classics would have compared them to the triumvirate Lepidus, Mark Anthony, and Octavius, who divided the empire among themselves, a comparison quite perfect even in respect to the baseness and cruelty of the Argentine Octavius. The three leaders were now in their element, and refreshed themselves with a bit of true gaucho life; scouring the pampas daily, and making trials of skill in racing, lassoing horses, and fighting; in all of which Rosas was usually victorious. He one day invited Lopez to have a bout, but Lopez said, "No, comrade, you are too rough for me." And in fact he had left them pretty well covered with cuts and bruises.

Quiroga crossed the pampas by the same road by which, twenty years before, he had fled as an outlaw from Buenos Ayres. At the city of Rio Quarto he met with an obstinate resistance, was delayed three days by the marshes which served as a defense to the garrison, and was about to retreat when a traitor came to him with the information that they had no more cartridges. Thanks to this timely revelation, Facundo took the place without difficulty.

At Rio Quinto he had to contend with the brave Pringles, the veteran of the war of independence, who on one occasion, when he was met by the Spaniards in a narrow pass, spurred his horse into the sea, with the cry, "Viva la Patria!" This same Pringles, whom the viceroy Pezuela had loaded with presents, and for whom San Martin had struck off the singular medal, *"Honor to the vanquished of Chancai,"* was now to die by the hands of Quiroga's convicts.

Excited by this unhoped-for triumph, Facundo advanced upon San Luis, where little resistance was offered. Beyond this the road branched off into three, and Quiroga considered which to take. The one to the right led to the Llanos, the theatre of his early deeds, the cradle of his power; in this direction there were no forces superior to his own, but neither had he any resources there to fall back upon. The middle road led to San Juan, where there were a thousand men in arms, but unable to resist a charge of cavalry with Quiroga's terrible lance at its head. Finally, the road to the left led to Mendoza, where the real forces were under command of General Videla Castillo. There was a battalion of eight hundred trained men, commanded by Colonel Barcala; a squadron of cuirassiers, under command of Lieutenant-Colonel Chenaut, and also some militia-men, and pickets of cuirassiers of the Guard. Facundo had with him only three hundred undisciplined men, and was not in very good health himself. Which road should he take? He chose the road to Mendoza,—came, saw, and conquered. But how was this possible; was there cowardice or treachery? Neither. An unwise imitation of European strategy; an error in tactics in part, and in part an Argentine prejudice, caused the shameful loss of this battle. Videla Castillo knew that Quiroga was approaching, but did not believe, as no other general would have believed, that he would attack Mendoza; he therefore sent to the Lakes his veteran troops, who, with some other detachments from San Juan under the command of Major Castro, formed a force strong enough to resist an attack, and to force Quiroga to take the road to the Llanos. So far it was all right. But Quiroga did march upon Mendoza, and the whole army went out to meet him. In the place called Chacon there is an open field in which the army left its rear guard; but soon after, hearing the firing of a company in retreat, General Castillo ordered the army to fall back hastily, in order to occupy the level field of Chacon. This was a double error; in the first place, because a retreat at the approach of a formidable enemy paralyzes inexperienced soldiers, who do not understand the cause of the movement; and secondly, because the rougher and more broken the ground, the better it would have been for fighting Quiroga, who only had with him a small body of infantry. What could he have done in such a field against six hundred infantry with a formidable battery of artillery in front? But unfortunately the officers were all native Argentines, who were devoted to horses; for them there would be no glory except in a victory won by the sword, and therefore they thought an open field for cavalry charges was absolutely necessary; this is the mistake in Argentine strategy.

The battle began, and a squadron of militia was ordered to charge,—another Argentine mistake is this of beginning the fight with a charge of cavalry, a mistake which has lost to the Republic a hundred battles. And in addition to this error there was a misapplication of the European art of warfare. In Europe, where the masses of the troops are in column, and where the battle-field includes several towns or hamlets, the picked troops are kept in reserve until needed. In South America, a pitched battle generally takes place in an open field, the troops are not numerous, and the heat of the contest lasts but a short time, so that it is always desirable to rush in at once with the best men. In the present case, a cavalry charge was the worst possible beginning, but if it must needs be, it should at least have been made by the best troops, in order to rout at once the three hundred men who made up both army and reserve of the enemy. Instead of this, the old routine was followed: ordering to the front a large number of awkward militia, each man afraid of wounding himself with his own lance, and when the order to charge was given, they stood stock still, then fell back, and being charged upon by the enemy, gave way and embarrassed the best troops behind. In a moment all was confusion, and the battle lost; and Facundo passed on in triumph to Mendoza, without caring for the generals, infantry, and guns, which he left to his rear guard. This was the result of the battle of Chacon, which left exposed the flank of the army of Cordova at the moment it was about to march upon Buenos Ayres. Quiroga's inconceivable audacity was crowned with the most complete success. It was useless to try to drive him from Mendoza; terror and the prestige of victory gave him means of resistance, while defeat had left his enemies discouraged. He would only have hastened to San Juan, where arms and money were to be had, and commenced a useless and interminable war. The generals, therefore, went to Cordova, and the infantry and officers of Mendoza came to terms the next day. The Unitarios of San Juan emigrated to Coquimbo, to the number of two hundred, and Quiroga remained in peaceful possession of Cuyo and Rioja. These two cities had never suffered from all the evils Quiroga had hitherto brought upon them, as they did now from the interruption of business caused by such a large emigration of the wealthiest inhabitants.

But I must especially remark upon the still greater harm done to the spirit of civilization. Considering the inland situation of Mendoza, it had been a highly civilized city, with a spirit of enterprise and progress greater than any city of the Republic; it was the Barcelona of the interior. The spirit of progress had attained its height under the administration of Videla Castillo.

Two forts had been built towards the south with the double advantage of extending the boundaries of the province, and of securing it permanently from the savages. The swamps had been drained, the city ornamented, societies of agriculture, industry, mines, and of public education had been formed, and directed by intelligent, enthusiastic, and enterprising men; a manufactory of woollen and flax had been established which furnished clothing for the troops, and an armory for the making of swords, cuirasses, lances, and bayonets, with none of the work imported except some parts of the cannon. A French chemist, by the name of Charron, had put up a machine for moulding bullets, and types for the printing-press, and investigated the metals of the province. It is impossible to conceive of a more rapid development. These things would not have attracted so much attention in Chili or Buenos Ayres, but in an inland province with only the aid of native workmen, the progress was prodigious, and in ten years it might have been one of the most remarkable places in the country; but Facundo's army crushed this promising civilization, and the monk Aldao passed his plough over it and watered the earth with blood for ten years. What could remain?

But the progress of ideas was not entirely stopped with the occupation of Quiroga; the members of the mining society, who emigrated to Chili, there gave themselves up to the study of chemistry, mineralogy, and metallurgy. Godoi Cruz, Correa, Villanueva, Doncel, and many others, looked up all books treating the subject, and made a large collection of different metals from all parts of South America; they also examined the Chilian archives for information about the mines of Uspallata, and with much labor succeeded in establishing modes of operation by which these mines have become profitable, notwithstanding the scarcity of metal. From that time dates the new and profitable working of the mines of Mendoza. The

Argentine miners, not satisfied with these results, scattered themselves throughout Chili, which afforded a rich field for the experiments of their science, and they have accomplished much at Copiapo and other places by the introduction of new machinery and tools.

Godoi Cruz had another object in his researches: he endeavored, by introducing the cultivation of the white mulberry, to solve the problem of the possible future of San Juan and Mendoza, which depends upon the discovery of some production of great value, yet of small compass. Silk answers this condition, imposed upon these inland cities by their great distance from the seaports, and the high price of transportation. Godoi, not satisfied with publishing at Santiago a long and complete treatise on the cultivation of the mulberry, and the care of the silkworm and cochineal, had it distributed through the provinces free of cost, kept the question of the mulberry constantly before the public for ten years, urging its cultivation, and setting forth its advantages, while he carried on a correspondence with Europe, learning the current prices, and sending over specimens of the silk he had himself obtained, thus discovering the failings or excellences in quality, and also the best methods of spinning. The results of this great, patriotic labor, were all that he could hope for; now there are already some thousands of mulberry-trees, and the silk gathered by the quintal was spun, twisted, dyed, and sold in Buenos Ayres and Santiago, for the European market, at the rate of six or seven dollars a pound; for the silk of Mendoza was as glossy as that of the best quality in Spain or Italy.

The old man finally returned to his native place to rejoice in the sight of a whole city succeeding in a profitable change of employment, hoping that he might live to see a caravan depart for Buenos Ayres, bearing the valuable production which made the wealth of China for so many years, and for precedence in which the manufactories of Lyons, Barcelona, Paris, and all Italy still dispute.* Mendoza preceded all Spanish America in developing this useful branch of industry.

Have Facundo or Rosas ever done the least thing for the public good, or been interested in any useful object? No. From them come nothing but blood and crimes. I have given these details at length, because in the midst of horrors such as I am obliged to describe, it is comforting to pause on the few progressive impulses which revive again and again after being apparently crushed by savage barbarians. Civilization will, however feeble its present resistance, one day resume its place. There is a new world about to unfold itself, and it only awaits some fortunate general to put aside the iron heel which has so long crushed it. Besides, history should not be considered merely a tissue of crimes, and for this reason it is desirable to bring before the mind of a subjugated people a remembrance of past epochs. If they desire for their posterity a better record than they themselves have, let them not hope for it because the cannibal of Buenos Ayres is just now tired of shedding blood, and permits exiles to return to their homes. This fact is of no import in the progress of a people. The great evil to be dreaded is a government which fears the influence of thoughtful and enlightened men, and must either exile or kill them. This evil results from a system which gives one man such absolute power that there can be no liberty of thought or action, no public spirit—the desire of self-preservation outweighing all interest for others. Every one for himself, and the executioner for all without discrimination, this is the *résumé* of the life and government of an enslaved people.

Facundo, once more master of Mendoza, adopted his old methods of raising money and soldiers. One evening his agents

---

*The final result did not justify these flattering expectations. The cultivation of silk died out in Mendoza for want of encouragement.

were all over the city arresting the officers who had capitulated at Chacon; for what purpose it was not known, but the officers felt no great fear, confiding as they did in the good faith of the treaty. Nevertheless, a number of priests were also brought in and ordered to hear the confessions of the officers, who were then placed in a line and shot, one after another, under the direction of Facundo; the execution lasting about an hour. He afterwards gave as an excuse for this horrible violation of faith, that the Unitarios had killed General Villafañe. There was some foundation for the charge, but the revenge was monstrous. At another time he said, "Paz shot nine of my officers, but I have shot ninety-six of his." Paz, however, was not responsible for that deed, which he deeply lamented, and which was also an act of retaliation.

But the system of giving no quarter, so tenaciously followed by Rosas, and the constant violation of all customary forms, treaties, capitulations, etc., are the result of causes not depending on the personal character of the provincial leaders. Acknowledgment of individual rights which lessens the horrors of war, is the result of centuries of civilization, and was not to be expected among the semi-barbarians of the pampas. The savage kills his prisoner, and respects no compact when he has occasion to violate it.

The death of Villafañe had happened in Chili, and had already been avenged "eye for eye, tooth for tooth," in accordance with the *lex talionis*. The perpetrator of this deed was a remarkable specimen of the class of men I have been endeavoring to describe, and is therefore worthy of mention. Among the San Juan emigrants who went to Coquimbo, there was a Major Navarro, from the army of General Paz. This man, who came of a distinguished family of San Juan, was small in size, with a thin, flexible body, and celebrated in the army for a rash courage. At the age of eighteen he mounted guard as lieutenant of militia on the night when (in 1820) the battalions of the first division of the army of the Andes revolted, and, forming in four companies before the guard-house, ordered the city militia to surrender. Navarro alone remained in the guard-house, and defended the entrance; and then, holding one hand over three wounds in his thigh, covering with the other arm five wounds in his breast, and blinded by the blood streaming from his head, made his way home, where he was six months recovering his strength; a cure altogether unhoped for and well-nigh miraculous. Thrown out of his place by the disbanding of the militia, he devoted himself to trade, but a trade accompanied with dangers and adventures. At first he was engaged in introducing contraband goods into Cordova; afterwards he carried on a trade with the Indians, and finally married the daughter of a cacique, lived with her faithfully, took part in the wars of the savages, and accustomed himself to eat raw meat, until, in the course of three years, he became a thorough savage. While there he heard that the war with Brazil was about to commence, and leaving his beloved savages, entered the army with his old rank of lieutenant, where his bravery was so conspicuous that he soon became a captain and brevet major, and one of Lavalle's chosen men. At Marquez the whole army was astonished at his daring. After these expeditions he remained at Buenos Ayres with Lavalle's other officers, Arbolito, Pancho el ñate, and other chiefs, who displayed their bravery in coffee-houses and hotels. The animosity against the officers of the army became greater every day, and on one occasion they were drinking to the death of Lavalle, when Navarro heard them, and stepping up, poured out a glass and drank, saying in a loud voice, "To the *health* of Lavalle." A duel followed on the spot, and Navarro, who killed his man, fled from the city, and overtook the army before it reached Cordova. Before reëntering the service, he went in the interior to see his family, and learned with regret the death of his wife. Taking leave of his friends,

he went back to the army accompanied by two young men—
his cousin and nephew.

In the battle of Chacon he got a shot in his breast which
burned off his beard, and blackened his face with powder; and
in this condition he emigrated to Coquimbo, still accompanied
by his young relatives; but every day he felt a strong desire to
go back, and could hardly be prevented from doing so. "I am
a true son of the army," he would say, "and war is my element;
the first drop of blood shed in the civil war was from my veins;
and from them should come the last." At other times he said,
"I cannot go a step farther; I am getting farther and farther
from the epaulets of a general. What would my friends say if
they knew that Major Navarro was treading a foreign soil without a squad behind him?"

The day they crossed the boundary ridge, there was quite a
pathetic scene. They were obliged to give up their arms, and
the Indians could not conceive of a country where one was
not permitted to go about lance in hand. Navarro explained in
their own language, while two great tears rolled down his
cheeks; they then laid their arms upon the ground, with much
emotion, and even after starting on, went back and rode slowly
around them as if bidding them farewell.

It was in this state of mind that Major Navarro passed into
Chili, and took up his lodging at Guanda, a place situated at
the beginning of the road which leads to the cordillera. There
he learned that General Villafañe was going back to join Facundo, and openly announced his intention of killing him. The
emigrants, who knew what these words meant coming from
Navarro, left the neighborhood, after trying in vain to dissuade
him from his purpose. Villafañe was warned beforehand, and
asked protection from the public authorities, who gave him
some militia, by whom he was abandoned as soon as they
learned what was the trouble. But Villafañe was well armed,

and accompanied by six natives of Rioja. Just as he was passing through Guanda, Navarro appeared before him, with only a brook between them, gravely declared his intention, and then returned quietly into the house where he was breakfasting. That night Villafañe was so imprudent as to lodge at Tilo, a place only about four leagues off. In the night Navarro armed himself and took with him a company of nine men, whom he left at a convenient place near Tilo. He then approached by moon-light, entered the court-yard, and called out to Villafañe, who was sleeping with his men in the corridor, "Villafañe, arise! those who have enemies should not sleep." Villafañe seized his lance, but Navarro attacking him with his sword, ran him through the body. He then fired off a pistol, the signal agreed upon with his companions, who came up and falling upon Villafañe's men, killed or dispersed them. They then took horses and equipments and set out for the Argentine Republic to join the army. Mistaking the road, they found themselves after a while at Rio Quarto, where they encountered Colonel Echevarria, who was pursued by enemies. Navarro hastened to his aid, and the horse of his friend falling at that moment, begged him to get up behind himself; but Echevarria would not consent, and Navarro, determined not to fly without him, dismounted, shot his own horse, and both men soon shared the same fate. It was three years before his family knew what had become of him, the story being told by the men who had killed him, and who, by way of proof, dug up the skeletons of the two friends.

During Major Navarro's short absence, events had taken place which entirely changed the condition of public affairs. The famous capture of General Paz, who was caught at the head of his army by a lasso, decided the fate of the Republic. It may be said that the constitution failed to be established at that time through a singular accident; for Paz with an army of four thousand trained men, and a wisely arranged plan of operations, was sure of conquering the army of Buenos Ayres. Those who have since seen him triumphing in every direction, can judge if he was very presuming to take this conquest for granted. We might chime in with the moralists who so often attribute the fall of empires to the merest accidents; but if it was an accident to catch a great general with a lasso, it was not accidental that the men who did it should have used such means, being as they were of true gaucho nature, though converted into a political element.

Facundo, having so cruelly revenged the death of General Villafañe, marched upon San Juan to prepare an expedition against Tucuman, where the army had retired after the loss of its general had destroyed all hope of accomplishing anything. On his arrival, all the Federal citizens went out to receive him as they had done in 1827; but Facundo was not fond of repetitions. He therefore sent one company in advance of the assembled citizens, and another behind them; then entered the city himself by a different route, leaving his officious hosts prisoners in the street, where they passed the whole day and night, lying down among the horses' feet if overpowered with sleep.

When he reached the public square, he stopped his carriage, put an end to the noise of the bells, and ordered all the furniture of the house provided for him by the city, to be thrown into the street, carpets, curtains, chairs, tables, mirrors,—all heaped in confusion in the middle of the square; nor would he go in until sure that nothing remained but the bare walls, a little table, a single chair, and a bed. While this was going on, he called a child who was passing by his carriage, and asked him what his name was, and when he answered "Roza," said, "Your father, Don Ignacio Roza, was a great man; give my compliments to your mother."

The next day a bench was prepared for the shooting of his usual victims. Who were they to be this time? The Unitarios had fled in great numbers, and many timid people not Unitarios. But Facundo began to impose contributions upon the women whose husbands, fathers, or brothers were absent, and the results were quite satisfactory, and accompanied by the usual circumstances,—sobs and cries of women threatened with the lash, some actually whipped, two or three men shot, one lady compelled to cook for the soldiers, and other nameless outrages. There was one especial day of horror to be remembered; it was when Facundo was about to depart for Tucuman; the divisions were filing off one after another, and the muleteers were taking care of the baggage, when a mule broke loose, and in trying to get away ran into the church of Santa Anna. Facundo ordered them to catch it; the muleteer went in for this purpose, and at the same moment an officer, by command of Quiroga, entered on horseback, tied both man and mule, and brought them bound together, the unfortunate muleteer suffering from the kicks of the animal. Just then it appeared that something was not quite ready for the departure, and Facundo ordered the negligent authorities before him. His Excellency the Governor and Captain General of the Province received a buffet, the chief of police narrowly escaped a bullet as he ran, and all reached their offices as quickly as possible to give the neglected orders.

A little later, Facundo, seeing an officer strike two soldiers who were fighting, with the flat of his sword, called him up and attacked him with his lance; the officer used his own for the defense of his life, and presently disarmed Quiroga, whose lance he then picked up and returned respectfully. Quiroga again attacked him; there was another encounter, and he was again disarmed. He then called six men, had the officer seized, and stretched across the window-frame with his hands and feet tied fast, and ran him through with a lance again and again, until life was entirely extinct. His rage was without bounds; General Huidobro, his second, was also threatened with his lance, and prepared to defend his life.

And yet Facundo was not cruel or blood-thirsty in comparison with other barbarians; he was only a barbarian, who did not know how to restrain his passions, and these once aroused were without limit, without restraint; he was a terrorist who, on entering a city, shoots one, and perhaps lashes another, but for a reason. The person shot is blind, or paralyzed; the unhappy victim of the lash is a respectable citizen, a young man of one of the first families. His brutalities to women come from a want of delicacy; the humiliations imposed upon the citizens from the coarse desire to ill-treat and to mortify the self-respect of those by whom he feels himself to be despised. It is the same motive which makes terror a means of government. What would Rosas have done without it in a society like that of Buenos Ayres? How else could he have commanded from an intelligent people that respect which they never willingly show for persons who are in themselves low and contemptible? It is incredible what an accumulation of atrocities is necessary to pervert a people, and nobody knows the amount of close observation and sagacity employed by Don Manuel Rosas in order to subject the city to that magical influence which destroyed in six years all knowledge of the just and the good; which broke the bravest spirits and put them under the yoke.

Terror in France in 1793 was an effect and not a means. Robespierre did not guillotine nobles and priests to create a reputation, nor to elevate himself upon the heaps of the slain. He was a stern man, who believed that he must remove from France all her aristocratic members to insure the object of the rebellion. "Our names," said Danton, "will be execrated by posterity, but we shall have saved the Republic." With us, terror is a method of government invented to crush out knowledge, and force men to recognize as a thinking head, the feet which are upon their necks; it is the compensation an ignorant man in power takes for the contempt which he knows his insignificance inspires in a people infinitely superior to him.

This is why we have in our times a repetition of the extravagances of Caligula, who caused himself to be worshipped as a god, and associated his horse with him in the government. Caligula knew that he was the very lowest of those Romans whom he nevertheless held under his foot. Rosas caused his sacred likeness to be placed in the churches, and borne through the streets on a car, to which were harnessed officers and even ladies, for the purpose of giving celebrity to his name. But Facundo was only cruel when in a passion. His deliberate acts were limited to shooting or lashing a man. Rosas, on the contrary, was never in a passion. He made his plans in his closet, and gave his orders to his emissaries.

CHAPTER XII

Social War

CIUDADELA

The expedition departed, and the people of San Juan breathed
once more as if awakening from a horrible nightmare. Facundo
displayed in this campaign a spirit of order and a rapidity of
march which showed how much he had learned from past disasters. In twenty-four days he passed over with his army about
three hundred leagues; so that he came near surprising some
squadrons of the enemy which only became aware of his approach when he took up his quarters at Ciudadela, an old encampment of the patriot armies under Belgrano. It would be
inconceivable how such an army as that commanded by Madrid, at Tucuman, with brave officers and experienced soldiers,
could be conquered, if moral causes and prejudices against strategy did not solve the enigma.

General Madrid, commander-in-chief, had under him
Colonel Lopez, a provincial leader from Tucuman, who was
personally opposed to him; and, besides that, a retreat demor-
alizes troops. General Madrid was not the man to govern inferior officers. The army went into battle half-federal and
half-montonero in spirit, while that of Facundo had the unity
produced by terror and obedience to a leader who is not a
cause but a person, and who on this account overcomes free-

will and destroys individuality. Rosas triumphed over his enemies by that power, which made all his satellites passive instruments and blind executors of his supreme will.

The evening before the battle, Colonel Balmaceda asked of the general-in-chief permission to make the first charge. If it had been allowable for a battle to begin with a cavalry charge, or for an inferior officer to take the liberty of suggesting it, the battle would have been gained; for nothing in Brazil or the Argentine Republic had ever been able to withstand the charges of the second regiment of cuirassiers. The General acceded to the demand of the commander of the second; but Colonel Lopez declared that this would take away some of his best men; for to him the select troops had been given in charge, which, according to rule, form the reserve; therefore the general-in-chief, not having sufficient authority to stop these disputes, sent back to the reserve the invincible battalion, and the brave officer commanding it.

Facundo deployed his men at such a distance as to shelter them from the infantry commanded by Barcala, and to weaken the effect of eight pieces of artillery directed by the intelligent Arengreen. Could Quiroga have foreseen what his enemies were first doing? In a previous battle he had shot his own victorious officer for not pursuing with an inferior force the defeated enemy.

From one end to the other of Quiroga's line the soldiers trembled with terror, not of the enemy, but of their chief, who walked up and down behind the line, brandishing his lance. They could only hope to escape from this oppressive terror by throwing themselves upon the enemy. They rushed forward, broke the line of bayonets merely to put something between them and the image of Facundo, which pursued them like a phantom. Thus on one side reigned terror, and on the other anarchy. At the first attempt to charge, the cavalry of Madrid gave way, the reserve followed, and there only remained five officers, with the artillery, whose discharges became fainter and fainter, and the infantry, which rushed to a hand-in-hand fight with the enemy. But why say more? The victor should give the details of a battle.

Consternation reigned in Tucuman; immense numbers emigrated, for this was Facundo's third visit. The following day a contribution was levied. Quiroga, knowing that there were valuables hidden in a church, questioned the sacristan, who, being a silly fellow, answered with a laugh, for which he was shot on the spot. The chests of the general were soon filled with gold; therefore it is not strange that the guardian of San Francisco and the priest Colombres, were the next victims of the lash. Facundo then visited the prisoners, counted out the officers, and retired to rest after his fatigue, leaving orders for them to be shot.

Tucuman is a tropical country, where Nature has displayed its greatest pomp; it is the Eden of America, and without a rival on the surface of the earth. Imagine the Andes covered with a most luxuriant vegetation, from which escape twelve rivers at equal distances, flowing parallel to each other, until they converge and form a navigable stream, which reaches to the heart of South America. The country watered by these branches comprises more than fifty leagues. Primeval forests cover the surface, and unite the gorgeousness of India with the beauties of Greece.

The walnut interlaces its long branches with the mahogany and ebony; the cedar and the classic laurel grow side by side, and beneath these the myrtle consecrated to Venus; still leaving space for the fragrant spikenard and the white lily.

A belt of odoriferous cedar allows a passage through the forest, which is everywhere else impassable because of the thick and thorny rose-bushes. The old trunks are covered with various species of flowering mosses, and the bindweed and other vines festoon and entwine all these different trees.

Over all this vegetation, which defies the brush of fancy in combination and richness of coloring, fly myriads of golden butterflies, brilliant humming-birds, green parrots, blue magpies, and orange-colored toucans. The sound of these noisy birds greets one all day long like the roar of a cataract.

Major Andrews, an English traveller, who has devoted many pages to the description of these beauties, relates that he used to go out every morning to enjoy the sight of this magnificent vegetation, and that he often penetrated far into the thick, aromatic forests, so enraptured that only after his return home did he know that his clothes were torn, and his face scratched and bleeding. The city is surrounded for many leagues by a forest of orange-trees, rounded to about the same height, so as to form a vast canopy supported by millions of smooth columns. The rays of the torrid sun have never shone upon the scenes which are enacted under this immense roof. The young girls of Tucuman pass the Sundays there, each group choosing a convenient place. According to the season, they gather fruit or scatter blossoms under the feet of the dancers, who are intoxicated with the rich perfume and the melodious sounds of the guitar. Perhaps one might believe this description to be taken from the "Thousand and One Nights," or other Eastern fairy tale; but I cannot half describe the voluptuous beauty of these damsels, daughters of the tropics, as they recline for their siesta beneath the shade of the myrtles and laurels, enjoying such odors as would bring asphyxia upon one unaccustomed to the atmosphere.

Facundo went into one of these recesses formed by shady branches, perhaps to consider what he should do to the poor city fallen into his hands, like a squirrel into the paw of a lion. Presently a deputation of young girls, radiant with youth and beauty, approached the place where Facundo was lying upon his poncho. The bravest and most eager led the way, hesitating from time to time. Those who followed urged her forward;

then all paused, seized with fear. They glanced at one another for encouragement; then, advancing timidly, stood before him. Facundo received them kindly, made them sit down around him, and asked the object of their visit. They came to beg for the lives of the officers who were to be shot. Sobs, smiles, all the little fascinations of women were put in requisition to obtain their charitable end. Facundo seemed deeply interested, and smiled benignantly; he wished to hear from each one, of their families, their homes, a thousand details which seemed to please him; and thus passed an hour of expectation and hope. At last he said to them, with the greatest complacency, "Do you hear those guns? It is too late: they are shot." A cry of horror arose, like that which escapes from a flock of doves pursued by a falcon. They had indeed been shot—and how? Thirty-three officers, from the rank of colonel upwards, received the fatal balls entirely naked. Two brothers, sons of one of the first families of Buenos Ayers, embraced each other at the last moment, so that the body of one prevented the ball from reaching the other. The latter cried, "I am saved." A mistake, unfortunate one! How much he would have given to live. While confessing, he had taken a ring from his mouth, where it was concealed, and had charged the priest to give it to his betrothed; who, on receiving it, lost her reason, and never again recovered it.

The cavalry took charge of the corpses, and dragged them to the cemetery; so that bits of brain, arms, and legs remained on the square of Tucuman, and served as food for the dogs. How many victories are thus tarnished!

Don Juan Manuel Rosas had killed in the same manner and almost at the same time, at St. Nicholas de los Arroyos, twenty-eight officers, not to speak of more than a hundred assassinations. If anything can add to these horrors, it is the fate of Colonel Arraya, the father of eight children, and a prisoner, with three lance wounds in his shoulder. He was forced to enter Tucuman on foot, naked, bleeding, and loaded with eight guns. Exhausted with fatigue, a bed was allowed him in a private house. At the hour appointed for his execution, which was to take place on the public square, some musketeers forced their way into the house and pierced him with balls in his bed; leaving him to die in the flames of the burning sheets.

Colonel Barcala, the celebrated negro, was the only chief saved from this butchery. He was the ruling spirit of Cordova and Mendoza, and the civic guard idolized him. He was an instrument that they might preserve for the future.

On the following day a process was commenced throughout the city, called sequestration. It consisted in placing sentinels at the doors of all the shops, warehouses, leather and tobacco stores, tanneries, indeed everywhere, for there were no Federals. Federalism is a plant which grew there only after the soil was three times watered with blood by Quiroga, and once more by Oribe. Now it is said there are some Federals, as is proved by their ribbon, upon which is written, "Death to the savage Unitarios."

All movable property, and the flocks and herds, were claimed by Facundo. Two hundred and fifty carts, each loaded with sixteen beeves, were sent to Buenos Ayres. The European goods were gathered to be sold at auction by the commanders. Everything was offered for a low price. Facundo himself sold shirts, women's skirts, and children's clothes, unfolding and showing them to the crowd; any bid was received; the sale was soon finished; the affair was a success,—the crowd was dense.

After a few days, however, purchasers were scarce, and embroidered handkerchiefs were offered in vain for four reales—there was nobody to buy. What had happened? Did the people repent? Not at all; but there was no longer any money in circulation. The contributions on one hand, sequestration on the other, the auction finally, had taken the last medio in the province. If indeed a few still remained in the hands of the officials, the gaming-table emptied their purses. Leather bags filled with money were piled in front of the general's house, and remained there all night unguarded; for the passers-by did not even dare to look at them.

And yet the city had not been abandoned to pillage, nor had the soldiers had that immense booty. Quiroga used to say to his friends in Buenos Ayres that he never permitted his men to pillage, because of the immorality of the thing. A farmer once complained to him that some soldiers had stolen his fruit, and ordering the regiment before him, he discovered the guilty ones, who each received six hundred lashes; the terrified old man begged that the victims might be spared, and was threatened with a share of the punishment. This is the gaucho nature: he kills because his leader commands him to kill, and does not steal because he is not commanded to steal. It might seem strange that these men should not rebel and throw off the dominion of one who gave them nothing in exchange for their valor or their lives, did we not know from Don Juan Manuel Rosas how much terror can do, not only with the poor gaucho, but with the illustrious general and the proud, wealthy citizen. As I have already said, terror produces greater results than patriotism.

A colonel of the army of Chili, Don Manuel Gregorio Quiroga, Federal ex-governor of San Juan, and, at that time, a major-general in Quiroga's army, perceived that this booty of half a million was destined for the general alone, who would not hesitate to box the ears of an officer for keeping a few reales from the sale of a handkerchief. He therefore conceived the idea of obtaining his pay by abstracting several valuable rings from the general stock. But Facundo found out the theft, and had him tied to a post to be publicly humiliated; and when the army returned to San Juan, the major-general went on foot over almost impassable ground yoked with a bull. The companion of the bull expired at Catamarca without attracting any notice. At another time Facundo, having found out that a young man by the name of Rodriguez, of high standing in Tucuman, had received letters from the exiles, had him arrested, conducted him to the square himself, tied him up, and ordered him to receive six hundred lashes. But the soldiers did not administer the punishment skillfully enough, and Quiroga took the leather straps used for the purpose, and swinging them through the air with his mighty arm, gave fifty lashes by way of example. At the end of the performance he himself poured salt water over the back, and picked off the bits of skin from the wounds. This done, he went home and read the intercepted letters, in which were messages from husbands to wives, charges not to be uneasy about them, together with receipted bills for merchants, etc., but not a word of politics. Quiroga then asked for Rodriguez, but hearing that he was dying, sat down to cards, and won immense sums. Don Francisco Reto, and Don N. Lugones, were heard murmuring at the horrors they witnessed, and each received three hundred lashes, with an order to walk home through the streets naked, their hands over their heads, and their backs dripping blood; armed soldiers following at a little distance to see the sentence duly executed. To what a degree of indifference men may be brought by an infamous tyrant against whom there is no appeal, was shown by Don Lugones, who, turning to his companion in punishment, said, "Hand over a cigar, and let's have a smoke."

Dysentery prevailed at that time in Tucuman, and the physicians said there was no remedy for it, that it came from mental causes, from terror, a disease for which no remedy has yet been found in Buenos Ayres. One day Facundo presented himself before the house of a young widow who had taken his fancy, and asked some children who were playing at the door, where the lady was; one of the boys answered that she was not in. "Go tell her I am here," said Quiroga. "What is your name?" asked the boy, who, when the other replied, "I am Facundo

Quiroga," fell down senseless, and has only recently recovered his reason.

A young girl having excited his admiration, he proposed to take her to San Juan. It can be imagined how the poor girl received this proposition from a tiger. Stammeringly she said that she could not; that her father—. Facundo went to the father, and the miserable man, trying to conceal his horror, took courage to say that perhaps he would abandon his daughter, and she would be unprotected. Facundo declared that he should have no cause for that objection; and the unhappy father, still hoping to put him off or to gain time, proposed that a paper should be drawn up and signed; but Facundo immediately wrote and signed the required document, and passed it to the other for his signature. At the last moment the father asserted himself in the man, and he cried, "Kill me! but I will not sign." "Ah, old rascal!" cried Facundo, leaving the house in a rage.

Quiroga, the champion of the provinces, as he called himself, was barbarous, avaricious, lustful, and gave himself up to his passions without restraint; his successor did not rob cities, nor outrage women; he had only one passion,—the thirst for human blood and despotism. Instead, he knew how to use words and forms which satisfy the indifferent, such as: *the savages, the bloodthirsty creatures; perfidious, wretched Unitarios; the perfidious minister of Brazil; the dirty money of France; the iniquitous claims of England;*—words thus sufficing to cover the longest and most frightful series of crimes that the nineteenth century has witnessed. Rosas! Rosas! I bow before thy mighty wisdom. Thou art as great as the Plata, as the Andes! Thou alone hast discovered how contemptible are the liberties, the knowledge, and the pride of mankind. Trample upon them all; let all the governments of the civilized world honor thee, the more insolent thou art. Abuse them! thou wilt always find dogs to snatch up the spoils thrown to them!

In Tucuman, Salta, and Jujui, a great, progressive, industrial movement was interrupted by the invasion of Quiroga. Dr. Colombres, whom Facundo loaded with manacles, had introduced and encouraged the cultivation of sugar-cane, for which the climate is so well adapted. He had bought plants from Havana, sent agents to the mills of Brazil to study the processes and apparatus; succeeded in distilling the molasses; and did not rest until ten mills were established and in successful operation. But this was scarcely accomplished when Facundo turned his horses into the fields of cane, and destroyed the mills.

An agricultural society was already publishing its proceedings, and preparing to attempt the cultivation of indigo and cochineal. At Salta, looms and workmen had been brought from Europe for weaving woolen goods, cloth, carpets, etc., all of which had turned out profitably. But what particularly occupied the attention of those cities was the navigation of the Bermejo, the great stream which flows between the two provinces, unites with the Paraná, and thus provides an outlet for the valuable productions of that tropical country. The future prosperity of those beautiful provinces depended upon turning their streams to the uses of commerce; from poor inland cities, with small populations, their capitals might in ten years be converted into great centres of civilization and wealth, if, under the protection of an able government, their inhabitants could devote themselves to removing the slight obstacles in the way of their progress. Nor are these chimerical dreams of a possible but distant future.

In North America, not only hundreds of large, populous cities, but even whole States have sprung up throughout the region watered by the Mississippi and its branches, in less than ten years. And the Mississippi is not more available for commerce, than the Parana; nor do the Ohio, Illinois, or Arkansas water a larger or richer territory than the Pilcomayo, Bermejo, Paraguay, and so many other great rivers which designate the path to be taken by the people who shall hereafter inhabit the Argentine Republic. Rivadavia considered the navigation of the inland rivers of the greatest importance; an association was formed at Salta and Buenos Ayres with a capital of half a million dollars for this purpose, and Sala had made his voyage and published a map of the river. How much time has since been lost from 1825 to 1845! And how long will it still be before God shall destroy the monster of the pampas?

For Rosas, in so obstinately opposing the free navigation of rivers, in pretending to fear European intrusion, in keeping up the hostility of the inland cities and leaving them to their own resources, does not simply obey the instinctive prejudice against foreigners, nor even the impulse of the ignorant native of the port who, possessing the seaport and the general custom-house of the Republic, does not care for the development of civilization and wealth of the whole nation, or see that this would fill the harbor with ships bearing the products of the interior, and the custom-house with merchandise. He follows, rather, the natural instinct of the gaucho of the pampas, who has a horror of water, a contempt for ships, and knows no greater delight than riding a good horse. What does he care for mulberry-trees, sugar, indigo, the navigation of rivers, European immigration, or anything beyond the narrow circle of ideas in which he has lived? What does he care for the progress of the interior when he himself is in the midst of wealth, possessing a custom-house which brings in two millions a year without any trouble on his part?

Salta, Jujui, Tucuman, Santa Fé, Corrientes, and Entre Rios, would now rival Buenos Ayres if the industrial movement so eagerly begun, could have continued. As it is, some of its results remain: Tucuman now has large sugar-presses, and distilleries, which would bring great wealth if the products could be carried with less expense to the coast and exchanged in Buenos Ayres for merchandise. But no evils are eternal, and a day must come when the eyes of this people will be opened, who are now denied all liberty of progress, and are deprived of all capable and intelligent men, who could carry on the great work, and bring about in a few years the prosperity for which Nature has destined this now stationary, impoverished, devastated country. Why are such men persecuted? Brave, enterprising men, who employed their lives in various social improvements, encouraging public education, introducing the cultivation of the mulberry and the sugar-cane, exploring the water-courses, with only the national interest at heart, and desiring no other reward than the satisfaction of serving their fellow-citizens! Why do we not see again arising the spirit of European civilization which, however feeble, did once exist in the Argentine Republic? Why has the present government—more truly Unitarios in spirit than ever Rivadavia intended—never given a thought to the investigation of the inexhaustible and yet untouched resources of a favored soil? Why has not even a twentieth part of the millions employed in a fratricidal war been used to educate the people or to facilitate trade? What has been given to this people in exchange for its sacrifices and sufferings? A red rag! This is the extent of the government's care of them for fifteen years; this is the only measure of the national administration; the only relation between master and slave, the mark upon the cattle!

CHAPTER XIII
Barranca—Yaco!!!

The fire which burnt Albania so long was at last extinguished. All the red blood has flowed, and the tears of our children have been wiped away. Now we hold the cord of federation and friendship.
— COLDEN's *History of the Six Nations*

The conqueror of Ciudedala had driven the last supporters of the Unitario system beyond the confines of the Republic. The guns were hushed, and the tramp of cavalry was no longer heard on the pampas. Facundo returned to San Juan, and disbanded his army; but he restored the nominal value of what money he had taken from San Juan by the spoils of Tucuman. What more was there to do? Peace was then the normal condition of the Republic, as war had been before.

The conquests of Quiroga had destroyed all feeling of independence in the provinces, all regularity of administration. Liberty had ceased, and Quiroga's name took the place of law. In this portion of the Republic all leaders were united in one, and Jujui, Salta, Catamarca, Tucuman, Rioja, San Juan, and Mendoza, remained under the sole influence of Quiroga. In a word, the Federals had disappeared as well as the Unitarios, and the most complete unity existed in the person of the conqueror. Thus the undivided organization of the Republic which Rivadavia had attempted, and which had occasioned the contest, was realized in the interior at least, unless we can admit the existence of a *confederation* of cities which have lost all free will, and are at the mercy of a single leader. But in spite of the misapplication of common terms, the facts are too plain to be doubted. Facundo even spoke contemptuously of the much talked-of Confederation; proposed to his friends that they should choose a provincial for President of the Republic, and suggested Dr. José Santos Ortez, ex-governor of San Luis, his own friend and secretary. "He is not a rough gaucho like myself," he said, "but a scholar and an honest man; the man who knows how to do justice to his enemies, is worthy of confidence."

Thus it appears that Quiroga, after routing the Unitarios, went back to the old idea he entertained before the struggle— the advocacy of a presidency and the necessity of putting in order the affairs of the Republic. Yet some doubts troubled him. "Now, general," some one said to him, "the nation will be governed by Federal principles." "Hum," he answered, shaking his head, "there are still some obstacles in the way," and he added, with a significant look, "our friends below [Buenos Ayres] do not wish for a constitution."

When communications from Buenos Ayres came, and journals which gave the promotions of various officers who had commanded in the useless army of Cordova, Quiroga said to General Huidobro, "You see they have no titles to bestow upon my officers after all we have done here; we should belong to the port, to get anything." Knowing that Lopez was in possession of his Arabian horse, and did not send it to him, he was very angry, and exclaimed, "Ah, gaucho-stealer of cows, you will pay dearly for the pleasure of being well mounted!" And he continued his threats and abuse until his friends were alarmed at his indiscretion.

What did Quiroga intend to do now? He was governor of no province, and had no army under his command; nothing remained to him but his arms and the terror of his name. On his way to Rioja he had left hidden in the woods all the guns, swords, and lances which he had collected in the eight cities he had overrun, numbering more than twelve thousand. He deposited in the city twenty-six pieces of artillery, with plenty of baggage and ammunition, and moreover he had sixteen hundred fine horses at pasture in the ravines of Cuyo. Rioja was the cradle of his power, the very centre of his influence in the provinces; at a signal its arsenal would equip twelve thousand men for war. Some may incline to doubt these facts, but even as late as 1841 arms were dug up that had been concealed at that time. In 1830 General Madrid took possession of a treasure of thirty thousand dollars belonging to Quiroga, and soon after it was said that fifteen more had been found. Quiroga wrote to him charging him with having taken thirty-nine thousand dollars; and doubtless much more had been buried before the battle at Oncativo, during the time when so many cities were despoiled. As to the real amount concealed in those two parcels, Madrid afterwards thought that Quiroga gave it rightly, for the discoverer of the last parcel, having been taken prisoner, offered ten thousand dollars for his life, and when this was not accepted, committed suicide by cutting his throat.

Thus the interior had now a chief; he who had been conquered at Oncativo, and who had in Buenos Ayres only been entrusted with a few hundred convicts, was now the second, if not the first in power. To make the division of the Republic into two parts more decided, the provinces bordering on the Plata had made a league or confederation by which their liberties and independence were mutually assured; though a certain kind of feudalism still existed in the persons of Lopez of Santa Fé, Ferré, and Rosas,—leaders sprung from the people whom they governed. Rosas had already begun to influence public affairs very decidedly. After the victory over Lavalle, he was made governor of Buenos Ayres, and until 1832 filled the office as well as any other would have done. I must not omit a significant fact. From the first, Rosas demanded to be invested with absolute power, but was strongly opposed by his partisans in the city. By persuasions and deceptions he succeeded in obtaining it during the war of Cordova, and when that was ended, he was eagerly desired to give up this unlimited power. The city of Buenos Ayres did not then imagine that it could exist as an absolute government, whatever the principles of its political parties might be. Rosas, however, resisted, gently but ably. "It is not that I wish to make use of such power," he said, "but, as my secretary, Garcia Zuñiga, says, the schoolmaster must hold his whip in hand that his authority may be respected." He considered this comparison entirely appropriate, and repeated it frequently,—the citizens were the children, the governor, man and master.

Rosas was obliged to yield; but the ex-governor had no intention of becoming a mere citizen; the labor and patience of many years were about to bring their reward. During his legal term of service he learned all the entrances to the citadel, and all the ill-fortified points; and if he then left the government, it was only to take it by assault from the outside, without any constitutional restrictions, without being fettered by responsibility to any one. He laid down the truncheon to take up first the sword, and afterwards the battle-axe. Not long before he resigned the government, a great expedition, led by himself, was prepared to extend and protect the southern boundaries of the province which were exposed to frequent invasions of the savages. Everything was arranged on a large scale: an army composed of three divisions was to form a line of four hundred leagues, from Buenos Ayres to Mendoza. Quiroga was to command the forces of the interior, while Rosas, with his division, followed the Atlantic coast. The magnificence and utility of the enterprise concealed from the eyes of the people the political manoeuvre hidden under this plausible pretext. For what could be more desirable than to secure the southern frontier by making a large river the boundary between it and the Indians, and protecting it with a line of forts; a very practicable design, which had already been clearly marked out in the voyage of Cruz from the city of Conception, in Chili.

But Rosas had no idea of engaging in any enterprise which tended only toward the good of the Republic. His troops marched as far as Rio Colorado, moving slowly, and making observations on the soil, climate, and other circumstances of the country through which they passed. They destroyed some Indian huts, and took a few poor prisoners; and this was all that was effected by the great expedition, which left the frontier as defenseless as it had been before, and is still. The divisions of Mendoza and San Luis returned equally unsuccessful from the deserts of the south. Rosas then raised for the first time his red flag, like that of Algiers, and assumed the title of *Hero of the Desert*, in addition to that already acquired, of Restorer of the Laws—those same laws which he was now about to destroy.

Facundo, too keen to be deceived as to the object of the expedition, remained at San Juan until the divisions of the interior returned. The division commanded by Huidobro, which had been in the desert opposite San Luis, marched towards Cordova, and its approach put a stop to a rebellion headed by the Castillos, the object of which was to take the government from the Reinafes who were under the influence of Lopez. This rebellion was evidently gotten up at the instigation of Facundo; its leaders were from San Juan, the residence of Quiroga, and their supporters were his well-known partisans. The journals of the time, however, say nothing about Facundo's connection with that movement; and when Huidobro retired to his provincial home, and Arridondo, with other leaders of the rebellion, was shot, there was nothing more to be said or done; for the war about to begin between the two parties of the Republic, between the two leaders who were contending for supremacy, was to be a war of ambuscades, snares, and treachery. It was a silent combat; not a trial of strength between armies, but between audacity on one side, and skill and cunning on the other. This struggle between Quiroga and Rosas is but little understood, though it lasted five years. Each hated and despised the other, and neither lost sight of the other for a moment, for each felt that his life and success depended on the result of this terrible game.

Perhaps it will be well to make a political chart of the Republic from 1822, that the reader may better comprehend the following operations.

Argentine Republic

Region of the Andes	Borders of the Plata
Unity—	Confederation under
under the influence of Quiroga	the League of the Plata

Jujui	Rioja	Corrientes—Ferré
Salta	San Juan	Entre Rios ⎫
Tucuman	Mendoza	Santa Fé ⎬ Lopez
Catamarca	San Luis	Cordova ⎭
		Buenos Ayres—Rosas

Feudal Faction
Santiago del Estero—Ibarra

Lopez, of Santa Fé, extended his influence by means of Echague, a creature of his, and over Cordova through the Reinafés. Ferré, a man of independent spirit, kept Corrientes out of the struggle until 1839. Under the rule of Beron de Astrada, that province turned against Rosas, who, with his increase of power, had regarded the League as of no effect. This same Ferré was led by his narrow provincial spirit to denounce Lavalle as a deserter in 1840, for having crossed the Paraná with the army of Corrientes; and after the battle of Chaaguazu he took the victorious army from General Paz, thus losing the important advantages which might have been secured by that victory. Ferré in these proceedings and others, was actuated by the spirit of provincial independence which had grown up during the war with Spain. Thus the same feeling which had thrown Corrientes into opposition to the Unitario constitution in 1826, made it in 1838 oppose Rosas, who was attempting a centralization of power. Thence came Ferré's mistakes, and the misfortunes which followed the battle of Chaaguazu, making it of no use to the Republic, the general, or the province itself; for if the rest of the Republic should be consolidated under Rosas, Corrientes could not maintain its feudal and federal independence.

The southern expedition being ended, or rather stopped, for it had neither plan nor end, Facundo marched to Buenos Ayres with Barcala and his chosen band, and entered the city without taking the trouble to announce his arrival. Such neglect of ordinary forms might be commented upon were it not entirely characteristic. What brought Quiroga to Buenos Ayres at this time? Was it another invasion like that of Mendoza in the very stronghold of his rival? Or did this barbarian at last desire to live amidst the luxuries of civilization? It is probable that all these causes urged Facundo to his ill-advised journey to Buenos Ayres. Power instructs, and Quiroga had all the high qualities of mind which enable a man to adapt himself to any new position, whatever it may be. He established himself in Buenos Ayres, and was soon surrounded by the principal men of the place; he bought shares in the public funds to the amount of six hundred thousand dollars; played for various stakes; spoke contemptuously of Rosas; declared himself a Unitario among Unitarios, and talked continually about the constitution. His past life, his barbarous deeds, little known at Buenos Ayres, were explained and excused by the desire of conquest, and the necessity of self-preservation. His present conduct was temperate, his manner dignified and imposing, though he still wore the *chaqueta*, the striped poncho, and long hair and beard.

During his residence at Buenos Ayres, Quiroga made some trials of his personal strength. As he was walking, wrapped up as usual in his poncho, he saw a man with his knife drawn, refusing to yield to a policeman; and seizing the fellow, disarmed him, and carried him to the station; he had not given the policeman his name, but was recognized at the station by an officer, and next day the papers all related the story. He heard one day that an apothecary had spoken contemptuously of his barbarity in the provinces, and went to his office to inquire about it, but this time was not very successful; the physician, nothing daunted, told him that he would not be able to ill-treat people in Buenos Ayres as he had done in the provinces, and the story was circulated with great satisfaction in the city. Yet this Buenos Ayres, so proud of its institutions, was, before the end of a year, to be treated with greater barbarity than the interior had ever received at the hands of Quiroga. The police once went to Quiroga's house in search of him, and he overcame his first impulse to defend himself, feeling that there was a greater power than his, and that he might at any time be imprisoned should he take his defense into his own hands. Quiroga's sons were in the best schools, and he made them wear the European dress; and when one of them insisted on leaving his studies for the army, he was placed by his father in one of the regiments as drummer, until he should repent of his folly.

Quiroga used to declare that the only writers good for anything were the Varelas, who had abused him so much, and that the only honest men in the Republic were Rivadavia and Paz. To the Unitarios he said that he only wanted a secretary like Dr. Ocampo,—a politician who could write out a constitution, and he would march with it to San Luis, and thence show it to the whole Republic at the point of a lance. Quiroga represented himself as the leader of a new attempt to organize the Republic, and he might be said to have conspired openly had he done more than talk. His natural habit of idleness, and of expecting everything from terror, and perhaps the novelty of surrounding circumstances, prevented him from acting with energy, and at last put him in the power of his rival. There is no proof that Quiroga proposed any immediate action, unless it be found in his understanding with the governors of the interior, and his indiscreet words, repeated by both parties, though the Unitarios did not dare to trust their cause to such hands, and the Federals looked upon him as a deserter from their ranks.

While he thus gave himself up to dangerous indolence, the serpent which was to crush him in its folds, drew nearer and nearer. In the year 1833, Rosas, while nominally occupied with the great expedition, kept his army in the south, and narrowly watched Buenos Ayres and the progress of Balcarce's government. The province of Buenos Ayres soon presented a most singular spectacle. Imagine what would happen if a large comet should approach the earth: first a general disturbance, then deep, far-off rumblings, then oscillations of the earth attracted from its orbit, then a mighty convulsion followed by the upheaval of mountains, and finally the deluge and chaos that have preceded the successive creations on our globe. Such was the influence exerted by Rosas in 1834. The government of Buenos Ayres became more and more restricted, more embarrassed in its movement, more dependent on the "hero of the desert." Every communication from him was a reproach to the governor, exorbitant requisitions for the army or some unprecedented demand. Soon the civil authorities lost all influence over the country population, and complaint was made to Rosas, who was supposed to control the peasantry; but in a short time the same disregard of authority spread rapidly over the city itself, until it became no uncommon thing for armed men to ride through the streets, now and then firing upon the citizens. This disorganization of society increased daily, and it was not difficult to trace an influence from the camp of Rosas to the country districts,—from these to the suburbs of the city, and thence to a certain class of men within the city. The government of Balcarce succumbed to this power from without, and the partisans of Rosas worked hard to open the way for him, but the Federal party of the city made constant opposition. The chamber of representatives assembled in the midst of the confusion caused by the resignation of Balcarce, and chose General Viamont governor, who readily accepted the office.

For a short time order seemed to be reëstablished, and the city once more breathed freely, but soon the same confusion began again, and the same outrages were committed in the streets. It is impossible to describe the state of constant alarm in which the people lived during two years of this strange and systematic persecution. Frequently, without any apparent cause, people were seen running through the streets, the noise of closing doors was heard from house to house; some whisper had passed around—some one had observed a suspicious looking group of men, or the clatter of hoofs had been heard.

On one of these occasions Quiroga was passing by a street, and seeing well-dressed men running without knowing for what, he looked contemptuously at a group of armed ruffians, and said, "It would not have been so, had I been here."

"And what would you have done, general?" asked his companion, "you have no influence over these people."

Quiroga raised his head, and with flashing eyes, answered, "Look you, if I should go into the street, and say to the first man I met, 'Follow me,' would he not follow?"

There was such an overpowering energy in Quiroga's words, and his figure was so imposing, that they rarely failed to impress strongly.

General Viamont resigned at last, because he saw that he could not govern; that there was a powerful hand holding the reins of the administration; and no one could be found to succeed him, none dared accept the office. After awhile, however, Dr. Maza was placed at the head of the government, and as he was the old master and friend of Rosas, it was hoped that a remedy had been found for the evil. A vain hope, for the distress increased rather than diminished. Anchorena petitioned the governor to repress the social disorders, knowing that this was not in his power, that the police force would not obey; that the real power came from without.

General Guido and Dr. Alcorta, in the chamber of representatives, earnestly protested against the violent commotion in which the city was kept, but the evil still increased, and to aggravate it, Rosas, from his camp, reproached the governor with the disorders which he himself had fomented. Finally a committee of representatives went to offer him the government, saying that he alone could put an end to the suffering which they had endured for two years. But Rosas refused, and then there were new commissions, and new persuasions, until Rosas consented to do the people the favor of governing them, on condition that the legal term of three years should be extended to five years, and that the "highest public power" should be given him; an expression invented by himself, he alone understanding its meaning.

In the midst of these arrangements between Rosas and the city of Buenos Ayres, news came of a difficulty between the governors of Salta, Tucuman, and Santiago del Estero, which might result in war. Five years had passed since the Unitarios disappeared from the political world, and two since the city Federals had lost their influence in the government, but had courage to exact conditions which made capitulation tolerable. While the *"city"* surrendered at discretion, with its institutions, its liberties, etc., Rosas was carrying on complicated machinations outside. He was evidently in communication with Lopez of Santa Fé, and there was even a conference between the two leaders. The government of Cordova was under the influence of Lopez, who had placed the Reinafés at its head. Facundo was now invited to go and use his influence to settle the difficulties which had arisen in the northern part of the Republic, no one else being chosen to aid him in this mission of peace. He refused at first, then hesitated, and finally accepted.

It was on the 18th of December, in 1835, that Facundo took leave of the city, saying to his friends, "If I succeed, you will see me again, if not, farewell forever." At the last moment this intrepid man was assailed by dark presentiments; it will be remembered that something similar happened to Napoleon when he was leaving the Tuilleries for Waterloo.

He had scarcely made half a day's journey when a muddy brook stopped his carriage. The travelling attendant came up and tried to get it over; new horses were put in, and every effort made to move the carriage, but in vain, and Quiroga falling into a rage, ordered the man himself to be harnessed to the vehicle. His brutality and terrorism appeared again as soon as he found himself without the city. This first obstacle being overcome, he went on across the pampas, always travelling until two o'clock in the night, and starting again at four. He was accompanied by Dr. Ortez, his secretary, and a well-known young man, who had been prevented from continuing the journey in his own carriage by the loss of a wheel soon after starting.

At every post Facundo eagerly asked how long it was since a courier from Buenos Ayres had passed; the usual answer was, "about an hour," after which he called hurriedly for horses, and drove on rapidly. Their comfort was not increased by the rain, which fell in torrents two or three days. On entering the province of Santa Fé, Quiroga's anxiety increased, and it became absolute agony when, on reaching the post at Pavon, he found that the post-master was absent, and that there were no horses to be had immediately. His companions saw no cause for this mood, and were astonished to find this man who was a terror to the whole Republic, a prey to what seemed groundless fears.

When the carriage once more started, he muttered in a low tone to himself, "If I only get beyond the boundaries of Santa Fé, it is enough."

At last they arrived at Cordova, at half-past nine at night, just an hour after the courier from Buenos Ayres, who had preceded them all the way. One of the Reinafés hastened to the post-station where Facundo still sat in his carriage calling for horses, and greeting him respectfully, invited him to pass the night in the city where the governor had already prepared for his reception. But to each renewed offer of hospitality, Quiroga only answered by a call for horses, until Reinafé retired mortified, and Facundo set out again at twelve o'clock at night.

Meanwhile the city of Cordova was filled with mysterious rumors; the friends of the young man who had by chance come with Quiroga, and who stopped at Cordova, his native place, went to see him in crowds, seeming to be much astonished at finding him alive. They informed him that he had a narrow escape; that Quiroga was to have been assassinated at a certain place; that the assassins were engaged and the pistols purchased; but he had escaped them by his haste, for the courier had scarcely arrived and announced his coming, when he appeared himself, frustrating all their plans. Never was such a thing undertaken with so little secrecy; the whole city knew all the particulars of the crime intended by the government, and Quiroga's assassination was the only subject of conversation.

Quiroga arrived at his destination, settled the difficulties between the hostile governors, and started back to Cordova, in spite of the reiterated entreaties of the governors of Santiago and Tucuman, who offered him a large escort, and advised him to return by way of Cuyo. It would seem that some avenging spirit made him obstinately persist in defying his enemies, without escort, and without any means of defense, when he might have gone by the Cuyo road, disinterred his immense deposit of arms at Rioja, and armed the eight provinces which were under his influence. He knew all; had received repeated intimations in Santiago del Estero; he knew the danger he had escaped by his rapid progress; knew the greater one which awaited him, for his enemies had not given up their design. "To Cordova!" he cried to the postilion, as if Cordova was to be the end of his journey.

Before they reached the post-station of Ojo del Agua, a young man came out of the woods into the road, and asked at the carriage for Dr. Ortez, who got out and heard from the young man, that Santos Perez with a military company was stationed near a place called Barranca-Yaco; that as the carriage passed they were to fire into it from both sides, and afterwards kill the postilions; no one was to escape; the orders were positive. The young man, who had formerly been befriended by Ortez, now came to save him, and had a horse ready at a little distance for him to ride. The secretary, astounded by this news, told Quiroga what he had heard and urged him to save himself. Facundo questioned the young man again, and thanked him for the information, but told him he might make himself easy, adding in a loud voice, "The man is not born who will kill Quiroga; at a word from me to-morrow, that whole company will put itself under my command, and escort me to Cordova."

These words of Quiroga, which I have but recently learned, explain why he so strangely persisted in defying death. Pride and faith in the terror of his name, urged him on to the fatal catastrophe. I had already so accounted for it in my own mind, before I had the confirmation of his words.

The night which the travellers passed at the post-station of Ojo del Agua, was one of great agony to the unhappy secretary, who was going to a certain death without the half-savage valor and rashness which inspired Quiroga; death never seems more terrible than when imposed by the senseless bravado of a friend, and when there would be no dishonor in avoiding it. Dr. Ortez took the post-master aside and asked him about the report he had heard, promising not to abuse his confidence; he was told that Santos Perez had been there with his company of thirty men not an hour before, and they were then stationed at the appointed place, fully armed; that all who accompanied Quiroga were to be killed, as Perez himself had said. This corroboration of the information before received did not alter the determination of Quiroga, who, after taking a cup of chocolate, as usual, slept profoundly; unlike Ortez who lay awake thinking of his wife and children whom he would see no more, and only because he could not incur the charge of disloyalty to his friend,—a friend more to be feared than many enemies. At midnight, his agony becoming insupportable, he got up with a faint hope of receiving some comfort from the post-master. But the man could only repeat what he had already told, and showed unfeigned anxiety himself, for, as he said, the two postilions he was obliged to provide would have to share the same fate. Ortez then aroused Quiroga, and made one more attempt to dissuade him from his purpose, saying that he could not accompany him if he persisted. Quiroga laughed at his fears, and gave him to understand that his own anger would be more dangerous than anything he could meet at Barranca-Yacco; so that the unfortunate man could only submit. Quiroga then called his strong negro servant and set him to cleaning some arms; this was all he could be induced to do in the way of precaution.

Daylight came at last, and the carriage started, accompanied by two postilions, one of whom was a mere lad and nephew of one of the company which lay in wait for them; two couriers who accidentally joined the party, and the negro who went on horseback. They soon reached the fatal spot, two discharges were fired into the carriage from each side of the road, but without wounding any one; then the soldiers rushing up sword in hand, disabled the horses in a moment, and cut to pieces the driver and couriers. Quiroga meanwhile put his head out of the window and said to the commander of the company, "What is all this?" His only answer was a ball through his head. Santos Perez then passed his sword several times through the body, and when the butchery was completed, had the carriage filled with dead bodies, and dragged into the woods, with the murdered postilion still on his seat. The young lad alone was alive, and Perez seeing him, asked who he was. His sergeant replied, that the boy was a nephew of his, and that he would answer for him with his life. Without a word, Perez walked up to the sergeant, shot him through the heart, and then seizing the boy by the arm, threw him on the ground and cut his throat in spite of his childish cries for mercy. Yet in after life the death cries of this lad became a pursuing torment to him, and sounded in his ears, sleeping or waking, wherever he might be. Facundo had said of all the deeds he had committed, but one remorse troubled him, which was for the death of the twenty-six officers shot at Mendoza.

This Santos Perez was a gaucho-outlaw, celebrated in all the Sierra and city of Cordova for the many murders he had committed, for his bold audacity and extraordinary adventures. While General Paz was at Cordova this man had gathered about him a large band of the most lawless men, and occupied one of the wild mountain districts. With higher ideas, he would have been equal to Quiroga; as it was, he was only his assassin. He was very tall, had a pale, handsome face, with a curly black beard.

Perez was long pursued as a criminal by the government, and more than four hundred men were sent out to look for him. Once he narrowly escaped being poisoned by Reinafé; at another time a party sent to take him was commanded by an old friend of his, who sent for him under pretense of having something to say to him. Perez went down to him, saying, "Here I am, what is wanted?" and when the captain hesitated a moment with embarrassment, he turned on his heel, saying contemptuously, "I knew you wanted to betray me, and only came to make sure of it;" and before they could seize him, he had disappeared. After numerous escapes of this kind, he was at last delivered up to justice through a woman's revenge. He had beaten his mistress one night, and when he had fallen asleep, she went out and told some policemen where he was, having first removed his pistols from beside his pillow. Being suddenly awakened, and seeing himself surrounded by armed men, he reached out his arm, and then said, quietly, "I surrender, they have taken my pistols."

An immense crowd assembled in the streets when he was carried into Buenos Ayres, and showered upon him every kind of abusive epithet, but he only held his head the higher, and murmured disdainfully, "If I but had my knife." He was followed with execrations as he walked to the scaffold, and his gigantic form, like that of Danton, towered above the crowd around him.

The government of Buenos Ayres gave great solemnity to the execution of Quiroga's assassins; the blood-stained, ball-pierced carriage was long exposed to public view, and lithographs of Quiroga, and of those executed on the scaffold, were distributed among the people. But the impartial historian will one day expose the real instigator of the assassination.

CHAPTER XIV
Friar José Felix Aldao,
Brigadier-General and Governor

On the 4th of February, 1817, the following incident happened in a deep, narrow valley of the Andes, through which the river Aconcagua rushes from rock to rock in its sudden descent. It was near sunset as the vanguard of the division, commanded by Colonel Las Heras, marched silently down the mountain towards Chili, by the rough, rocky road leading through Uspallata. The fort, known by the name of "La Guardia Vieja," was visible far down in the valley, and had the appearance of being entirely unoccupied, but a detachment of Spanish soldiers was concealed within, watching the approach of the insurgents, and prepared for a combat. Presently two discharges were fired from the fortifications; a company of the eleventh rebel regiment immediately advanced, firing, from the bank of the river to within twelve paces of the fort, while another defiled along the mountain side to prevent all possibility of the escape of the Spaniards. A moment afterwards they carried the walls at the point of the bayonet, and wherever the contest was most desperate, were seen flashing the swords of thirty grenadiers, under Lieutenant José Aldao. Among these was a strange figure dressed in white, like some phantom, and dealing blow after blow with wild ferocity. This was the chaplain of the division, who, carried away by excitement, had obeyed the order to charge, which, when given to the conquerors of San Lorenzo, was sure to be followed by a battle in which no quarter was given.

When the victorious vanguard returned to the fortified encampment occupied by Las Heras and the rest of the division, the commander saw by the blood-stains on the scapulary of the chaplain, that he had been increasing the number of the dead instead of comforting the dying, and signified to him that he would do better to keep to his breviary and leave the sword to warriors. The hot-tempered chaplain could ill-brook this reproof, and turned hastily away with flashing eyes and compressed lips. On dismounting at his lodgings, he grasped the sword still hanging at his side, saying to himself, "We shall see." Thus was formed an irrevocable resolution. That evening's combat had revealed his natural instincts in all their strength, proving how little fitted he was for a profession requiring mildness and brotherly love; he had felt the pleasure in shedding blood which is natural to those who have the organ of destructiveness strongly developed; war attracted him irresistibly; he wished to rid himself of the troublesome gown he wore, and to win the laurels of the soldier in place of the symbol of humiliation and penitence; he therefore determined that he would be no longer a priest, but a soldier, as were José and Francisco, his brothers. The fear of scandal would not deter him, for he could cite many examples in his favor; the celebrated engineer Beltran, who had lighted with resinous torches the dangerous passes of the Andes, and who afterwards prepared at Santiago congreve rockets to be thrown into the forts of Callao, was also a priest who had laid aside the gown, finding that he was able to serve his country more effectually than the church. In all parts of America, especially in Mexico, priests and monks had led the insurgents, taking advantage of the influence which their priestly office gave them over the common people. However, the chaplain Aldao was not troubled with a scrupulous conscience, and would not have been deterred from his resolution even without the excuse of such examples. He belonged to a poor, but honorable family of Mendoza, and had shown from his infancy such willfulness and disregard of authority, that his parents educated him for the priesthood, in the hope that its solemn duties would reform his evil tendencies; a fatal mistake, for his novitiate was, like his childhood, a continued course of violence and immorality. Notwithstanding this, he received sacred orders in Chili, in 1806, under the episcopacy of Meran, and the patronage of the reverend father Velasquez, who assisted him at his first mass at Santiago, and who was greatly scandalized at seeing the newly made priest after the battle of Chacabuco in military costume, and with the martial bearing of a soldier. "Thou wilt repent of this," cried the good priest, in his horror at this profanation; but unfortunately for the Argentine people the prophecy was not fulfilled, for the apostate, though unmourned, died a natural death, and with the honors of a victorious general.

Colonel Las Heras, in his official report of the battle of La Guardia Vieja, made favorable mention of the priest, for capturing two officers, which, according to military rule, gives a claim to promotion; and consequently, the priest who had made his first experiment in fighting at Guardia Vieja, appeared at the battle of Chacabuco in the uniform of a lieutenant of grenadiers, and won a soldier's laurels. Though he could never rid himself of his priestly title, he soon proved in his new career that he did not wear the sword in vain, and became renowned as a formidable warrior and an implacable enemy; known to the army and the public generally, as "El fraile," or the monk.

I will mention one of the many remarkable deeds performed by him at that time. In the pursuit after the battle of Maipu, a Spanish grenadier of gigantic stature was cutting his way through the surrounding enemies, and with each blow of his mighty sword stretching a lifeless body on the ground; the brave Lavalle attempted to approach him, but felt his eager valor cool whenever the confusion of the struggle brought them together. Aldao, seeing this, made his way up to the giant, and, instead of falling with the many other victims, beat aside the terrible sword and passed his own again and again through the body of the huge Spaniard, amidst the loud acclamations of his party.

But whatever honorable deeds in arms the recreant priest may have accomplished, his conduct would at any other time, or in any other circumstances, have covered him with opprobrium. Freed from the restraint hitherto imposed upon his inclinations by the priestly office, eager for pleasure, and perhaps impelled to excesses by the necessity for excitement in which men often seek to drown any possible remorse for a wrong step in life, the monk henceforth became famous for his disorderly habits; his private life being devoted to intoxication, cards, and women. But perhaps even these vices would have been forgiven, had they not outlasted the first excitement of unrestrained youth, and followed him to the end of his life. He abused even the large indulgence with which his companions in arms regarded his conduct, and though his commanders were very willing to make use of his courage, they took care to send him to a distance whenever it was possible to do so with advantage. Whatever differences of opinion there may be among men, all feel a repugnance at seeing a priest stained with blood, and given over to intoxication and vice.

Aldao had the rank of captain in the army which left Valparaiso under command of San Martin, to deliver Peru from the Spanish dominion. In that country, where the main body of Spanish forces was stationed, the insurgent army needed auxiliaries to harass the enemy on all sides, and act as reserve forces. For this purpose bands of guerrillas were organized in the mountains, which kept the royalists in continual alarm. These bands required bold, fearless commanders, who would risk everything to attain their ends, and who shrank from nothing, not even pillage and assassination. After taking part in the contests at Lacca and Pasco, Captain Aldao was sent to raise one of these bands and to act on his own responsibility, as circumstances should suggest. His own master, and within reach of no higher authority than himself, it can easily be conceived that his violence and unrestrained passions found plenty of victims among a timid people quite incapable of resistance. A characteristic incident soon happened. Aldao had determined to defend with his troop of Indians the bridge of Iscuchaca, but at the approach of a detachment of Spaniards, more than a thousand natives fled, thus losing their advantageous position, and without resistance delivering to the enemy an important post. Their furious leader, unable to prevent their flight, fell upon them as upon a flock of sheep, and did not cease slaying until a large heap of dead and wounded had fallen under the repeated strokes of his sword. However bloody might have been a contest at the bridge, and however deadly the fire of the Spaniards, fewer Indians would have fallen than thus lay on the ground, the victims of one man's anger.

The circumstances which occasioned the disbanding of San Martin's army, made it unnecessary for Aldao to remain longer in the mountains, and with the rank of lieutenant-colonel, he went to Lima, where fortune favored him at cards, until he had gained a large fortune, and then he left for Pasto. He there met a beautiful young girl of respectable family, with whom he became violently enamored, and who returned his passion. This was no passing fancy, but a deep, lasting feeling on both sides, only strengthened by the impossibility of a lawful union, which would ever be prevented by his priestly vows. Fortunately for him, she was unselfish enough to consent to be the mistress of a soldier whose epaulets could not conceal the stain of apostasy, and, leaving friends and country, she fled with him where the humiliation of her social position would be less known.

Aldao established himself at San Felipe, capital of the province of Aconcagua, where he became a merchant, and lived respectably; but the unfortunate pair were condemned to suffer the inevitable consequences of their false position, and the church which he had repudiated, would not quietly see him in the arms of another mistress. The curé Espinosa threatened to send him to Santiago to the tender mercies of the order he had abandoned, and finally forced him to remove to Mendoza, his native place, and carry there the scandal of his unlawful union. The church is ever bitter against those who have left her for social positions. If the monk Aldao could have married lawfully, perhaps his passions might have been moderated by the pleasures of home, and he might have been saved from the crimes of his after-life.

On recrossing the Andes, his reflections must have been strange, and anything but pleasant, for the mountain ridge which separated two provinces, was also a dividing line between the two phases of his existence: on one side he had been the chaplain,—the Dominican friar,—on the other, he was the Lieutenant-Colonel Felix Aldao, with an unwedded wife at his side. The people of Mendoza, who had been accustomed to see him with gown and rosary, would now see him with sword and epaulets, and women and children would point mockingly at "the Fraile," a name which came to be a more painful wound than any received in battle. He avoided society, and secretly nourished a sort of hatred for all mankind, which was the more bitter because suppressed.

On his arrival at Mendoza, in 1824, he took a farm at a little distance from the city, where he labored with commendable industry and intelligence, and where the only drawback to his happiness was the remembrance of the detested tie which still bound him to the church. In this retirement Aldao might have lived quietly to the end of his days, but unfortunately for himself and his country, echoes of arms and civil war once more resounded throughout the land, and he was drawn into that public life from which he was to escape only by death, loaded with crimes and pursued by endless maledictions.

The elements of destruction existing in the Argentine Republic were then in motion, and were soon to develop the cruel and despotic government which now crushes it. The brilliant but artificial government established by Rivadavia at Buenos Ayres, fascinated its immediate supporters, but provoked jealousies and opposition in the interior; divers ambitions were developing: the *Caudillos*★ were soon to appear; parties were just forming; the envy excited by a rich, powerful city in her poorer neighbors, clamored for a confederation; Spanish prejudices caused many men to oppose all reform; the presidential government seemed to many a foreign domination; all was chaos; the clouds preceding the hurricane gathered darkly on the horizon, and as the terror of birds indicates a coming storm, so the general uneasiness of men's minds signified that some mighty commotion was at hand.

Suddenly the storm burst upon San Juan with the cry of "Viva la Religion!" The government of Carril was overthrown, and in less than twenty-four hours a fiddler had become a general, a lame cobbler was making laws, and a clown deciding the fate of a country. One Maradona, a pretended old nobleman, was found to give some show of decency to the plebeian mob; and, unfortunately, deluded priests, believing it to be a question of religion, placed the cross at the head of this insurrection,—the beginning of the long series of crimes which brought the Republic to its present condition of barbarism. Two hundred citizens fled to Mendoza, and besought aid from the brave soldiers who had returned from Chili and Peru, Felix Aldao among the rest. He hesitated, and asked himself why he should leave the asylum in which both his glory and his shame were hidden; but finally consented, and under the command of his brother José, marched to San Juan at the head of a company which obtained an easy victory over the plebeian crowd, without a leader or officers capable of directing its enthusiasm.

★Country chiefs.

The Aldao brothers returned to Mendoza covered with laurels, and provided by their friends with money obtained by exorbitant contributions imposed upon their enemies. But the Aldaos had acquired in the expedition something more than fame and money,—the knowledge of their own power,—and formed a brotherly league for the purpose of obtaining their ends. All three were colonels, all brave, intelligent, and capable.

This triumvirate has exercised a most pernicious influence in the Argentine Republic, never yet fully appreciated. After reconquering Chili, San Martin sent the first regiment of the Andes to San Juan with orders to raise a company of dragoons, and then to join the army which was to invade Peru. But José and Francisco Aldao with other rebels, executed a military maneuver which deprived the army of this expected aid. Most of the officers were assassinated, and the two regiments, not having succeeded in occupying Mendoza, where Colonel Alvarado and other forces of the army were stationed, attempted a disastrous retreat to Tucuman, and dispersed with the shame of having deserted their banners.

The stragglers of the disbanded regiments, in passing through Rioja, met with a man already conspicuous in the provincial rebellions, and whose name was destined to become terrible in Argentine history. This gaucho with keen black eyes, and a pale face, almost covered with a thick, curly black beard, obtained from the deserters their arms. The dream of years was realized; Facundo Quiroga was in possession of arms, and provincial barbarism, the brutal passions of the multitude, plebeian ambitions and prejudices, the thirst for blood and pillage, had at last their partisan, their gaucho hero, their spirit personified. Facundo Quiroga had arms, and men would not be wanting; one cry from him resounding from forest to plain, would bring about him a thousand mounted gauchos.

Ah! when will an impartial history of the Argentine Republic be written? And when will its people be able, without fear of a tyrant, to read the terrible drama of the revolution,—the well-intentioned and brilliant, but chimerical government of Rivadavia; the power and brutal deeds of Facundo Quiroga; and the administration of Rosas, the great tyrant of the nineteenth century, who unconsciously revived the spirit of the Middle Ages, and the doctrine of equality armed with the knife of Danton and Robespierre. Had the defense of Montevideo gloriously ended the revolutionary period, we should have an epic poem in place of history, and in forty years should have passed through all the changes and elaborations which have been developed in Europe only with the lapse of many centuries. That we have made for ourselves a military reputation, witness Brazil, Chili, Peru, Bolivia, and the Indians to the south of us; our victorious arms have been carried to the farthest extent of the continent. We have had our institutions, and contests of ideas and principles. And our future destiny is foretold in our numerous rivers, the boundless pasturage of our plains, our immense forests, and a climate favorable to the productions of the whole world. If we lack an intelligent population, let the people of Europe once feel that there is permanent peace and freedom in our country, and multitudes of emigrants would find their way to a land where success is sure. No, we are not lowest among Americans. Something is to result from this chaos; either something surpassing the government of the United States of North America, or something a thousand times worse than that of Russia,—the Dark Ages returned, or political institutions superior to any yet known.

José and Francisco, after bringing disorder into the army which was to invade Peru, and exciting revolts in the interior, were taken prisoners and carried to Lima, where they would have received punishment for their misdeeds, had not the monk, chief of the mountain guerrillas, appeared and interceded for them with San Martin, urging as a consideration his own past services. Francisco, after the battle of Ayacucho, in which he served under Bolivar, returned to Chili, where he was engaged by Rivadavia's agents to go to Mendoza and organize a force to dislodge Facundo Quiroga, who had taken possession of San Juan. For Quiroga, having heard something of the agitation among the Catholics, lost no time in raising a black flag with a red cross upon it, and the words, "Religion or Death!" though it is very certain that he did nothing for the benefit of religion anywhere, and equally true that violence and death constantly followed his footsteps. It is singular to see how these restless Caudillos looked for some pretense to disguise their vague, undefined ambition.

A letter addressed to Quiroga by one of his partisans contains this statement: "We can't do anything more with 'Religion or Death,' general, it no longer makes an impression; *confederation* is the word for us now; let us have a Constitution, and we will carry it at the point of the bayonet." Yet Quiroga was assassinated while endeavoring to persuade the Unitarios to join him for the purpose of destroying Rosas and the Federals.

Francisco Aldao arrived at Mendoza with ten thousand dollars, which he had received beforehand for the enterprise against Quiroga; but a consultation with his brothers caused him to change his mind, and keeping the money, he joined with them in forming the military trio from which Mendoza suffered so many outrages. From this moment the Aldaos labored secretly for the attainment of their own ends, the field being open to all unprincipled ambitions. They received an order to raise a regiment for the army of Brazil, and accepted it, with the intention of using the men for their own purpose.

Their ambition, however, met with an obstacle in the person of a creole negro. This slave, who early showed the talent not unfrequent in descendants of the African race, had been carefully educated by his owners, and was in condition to make use of his natural endowments when occasion required. He began his career as his master's assistant, and was rapidly promoted, until he became commander of a battalion, which brought him in contact with the chief politicians of the time. Barcala was not only one of the most distinguished characters of the revolution, but his reputation was untarnished, and this could be said of very few in those lawless days. He was a man of refined manners, tastes, and ideas, and his success was owing to his own merit. He never forgot his color and origin. He acquired his fame in history through his rare talent for organization, and the gift which he possessed in a high degree of conveying ideas to the masses; the lower classes were transformed by the magic of his power; and the officers and soldiers of his training were remarkable for their good behavior, decent dress, intelligence, and love of liberty. It was long before the impression made by Barcala in Mendoza was effaced; and in the revolution of 1840, against Rosas, a large battalion of infantry in Cordova still bore his name upon their banner, and resisted Rosas to the last. He had been in Cordova in 1830, and had inspired its artisans and laborers with the love of liberty and equality, in the broadest sense of these terms; and, though he was now dead, his ideas remained in the hearts of the people.

Obscure men who rise to power through the chances of social revolutions, never fail to persecute in others the intelligence and knowledge which they have not themselves; when the ignorant rule, civilization is brought down to their own level, and woe to those who rise above it, be it ever so little. In France, in 1793, the sovereign people guillotined those who could read and write as aristocrats; in the Argentine Republic, men of culture were called *savages*, and had their throats cut, and though the name seems mere irony, it is something more when applied by the assassin, knife in hand. The Caudillos of the interior rid their provinces of all lawyers, doctors, and men of letters; and Rosas pursued them even within the walls of the university and private schools. Those who were allowed to remain were such persons as could be useful in getting up a repetition of the government of Philip II of Spain, and of the Inquisition.

Barcala felt himself to be a *gentleman*, and united a spotless reputation to great professional knowledge, and a talent for strategy which placed him among officers of the first rank. He made himself famous in the army of Brazil, and Paz and other officers of note regarded him with a respect amounting to veneration. Quiroga, who shot all the officers made prisoners at Ciudadela, spared him—the only one who had fought until the last of his men were surrounded, and retreat was impossible. When offered his life on condition of serving under Quiroga, he accepted only with the understanding that he was not to fight against his own party; and in him Quiroga gained a whole army.

Such was the man whom the Aldaos wished to put out of their way; not a very difficult undertaking, since Lavalle, the Aldaos, and Barcala himself were to unite in an expedition to overthrow Albin Gutierrez, who had declared against the national government. Barcala and Lavalle marched to join the army against the empire, and the Aldaos remained to oppress the people, and give themselves up to the pleasures of dissipation.

The triumvirate had made use of all parties, and had served all parties in order to rid themselves of influential men. The revolution in favor of the national government having succeeded, they joined with Quiroga for the purpose of destroying it. The Constitution arranged by the Congress of 1826, was offered for acceptance to the provinces. The agents of this Congress were received in a rather singular manner by Quiroga in behalf of San Juan, which he then occupied. Two or three hides, stretched over lances stuck down in the middle of a clover field, formed a tent to protect this caliph of the faithful—this *divinely commissioned helper*—from the rays of the sun; here Facundo was lying upon a black cloak, dressed in a crimson *chiripa*, red cloth mantle, and untanned boots.

Dr. Zavaleta, Dean of the Cathedral, and agent of Congress, was received in this palace, and stood embarrassed in the presence of the commander, who neither moved nor looked at him, until he stammered a few words about his mission. Facundo then stretched out his hand, received the paper containing the Constitution, and wrote in the corner in scarcely legible characters, *"Despachado,"* and there was an end of the matter.*

In Mendoza the result was no better. The agent from Congress pathetically expatiated upon the evils existing in the Republic, conjured all patriots to unite under a constitution which would insure universal order and harmony of government; but there was a threefold ambition to satisfy, so he made his touching speech with tears in his eyes in vain, and returned without having accomplished anything. The Constitution met with the same reception everywhere; not from the people, who were allowed no voice in the matter, but from the Caudillos, who desired to retain for themselves entire liberty of action. The Constitution would have restrained them, whereas they required an open field for their ambitions, and pretexts for war, —religion, confederation,—anything to disguise the universal ambition. Thus the national government fell, and the celebrated Dorrego assumed the government of Buenos Ayres. The old Unitarios could not understand that Dorrego, with all his ambition and his intrigues, was nevertheless the only person who might have organized the Republic under a parliamentary form, and prevented it from being brought by Rosas under the rule of a cruel despotism which was to destroy all civilization and prosperity. Dorrego owed his elevation to the parliamen-

*Subsequent information makes it certain that this scene was but a myth of the time, the only fact being that Facundo thus disposed of the Constitution sent to him.

tary chamber and the press of the opposition party, and he would never have destroyed the powers which had defeated the former presidency; but all were overthrown when the gaucho of the pampas came into power, who understood little, and cared less for liberty and individual rights. It was his way to accomplish his ends by cutting men's throats; and on this principle the Republic is now governed.

The 1st of December, 1828, and the fatal victory of Navarro, taught the Caudillos their own power, and one and all prepared for the struggle—the Aldaos in Mendoza, and Facundo in the Llanos. A regiment of auxiliaries was put in training at Mendoza under command of the monk-colonel, whose fame was not yet so great as that of his brothers. As soldiers of the War of Independence, they knew what discipline can accomplish, and the auxiliaries, thoroughly equipped and trained, occupied the right wing in the famous battle of Tablada, in which eight hundred veterans of the national army, commanded by the able General Paz, left three thousand enemies dead, after a two days' fight. Of the regiment of auxiliaries, sixty-five survived, with their colonel, who was wounded in the side.

While this monk-colonel was confined at San Luis, by his wound, he amused himself by reading atheistical books,—an apparently insignificant fact, yet it would seem to prove that there was a struggle still going on in his conscience, of which he would fain have relieved himself. Quiroga, after the defeat, fled to the Llanos; Aldao naturally went back to his brothers. But many changes had taken place in his absence: a division from San Juan marching to Cordova, revolted on the way, and joined the Unitarios, who were sanguine of success, but unskilled in the art of war. The two Aldaos then at Mendoza, pursued them, and after a few marches and countermarches, conquered them without firing a shot.

On returning to Mendoza, the victorious troops, hearing of the victory at Tablada, revolted and threw the power into the hands of the liberal party, which showed no more prudence than it had done at San Juan. These mistaken men persisted in immediately establishing their long-desired constitutional forms, respect for life being their great maxim, and parliamentary discussion their means of action. Their enemies took advantage of this infatuation to ridicule them, and to endeavor again to overthrow their plans, while a magnificent system of government was maturing under the direction of General Albarado.

The brothers José and Francisco were planning within their prison walls their reëstablishment in power; while the monk presented himself in the neighborhood, and with sixty men and the use of skillful intrigues, opened a campaign against a government dependent upon a fanatical people, two thousand men under arms, and a man of reputation at its head. The prisoners soon escaped, and the discussion of terms of conciliation by the feeble government, gave time and resources to the Aldaos. The die was cast, and the fate of Mendoza was decided. A month was sufficient for the army to be hemmed in, and even fired upon in the streets.

Facundo Quiroga sent several hundred gauchos from Rioja to aid the three colonels of Mendoza, who had assembled a considerable number of montoneros. The government troops were exasperated at the inactivity in which they were kept by Albarado, and rebelled, insisting upon being led to battle. Finally the very sufferings of those who had felt the power of the Aldaos aroused them, and they went out to seek their enemies. In "el Pilar," of sad memory, they found themselves surrounded, not having taken a good position. In the evening twenty thousand shots were fired, and a hundred cannonades were discharged by the surrounded troops, and the next day the firing continued until twelve o'clock, yet they had not made their way out. The Aldaos knew that the ammunition was exhausted, and entrenched their men behind breastworks.

Messages from Quiroga urged them to make no treaty, and to promise nothing. "We must," said he, "have as many enemies as possible to extort money from." But the people of Mendoza, hearing the incessant firing for two days, thought that by this time few survivors could remain, and the bereaved women ran through the streets entreating the priests and other influential persons to separate the combatants. A committee of priests approached the battle-field, selected neutral ground for a treaty, and it was agreed that all should submit to a government chosen by the people. The Aldaos must have laughed at the simplicity of their enemies, who were already conquered and prisoners, and yet maintained the proud bearing of free citizens. But Providence did not permit the farce to be enacted to the end, for it was to finish with a tragedy which filled even the actors with horror.

It was about half-past three in the afternoon when the treaty was completed; the soldiers stacked their arms, officers collected in groups congratulating themselves upon getting out of the difficulty so easily. Francisco Aldao came into the enemy's camp, where he was cordially received, and in the lively conversation which arose, many a jest was exchanged by men who had formerly been friends. At this moment an emissary from the monk presented himself, and demanded unconditional surrender, under pain of death. Cries of indignation burst from all sides, and Francisco was loaded with the most bitter reproaches, but he said with quiet dignity, "Sirs, there is nothing in all this; Felix has just dined, that is all." And he repeated these words with a peculiar emphasis, at the same time sending an aide to inform Felix that he was there, and that the slightest manifestation on his part would be a violation of the treaty.

The alarm spread rapidly, however, the cry of treason arose throughout the camp, and the officers were in vain calling upon the men to form, when six cannon balls were fired directly into the group in the midst of which Francisco Aldao stood. If the cannonade had been a moment later, José Aldao also would have been there, for he was just on the point of starting, when he was surprised by the discharge, and exclaimed, "That is the work of Felix,—he is drunk!" This was but too true, the monk was intoxicated, according to his usual afternoon custom; only a few days before they had been obliged to keep him in bed to save him from some gaucho enemies while in this condition.

Confusion prevailed everywhere, and reached its height at the approach of the Auxiliaries of Don Felix, and the Blues from San Juan. A moment after the monk himself came into the camp, and seeing a dead body lying upon a cannon wrapped in a cloak, a vague presentiment induced him to command the face to be uncovered; even then the fumes of the wine prevented him from recognizing it, and his attendants tried to make him withdraw, before he should perceive that it was his brother; but he again demanded sternly, "Who is it?" At the same instant he recognized Francisco, and struck his head violently with his fist, as if awakening out of a dream. Woe to the conquered! The carnage commenced, and he cried with a hoarse voice to his men, "Slay! slay them!" while he killed the defenseless prisoners about him. The officers were all cut down or left wounded and mutilated, without arms, without hands. Day closed before the butchery ceased, and the troops returned to the city, but every shot which broke the silence of the night, announced an assassination or the breaking open of some door. When the following day dawned, the pillage was still going on, and the sunlight revealed the outrages of the night.

The actors in this frightful tragedy were themselves stunned with the horror of their own work, and the monk became aware of all that he had done, and the death of his brother whom he had sacrificed. But he was not a man to show his remorse, and if he felt any he sought to stifle it by delivering himself up to intoxication and still further outrages. Thus the evil propensities which had been for a time under restraint, broke forth again; and revenge for his brother's death was an excuse for every excess. He had caused all the officers to be put to death on that uncontested battle-field; the next day he ordered the execution of all the sergeants, and on the next the corporals. Every time he became intoxicated his thirst for blood returned with redoubled fury, and there are still persons alive who heard him give orders for various assassinations, with minute directions as to the manner in which they were to be accomplished; that at such a spot, at such an hour, the legs of a certain victim were to be cut off; in another case the tongue was to be cut out, and in another the face was to be so mutilated as not to be recognized. Such deeds of barbarity were then unheard of and surpassed all imagination, but now they are common enough, and Buenos Ayres, Tucuman, Cordova, and Mendoza, have become familiar with still greater atrocities. Terror had then paralyzed the people, and when Quiroga arrived, he found it easy to obtain all the money he desired. There is still in existence an order which he drew upon the government for the payment of his gaming debts; for wherever he went the silence imposed by the terror of his name was only disturbed by rumors of punishments and executions for the purpose of obtaining means to carry on his games at the card-table. Mendoza remained under this evil influence, and a large army was prepared to resist General Paz.

During the monk's rage for blood, his wife or mistress saved the lives of many victims. His brother José, more considerate and more humane than himself, also tried to appease his fury, but with each evening came intoxication and unpremeditated outrages. From this time Aldao lived in a state of continual alarm, embittered by that horror of himself which was the only punishment he received in this world; for while his less criminal brother José was assassinated, he died a natural death, feared and obeyed to the last. But Providence works in secret and he will surely meet his deserts.

A new army commenced another campaign against General Paz. Aldao had filled up the vacancies in his company of aux-iliaries, and Facundo had gathered an undisciplined crowd of four or five thousand men. Aldao was accompanied by Don José Santos Ortiz, who was intrusted with the mission of trying to induce Quiroga to join with Paz in carrying on the war with Buenos Ayres, and it seems that Quiroga came near accepting the proposition. Paz on his part sent Major Pawnero,* a young man whose intelligence equaled his bravery, to make proposals of peace to Quiroga. But Quiroga's pride urged him to wipe out the mortification of his defeat at Tablado. The battle of Laguna Larga taught Quiroga that his heavy cavalry charges could not be always relied upon; a simple maneuver of the infantry on the other side decided the victory, and Quiroga fled to Buenos Ayres, leaving on the field his infantry, artillery, and baggage. During the pursuit of the fugitives, a stout man whose weight had exhausted his horse, was overtaken and thrown down by a lance. A soldier was about to make an end of him, when he cried, "Do not kill me, it is important to the nation that I should be taken alive to General Paz. I am General Aldao."

An officer took charge of him as far as Cordova, where a humiliating reception awaited him. Some officers from Men-doza, carried away by their desire for revenge, made him enter the town mounted upon a wretched animal, exposed to the insults of the people. "Wretch!" they shouted, "thou hast brought destruction upon thy country!" "I have also brought it much glory," replied the prisoner, with dignity, for the in-sults of his enemies had restored all his courage. He was then

*Now candidate for the Vice-Presidency of the Republic, 1868.

carried to prison, where he might reflect upon his past deeds in silence and solitude, and the retrospection became so intolerable that he excited the contempt of his jailers by his terror and childish exhibitions of alarm. He implored every one who came near him to tell him if anything was said about his death, and the ordinary noises about the prison filled him with fears, until at last he could no longer sleep at night, and never ceased his suspicious watch upon his jailers. Some priests undertook to reconcile him with the church, and whether through fear, or real repentance, he eagerly acceded to their propositions. One day while listening to Don José Santos Ortiz, he happened to look at a sentinel before his door, who knowing the terror he was constantly in, maliciously passed his hand across his own throat with a significant motion, and Aldao throwing the breviary from him, cried, "They will kill me to-day! they will kill me!"

His companion tried in vain to tranquillize him, by representing that he would have to be tried and legally condemned before he could be executed; he only became the more agitated, saying, "Ah, you have not done what I have done!" The soldier who had been famous for his bold, reckless audacity, did not dare to look death in the face, and showed the cowardice of a child.

In the mean time the people of Mendoza had again thrown off the yoke of the tyrants. Don José Aldao, unfortunately for himself, conceived the idea of escaping to the south, and trusting in the faith of the Indians; but the perfidious savages, having invited him and all his principal officers to a consultation, surrounded them; and though Don José succeeded in killing their chief, he and his friends, to the number of thirty, were all slain.

The people of Mendoza whom the monk Aldao had so terribly wronged, petitioned General Paz to deliver him up to them—and I mean the people in the largest sense of the word, for all had suffered by him more or less, and the craving for

revenge seemed to be a disease which seized upon the whole
community. No punishment could be invented severe enough
for him; but at least a gallows should be erected for him in the
field of Pilar, and it should be high enough for all the city to
see him expire in the midst of their execrations. One committee after another was sent to Cordova to press their claim to
the prisoner, as one connected in a peculiar manner with Mendoza, but General Paz was deaf to all these entreaties, and for
the time there was still a chance that Aldao might some day
escape from his prison.

The war recommenced about this time, and an accident
which only an Argentine can understand, took General Paz
from the head of his army. Having drawn up his men in a close
column, he rode forward to a small eminence to reconnoitre,
when, seeing a company of montoneros coming out of the
woods hard by, he supposed them to be some of his own troops
whom he had disguised as gauchos, and commanded an aide
to go and give them the necessary orders. The aide obeyed
unwillingly, being somewhat suspicious of the new comers, and
as he neared them was instantly shot, while at the same moment
Paz was caught in a lasso, thrown from his horse, and was
instantly in the hands of his enemies. The army, deprived of
the commander whose presence always insured victory, retreated to Tucuman, and sent into the city for the prisoners.

A squadron of cuirassiers had formed in the square at Cordova, in front of the state-prisons, from one of which came
frightful groans, breaking the silence of the night, and exciting
the compassion even of the oldest veterans. The prisoner of
Laguna Larga, the soldier of the War of Independence, was on
his knees, under the influence of unmanly fear, groaning and
sobbing in the belief that these nocturnal preparations were for
his death; the officer who went in search of him found him
with a wafer, which he had consecrated, and held in both hands
as a protection against his executioners. The prisoner, in his

hour of need, had resumed his priestly offices, and the theologians of the university of Cordova had a long discussion upon the efficacy of the consecration of the wafer as performed by him. Being quieted with much difficulty, the miserable man followed the army to Tucuman, and after the defeat at Ciudadela, he accompanied the fugitives to Bolivia, where they set him at liberty. Here ends one of the most eventful periods in the life of Don Felix, the only one of the trio then alive.

The battle of Ciudadela left the Republic once more at peace after the long previous struggle. The men who had been in favor of confederation had triumphed everywhere, from Buenos Ayres to Tucuman, and were now about to establish their form of government and to reconstruct the Republic. But instead of this, Facundo established a card-table in every city he visited; and with six hundred thousand dollars obtained by the year's conquests, went to Buenos Ayres to become the victim of another commander more astute than himself, who had determined to dispose of any man in the country who could in any way be his rival. The same indifference to the real interests of the people was manifested everywhere, and this state of things continued until 1840, though within the ten years Rosas established his power over the caudillos of the interior, while allowing them a nominal authority. The cities hoped than Facundo would reconstruct the Republic—a vain hope. They are now hoping that Rosas will be merciful to them if he succeeds in getting rid of his enemies.

Don Felix returned to Mendoza in 1832, and on his way through Rioja had an interview with Facundo, who had with him the noble Barcala. Aldao's first words were, "When are you going to shoot that negro?" Quiroga frowned and seemed ill-pleased; in fact he showed a haughty contempt for the monk, and wrote to the officers at Mendoza not to admit him into the army. But when Aldao presented himself, his personal influence was still too strong to be resisted, and the governor received him with offers of assistance, and bestowed upon him the title of commander-general of the frontier. He accepted the office, demanding at the same time that his salary should be paid from the date of his imprisonment at Tablado; he was evidently determined to secure for himself a comfortable and permanent establishment—the condition of the country seeming to promise peace and quiet for the present.

He took up his quarters in one of the southern forts, provided himself with a body-guard, and sent for a coarse, ignorant woman, by the name of Dolores, with whom he had become enamored in Rioja. Mendoza had for some time witnessed the jealous rivalry of his Lima mistress and this Dolores, and the latter being finally victorious, her rival went back to Chili, leaving two illegitimate children. An unfortunate influence for the people was this utter disregard of morality—vice in its most repugnant forms,—an apostate priest, unchaste women, illegitimate children, whose illegal birth was also sacrilegious. Aldao omitted no cares for his personal safety, and his body-guard never left him for a moment, not even when he sat at the card-table; and the fort from hall to cellar was one constant scene of dissipation. Excitement became more and more necessary to him, and when he visited the city he ordered preparations for card playing as if it were a regular part of public affairs. It is impossible to give an idea of the degradation into which this man had fallen, his debasing pleasures and entire forgetfulness of business. It is true that neither the Aldaos nor Quiroga ever really governed; they left to others the labors of the administration, while they reserved for themselves all the power.

Don Felix now governed Mendoza, through nominal governors who dared not displease him in anything; and his most casual remark uttered in his own fort, was enough to affect the government, and often became an absolute law. And this lasted for ten years, until constant intoxication brought his life to an end.

In 1832, Rosas prepared an expedition to the south, and invited the caudillos of the interior to coöperate with him for the protection of their respective frontiers, hoping by this means to make the pretext of an attack on the Indians cover an extensive military combination which he meant to use for his own elevation to power. Don Felix induced one tribe to attack another tribe, and deliver them prisoners to his troops; both tribes, however, united while on the way, and after putting to death sixty of the Mendoza soldiers, fled to the desert. Aldao followed and exterminated them, and this was all that was accomplished by the famous expedition; but Aldao made by it a valuable acquisition. Among the soldiers of his division was one Rodriguez, a man of great bravery, whom he took under his especial protection, and promoted to the command of a squadron. The monk was then becoming stout, incapable of action, and given up to intoxication, so that he would have been unable to sustain his power and reputation but for this Rodriguez, who, by proxy, still maintained the terror of his name.

Rosas having obtained absolute power in 1833, carefully studied the capacities of the various caudillos of the interior, that he might quietly bring them under submission; and this conquest of the provinces is one of the greatest acts of diplomacy accomplished by him. Soon afterwards he won over the auxiliaries of San Juan; had Quiroga put to death; got rid of his own tools, the Reinafés; deposed Cullen, of Santa Fé, and then had him shot; and made Benavides governor of San Juan in place of Yanzon. Barcala, the virtuous Barcala, was shot by the monk, who was now in the pay of Rosas. Brizuela, of Rioja, unrivaled for his brutality, was kept in command, notwithstanding the zeal of Benavides, his neighbor. Ibarra had quietly governed Santiago del Estero for eighteen years. In short, everything was arranged for the decline of the Republic into barbarism, when the despotic power of Rosas would be confirmed. Unfortunately there was no connected plan of resistance, no union, no leaders. Rosas had forbidden the passage of couriers throughout the interior, and the general want of confidence made any agreement between the cities impossible. The rebellion broke out, and the provinces joined in it one after another, but in the end were all forced to yield, paralyzed by the horrors of unheard-of outrages. Never was a revolution more universal or more ineffectual. Rosas would have lost his cause but for the weakness of his enemies.

Aldao together with Benavides now started on a campaign against Brizuela, who, unfortunately for the honor of their cause, had joined the patriots. It is hardly to be believed that a man in his position should make such a brute of himself as to remain intoxicated for six months at a time, without once seeing the light of day, or being for a moment in condition to receive the ambassadors from the different governors, or even Lavalle himself, who waited several days in vain for an audience. And Aldao behaved in the same way at San Luis, only not quite to the same extent.

The appearance of a small force commanded by the brave young Alvarez, caused the division of Benavides to disperse; while the monk retreated, and by a rapid march reached Mendoza in time to put down the rebellion of the 4th of November. The people looked for nothing else than a repetition of the slaughter of 1829, but Aldao contented himself with some persecution and imposition of taxes. His rage for shedding blood seemed to have ceased, and from this time no such wholesale murders would have taken place in Mendoza but for his disciples, who had profited but too well by his former example.

Aldao again joined Benavides, and with him conquered Brizuela, both of them then taking up quarters in Rioja, in order to intercept the army under Madrid, which was approaching from the north.

One day the news came to San Juan that a division from Tucuman was near at hand, and eight hundred men went out to meet them, but were repulsed. Then Acha, the immortal Acha, went with a handful of men to meet the united forces of Benavides, Aldao, and Lucero, amounting in all to twenty-five hundred men, with four pieces of artillery; and this battle of Angaco is the one glorious event amidst the errors, failures, and defeats of that period.

Acha's men were only about four hundred, little disciplined, and unacquainted with the country, but to make up for these disadvantages, he had with him a number of truly patriotic young men of high standing in the army, and their enthusiasm gave to the little company the strength of double their number. As the troops of the enemy quietly took their position, Acha stood playing with a little switch, and with a smile which was habitual with him, pointed to the enemy and cried, "Rascals! now for real work!" The battle commenced, and a deadly firing was kept up for five long hours, the infantry of Benavides being within three yards of Acha's company; for Aldao had fled, leaving his companion to take care of himself. The young Alvarez, who was seriously wounded early in the contest, left a vacancy which could not be filled; and presently, when the men became discouraged and wavered in their resistance, he had his wound hastily bandaged and returned to his place, animating his soldiers by his eager enthusiasm, till they rushed again into the fight with redoubled ardor. As evening came on, all order seemed lost, and each man fought on his own account; little groups of cavalry, of ten, twelve, or twenty men, charged upon the enemy from all directions, and at last when the noise lessened somewhat, and the smoke of the powder cleared away, Acha found, not without some surprise, that he had won the day. With his usual smile, he congratulated his weary soldiers, saying, "Did I not say there would be some work worth seeing?" It is a pity that this remarkable man should have somewhat lessened his reputation by a foolish carelessness, which at last cost him his life. On the other hand, Benavides gained his reputation by an act of bravery which would have done honor to any general in the army.

The victory of Angaco might have been the means of saving the Republic, had Acha done justice to the bravery and self-possession of his enemy. Benavides, thus conquered by a handful of men, returned to San Juan without showing the least discouragement, though his best officers had fallen, and all his stores were at the mercy of his victorious rival. He was retreating without haste to Mendoza, when he met a small reinforcement, and with this aid, little as it was, he conceived the possibility of a triumph, and determined to take immediate advantage of circumstances. Hastily returning, therefore, he attacked his unsuspecting conquerors, and after three days of vain resistance, took Acha himself prisoner, thus recovering all that he had lost, and winning as great renown as the battle of Angaco had given to his prisoner. When Madrid had been deprived of his vanguard, of the recruits which San Juan might have furnished, and of the chivalrous Acha,—a host within himself,—it was easy to strengthen the forces of Rosas under command of Pacheco. The battle of Rodeo del Medio was a corollary of the triumph at San Juan, and entirely owing to Benavides.

As to Aldao, his cowardly flight from the field of Angaco, had placed him in a humiliating position; all his former military fame seemed to have been transferred to Benavides, and in his own province he was regarded with open contempt. He made a journey to Buenos Ayres for the purpose of complaining to his master, and was rewarded by a magnificent reception. But this was followed by no attention from Rosas; he waited many months without obtaining an interview, and was then obliged to return to his own territory, which the army of Rosas had in the meantime despoiled of all implements of war. Henceforth Aldao had no other power than that obtained through Rodriguez and his band; this, however, was enough to enable him to rule Mendoza, which had learned by years of oppression to submit to him. Rosas had placed all real power in the hands of Benavides, whose prudence as well as bravery enabled him to keep it. The rivalry between these two commanders was encouraged by Rosas, as it insured his own safety.

Here ends the public career of Don Felix Aldao; the rest of his life was only the gradual decay of a constitution broken by dissipation and the hardships of war, and to the end he was pursued by the scourge of his own conscience and the maledictions of the people.

His harem had been increased by the acquisition of new mistresses; and the immoralities and scandal of his private life formed the common topic of conversation, where the shameful rivalry of these degraded women was openly exposed; and they not only taunted each other with their degradation, but laid violent hands on one another in the streets. And this state of things was the more abominable because the administration of the government was affected by it. Neither justice nor safety even was to be expected for those who should happen to offend the reigning favorite of the monk, and it was quickly known when a change of dynasty had taken place in the seraglio. Ladies of the first families suffered outrageous punishments for not treating these women with respect. One young girl was seated on a mule and whipped through the streets for speaking slightingly of one of the mistresses; and the principal inhabitants of Mendoza were compelled to meet them at a ball, where the young men strove for the honor of dancing with the coarse creature Dolores, who was the favorite at that time. On the death of one of the illegitimate children, Montero, the chief of the police, made the announcement publicly, inviting the citizens to attend the funeral, and the principal men of the place bore the coffin, which was richly decorated and accompanied by the chief magistrates, who walked before and behind it, while a military procession followed.

When Acha and Benavides were fighting at San Juan, Montero conducted Dolores to the barracks at Mendoza, where she aided him in arousing the enthusiasm of the troops destined to march, by showing them Aldao's children, and calling upon them to support and aid their general. What a loss this general was to Rosas! Montero only could supply his place. Rosas needed just such men to maintain quiet in the provinces. All the governors had some peculiar qualities by which they served the ends of the man whose tools they were. Brizuela was a sponge with vast capacity for imbibing brandy, a sort of wine-bottle, who governed admirably in Rioja. Some left the people to take care of themselves while they got up cock-fights and races; others shut up the government offices and passed months without making a decree or using any administrative forms whatever; others let things slide on easily, tolerating everything, but an intelligent lawyer or judge. They all involuntarily agreed upon one point, the gradual disappearance of the public roads. Highwaymen became numerous, schools were closed, trade languished, the administration of justice was given up to stupid or ignorant men, the press was filled with nothing but fulsome praises of the "Restorator;" manners were fast declining towards barbarism, learning was despised, talent persecuted, and ignorance became a title to honor. And these governors did well in acting thus if they desired to remain in favor, for whoever showed any real capacity, or any interest in promoting the public welfare, was soon put out of the way. The Dictator had arisen to power through the barbarism of the people; and the poverty and ignorance of the provinces secured him from all dangerous opposition. The best governed of the cities scarcely perceived the gradual decline, for despotism, even under its most favorable circumstances, is for a people what phthisis is for the body; the patient feels no pain, eats, sleeps, and enjoys himself without care; it is only the physician who sees death surely approaching. Rosas assumed for himself the care of thinking for all; he must be the head, and the governors of the provinces the arms, hands, and feet, to execute his will; each member to be used, according to its capacity, for anything but thought in behalf of the Republic: the construction of the government was to be his own work.

The life of Felix Aldao was now drawing to a close. For a year before his death he was troubled with a cancer on his face, which ate into his nose and eyes, until he became partially blind; while the odor was so offensive that his companions at the card-table could hardly endure it. His temper did not improve with sickness, and he became so suspicious of the physicians who attended him that they were obliged to flee, feeling that their lives were in danger. During this year of illness no one dared to propose a temporary governor, for those unfortunate people had come to believe that the government belonged of right to the caudillos, and that it would be treason to question their capability, even when ill. Aldao governed Mendoza to the last, and that without attending to anything but his own health. As his death approached, he would not remain alone for a moment, tormented as he was by the terrors of his imagination, and a number of the citizens were obliged to take turns in watching with him. One night he sprang from his bed and rushed in among them with a pair of pistols in his hands. They without waiting to see that the wretched creature was a prey to his own fears, and not attacking them, fled out of the house and the town, and could with difficulty be induced to return the next day. And these were the citizens of the Argentine Republic who had offended other states by their arrogant pride! These were the people who had irritated Bolivar by their overbearing manners! And now they stumbled over one another in their haste to run away from a sick monk!

At length, after months of acute suffering, the cancer caused the bursting of a vein, and the hemorrhage continued until he expired on the 18th of January—in retribution perhaps for the blood of the people which had flowed without stint at his command. Some say that he went back to the church and died penitent, leaving a large part of his wealth to the Dominican order, to which he had belonged. According to the obituary notices he made Rosas his testamentary executor; as the Roman proconsuls, dying in the provinces of the empire, used to leave their wealth to the emperor, together with the government of the provinces. These two contradictory statements prove at least one thing, that at his death there was still a question whether he was a monk or a general, but that matters little to him now. With the money acquired by oppressing the people of Mendoza, he left a home for each of his three families.

With so much that was bad, this man must have had some good qualities, for he had friends whose affection was never weakened by absence or death, and no one who inspired such devotion could be wholly bad. He was also beloved by his soldiers, many of whom remained with him for years. He was in the habit of sending large supplies of grain to the poor people south of Mendoza; and whenever he learned of the arrival of the Chilian families who frequently emigrated to Mendoza, he supplied them with provisions until they could establish themselves. And, lastly, those who saw him intimately, say that he was extravagantly fond of his children, whose caresses were his greatest pleasure.

The family of Aldao is now represented by the acknowledged children of three women, some other natural children, and the legitimate offspring of his brother Don José. All the Aldaos had met with a tragic end, though that of Felix was the least so. All Mendoza followed his body to the church within which he was buried. That evening the Almeda was crowded with persons of both sexes; until then, this promenade, the scene of much bloodshed when Pacheco was there, had been entirely unfrequented.

The only benefit which Mendoza received during the rule of this governor, was the settlement of its southern frontier by emigrants from Chili, who collected in villages under the protection of the fort of San Carlos, the habitation of Aldao, who always encouraged this emigration.

Mendoza is now without a governor; it remains to be seen who will obtain possession of it. When Rosas heard that the monk was about to die, he sent a sister of his with her husband, who was physician and also secretary for Aldao. After his death, when the choice of a new governor was discussed, Rodriguez was in favor of the secretary, but the people preferred a native of the city.

I have now concluded my self-imposed task, with the fear of not having been sufficiently impartial; yet it is my misfortune if the facts are not strictly correct. I have carefully consulted both his friends and enemies, and the old soldiers who were with him at the beginning of his career. I have thrown aside all that seemed doubtful, and endeavored to moderate everything that was exaggerated. For the rest, the life of such a man, who took part in so many political changes, should be brought before the public by a more powerful pen than mine. The biography of these tools of a ruler, shows what means he employs, and the end at which he aims.

APPENDIX

AUTHOR'S NOTICE
FROM THE 1845 EDITION

Once this work was published, I received from several friends a number of rectifications to events referred in it. Some inaccuracies had necessarily taken place in a job done quickly, far from the theater of events and on a subject matter about which nothing had been written until then. While coordinating episodes that had taken place in distant and remote provinces and in different epochs, verifying a point with an eye-witness, depending on manuscripts shaped without much care, or basing my research in my own personal recollections, it isn't altogether strange that on occasion the Argentine reader might not find something he had knowledge about, or that he might dissent on a proper name or date changed or placed out of context.

But I do have to declare that on the noble events I'm referring to that serve as basis to my explanations, there is an unquestionable exactitude to which any available public record will testify.

Perhaps there will come a moment when, having overcome the specific worries that gave birth to this little work, I will reshape it again using an altogether new plan, freeing it of all accidental digressions, and supporting its claims with official documents to which I only make passing reference in this version.

★ ★ ★

On ne tue point les idées.
—FORTOUL

Toward the end of 1840, I was leaving my homeland, a pitiful exile, ruined, full of bruises, kicks, and blows received the previous day in one of those bloody bacchanals of low soldiers and *mazorqueros*. As I passed the baths of Zonza . . . I wrote these words in charcoal:

On ne tue point les idées.

The government, which had been made aware of this, sent a commission in charge of deciphering the hieroglyph, which was said to contain base outpourings, insults and threats. Having heard the translation, they said, "So, what does it mean?" It meant simply that I was on my way to Chile, where freedom still shined, and that I had made up my mind to project the lighting that its printing presses emitted all the way to the other side of the Andes. Those who know my behavior in Chile know if I have been able to live up to my promise.

—Translated by I.S. and D.S.G.